Songs for the Spirits

Songs for the Spirits

Music and Mediums in Modern Vietnam

BARLEY NORTON

UNIVERSITY OF ILLINOIS PRESS

Urbana and Chicago

Library of Congress Cataloging-in-Publication Data
Norton, Barley, 1971–
Songs for the spirit : music and mediums in
modern Vietnam / Barley Norton.
p.   cm.
Includes bibliographical references and index.
ISBN 978-0-252-03399-5 (cloth : alk. paper)
1. Folk music—Religious aspects—Vietnam—
History—20th century. 2. Spirit possession—
Vietnam. 3. Mediums—Vietnam.
I. Title.
ML3921.8.F65N67   2009
133.9'109597—dc22   2008035441

For my parents, Margaret and Peter

Contents

Acknowledgments   ix

Note on Vietnamese Language   xi

DVD Contents   xiii

Introduction: Encountering Mediumship   1

1. Mediumship, Modernity, and Cultural Identity   21

2. Experiencing Spirit Possession   54

3. Songs for the Spirits   79

4. The Musical Construction of the Spirits   108

5. Musical Creativity and Change   131

6. Engendering Mediumship   155

7. Ritual and Folklorization in Late Socialist Vietnam   190

Epilogue: Thanking the Spirits   217

Appendix   225

Notes   229

Bibliography   237

Index   249

Acknowledgments

Any study based on field research is inherently collaborative, and this book would have been inconceivable without the generosity of numerous mediums and musicians who welcomed me into the world of mediumship and shared their experiences and thoughts with me. I am especially grateful to my *chau van* teachers, Pham Van Ty, Dang Cong Hung, and Le Ba Cao, for their musical inspiration, guidance, and friendship. While I cannot name everyone who contributed to this research, special mention should be made of Cao Mon, Duong Van Nguyen, Hong Van, Kim Lien, Le Thi Hoa, Le Tu Cuong, My Ha, Nguyen The Tuyen, Nguyen Thi Binh, Nguyen Thi Hang, Nguyen Thi Lai, Nguyen Thi Van, Nguyen Thi Xuan, Nguyen Thuy Hoa, Pham Quang Dat, Pham Van Mui, Thao Giang, Tran Viet Duc, Van Thi Doan, Vu Duc Quyet, and Xuan Khai. My research also benefited from the assistance of Ngo Duc Thinh at the Folk Culture Institute, Dang Hoanh Loan and Le Van Toan at the Vietnamese Institute for Musicology, and Tran Thu Ha at the Hanoi Music Conservatoire.

I owe a special debt to my dear friend, the multitalented musician Nguyen Manh Tien, whose presence looms behind much of this book. As well as providing invaluable practical help throughout my research, Tien was a constant source of inspiration and moral support—I will always cherish the many hours we spent playing and discussing music together. It was because of Tien and his wife, Huyen An, that the documentary *A Westerner Loves Our Music* came to be made. My thanks to Kim Huong, Huyen An, and the rest of the team at Vietnamese Television for making the documentary and to Laurent Van Lancker for filming the scenes of "a Westerner" in London. I also extend my sincere gratitude to my Vietnamese language teacher Trinh Thi Nhan for her kindness and openmindedness.

Friends in Vietnam did much to make my time there a pleasure. Frances House was the most charming host and friend during my stay in 1996–97, and I am grateful to William Smith and Ingo Schoeningh for their generous hospitality during my visit in 2004–5. A big *cam on* to Duong Bich Hanh, Gisa Jähnichen, Hoang Dao Hiep, Jonathan Birchall, Kirsten Endres, Lauren Meeker, Michael DiGregorio, Mila Rosenthal, Natasha Pairaudeau, Nguyen Trinh Thi, and Philippe Peycam. Thanks also to Peter, Mark, and Simon Hoosen, to Sweety Kapoor, to Marc Falconer, and to Karen Bayne and friends in the UK who helped me through the long, solitary hours of writing.

In an earlier incarnation this book was a dissertation, and I wish to express my thanks to my supervisor David W. Hughes for all his stimulating advice and support over the years. This book would also not have come to fruition without the guidance of Jonathan P. J. Stock, and I am grateful to Laurie Matheson, acquisitions editor at the University of Illinois Press, for her encouragement of my work. My sincere thanks to Katherine J. Hagedorn, Keith Howard, David W. Hughes, Shaun K. Malarney, Nguyen Thuyet Phong, and Jonathan P. J. Stock for their insightful comments on drafts of this research; to Andrée Grau at Roehampton University; to John Baily, Stephen Cottrell, and Keith Negus at Goldsmiths College; to Mary Lisa Gilonne for assisting with translating some of the French texts; and to Jim Copperthwaite for, among other things, co-composing the music track "Vina." I also owe a special musical debt to Rachel Swindells.

The completion of this book was made possible by a period of study leave from Roehampton University and a period of matched leave funded by the Arts and Humanities Research Council. Field research and the time for writing at various stages of this project were also funded by grants and scholarships from the British Academy, the School of Oriental and African Studies, and the Central Research Fund of the University of London. I gratefully acknowledge the support of these institutions. The DVD that accompanies this book was produced by Garry Nickols at Nest Films. Inclusion of the DVD book is made possible by a research grant from the Association of South East Asian Studies in the UK.

Finally, my heartfelt thanks to Katie Dyt, and I would like to thank my parents, Margaret and Peter, and my sister, Cherry, for their unconditional love and support.

Note on Vietnamese Language

Modern Vietnamese is written with a romanized script called *quoc ngu* (lit. "national script"). This script was initially devised by French and Portuguese missionaries in the seventeenth century and became the predominant script from the beginning of the twentieth century. The *quoc ngu* script replaced the older systems of writing Vietnamese with Chinese characters, *chu nho*, and with Vietnamese characters, *chu nom*, a system that is based on modified Chinese characters. Vietnamese is a tonal language, and the *quoc ngu* script includes diacritics to indicate the speech tones and to distinguish different vowel and consonant sounds. For the sake of simplicity and accessibility to non-Vietnamese-speaking readers, the Vietnamese words in this text are written without the use of diacritics, except for the musical transcription in Figure 5.1. The *quoc ngu* system is required in Figure 5.1 in order to illustrate the relationship between speech tones and melodic contour, and Figure 5.2 graphically represents the six speech tones used in standard Vietnamese. The six speech tones are indicated with the following diacritics (using the vowel "e"):

High rising (*sac*): é
Mid level (*khong dau*): e (i.e., no diacritic)
High broken (*nga*): ẽ
Low rising (*hoi*): ẻ
Low broken (*nang*): ẹ
Low falling (*huyen*): è

Vietnamese names are conventionally written with the family name first, followed by given names. This convention is adhered to in this book.

DVD Contents

The DVD features video extracts of mediumship rituals and folklorized performances of spirit possession. It also includes audio examples of *chau van,* revolutionary *chau van,* neotraditional compositions, and *ca tru.* It can be played on a DVD player or a computer with a DVD drive. The opening menu of the DVD lists the three main sections: "Ritual Songscapes," "Ritual as Theatre," and "Musical Examples." The first two sections contain video extracts, and the third consists of audio examples.

Ritual Songscapes

Incarnations of four spirits can be selected on the "Ritual Songscapes" menu: the Third Mandarin, the Second Lady, the Tenth Prince, and the Third Princess. Once a spirit is selected, incarnations of the spirit at one of two rituals, labeled Ritual 1 and 2, can be chosen. An overview of the progression of each spirit possession is provided in a table. The video extracts are embedded in the top row of the tables and are labeled Ext. 1 to 30. To play the video, an extract needs to be highlighted and selected. A translation of the song text appears after each video extract. To return to the main table, select "Back." The second row of the tables lists the sequence of songs performed, and the third row consists of a brief description of the medium's movements. Each song name appears in a separate column. When there is a change of song corresponding to the medium's ritual action, the song name and ritual action are aligned in the same column; when song changes are unrelated to the medium's movements, no columns are marked in the third row of the tables.

The relationship between songs and ritual action can therefore be observed at a glance. In the top row of the tables, the video extracts are aligned to make it clear which section of the ritual they correspond to. Most of the video extracts include performances of two or more songs, so the video-extract icons usually span across the columns in the second row.

I filmed both mediumship rituals with a Sony Hi-8 camcorder in Hanoi in 1997. Ritual 1 was recorded on April 24 at the Mulberry Temple (Den Dau). Ritual 2 was recorded at the An Tho Temple on July 8. Further details about the mediums and bands at these rituals are given in Chapter 3.

Ritual as Theatre

The "Ritual as Theatre" menu features video extracts taken from two folklorized performances of mediumship: *The Three Spirits* and *The Five Spirits*. The video extract of *The Three Spirits* consists of the entire performance of one of the spirits, the Little Young Prince. The video extracts of *The Five Spirits* features extracts of all five spirits: the Goddess Lieu Hanh, General Tran Hung Dao, Princess Cam Duong, The Tenth Prince, and the Young Princess or Little Princess of the Mountains.

The Three Spirits was performed by members of the Ha Nam Cheo Troupe in a courtyard outside the Lanh Giang Temple in Ha Nam Province about 100 kilometers south of Hanoi. *The Five Spirits* was performed by members of the Nam Dinh Cheo Troupe in the Cheo Theatre in the city of Nam Dinh about 120 kilometers south of Hanoi. I filmed *The Three Spirits* with a Sony Hi-8 camcorder on April 24, 1997, and *The Five Spirits* with a Panasonic mini-DV camcorder on December 9, 2004.

Music Examples

The "Music Examples" menu comprises twenty-eight audio tracks, all of which I recorded. These music examples are referred to as "track 1," et cetera, in the book. All of the tracks were on Digital Audio Tape (DAT), except numbers 19, 24, and 28, which were recorded on Hi-8 videotape.

Track 1. "Welcoming Vietnam's Great Victory" (Mung Viet Nam Dai Thang), performed by Kim Lien (voice), Nguyen The Tuyen (moon lute), and Pham Van Ty (percussion). Recorded December 2004.

Track 2. "Nam Dinh, My Home Town" (Nam Dinh Que Toi), performed by Hong Van (voice), Nguyen The Tuyen (moon lute), and Pham Van Ty (percussion). Recorded June 1998.

Track 3. "For the Fighters at the Frontier" (Gui Anh Chien Sy Bien Thuy), performed by Pham Van Ty (voice and moon lute) and Do Khac Huan (percussion). Recorded January 2005.

Track 4. "Hat Van Solo" (Doc Tau Hat Van), performed by Pham Van Ty (moon lute) and Do Khac Huan (percussion). Recorded January 2005.

Track 5. "Our Homeland" (Que Ta), performed by Bui Viet Hong (moon lute), Le Hai Phuong (dulcimer), and Do Khac Huan (percussion). Recorded January 2005.

Track 6. "Doc," performed by Pham Van Ty (voice and moon lute) with Pham Quang Dat (percussion). Recorded June 1997.

Track 7. "Con Giay Lech," performed by Pham Van Ty (voice and moon lute) with Pham Quang Dat (percussion). Recorded June 1997.

Track 8. "Con Oan," performed by Pham Van Ty (voice and moon lute) and Pham Quang Dat (percussion). Recorded in June 1997.

Track 9. "Xa Thuong," performed by Pham Van Ty (voice and moon lute) and Pham Quang Dat (percussion). Recorded June 1997.

Track 10. "Ho Hue," performed by Dang Cong Hung (voice and moon lute) and Chen (percussion). Recorded July 1998.

Track 11. "Xa Quang," performed by Dang Cong Hung (voice and moon lute) and Chen (percussion). Recorded July 1998.

Track 12. Three verses of "Phu Binh," performed by Pham Van Ty (voice and moon lute) and Pham Quang Dat (percussion). Recorded June 1997.

Track 13. "Phu Binh 'backbone,'" performed by Dang Cong Hung (voice and moon lute) and Chen (percussion). Recorded July 1998.

Track 14. Three verses of "Phu Binh," performed by Dang Cong Hung (voice and moon lute) and Chen (percussion). Recorded July 1998.

Track 15. One verse of "Phu Binh," performed by Dang Cong Hung (voice and moon lute) and Barley Norton (percussion). Recorded July 1998.

Track 16. Four verses of "Phu Noi," performed by Pham Van Ty (voice and moon lute) and Pham Quang Dat (percussion). Recorded June 1997.

Track 17. "Phu Noi 'backbone,'" performed by Dang Cong Hung (voice and moon lute) and Chen (percussion). Recorded July 1998.

Track 18. Two verses of "Phu Noi," performed by Dang Cong Hung (voice and moon lute) and Chen (percussion). Recorded July 1998.

Track 19. "Suoi Oi," performed by Pham Van Ty (voice and moon lute), Pham Quang Dat (voice and percussion), Trong Kha (voice), Truong Manh Linh (voice), Doan Nhuong (flute). Recorded April 1997.

Track 20. "Mua Dang," performed by Chen (voice and percussion) and Dang Cong Hung (moon lute). Recorded July 1998.

Track 21. "Cac Ban Tien," performed by Pham Van Ty (voice and moon lute) and Pham Quang Dat (percussion). Recorded June 1997.

Track 22. "Don," performed by Dang Cong Hung (voice and moon lute) and Chen (percussion). Recorded July 1998.

Track 23. "Doan Duc Dan's Don," performed by Dang Cong Hung (voice and moon lute) and Chen (percussion). Recorded July 1998.

Track 24. "Cao Mon's Xa" performed by Cao Mon (voice and percussion), Dang Cong Hung (moon lute and percussion), Le Tu Cuong (flute), Nguyen Ngoc Thu (percussion). Recorded July 1997.

Track 25. "Xa Tay Nguyen," performed by Pham Van Ty (voice and moon lute), Nguyen Van Mui (percussion), Nguyen Manh Tien (percussion), Thanh Hoai (voice), Nguyen Thuy Hoa (voice). Recorded April 1998.

Track 26. "Ty Ba Hanh," performed by the Ca Tru Thai Ha Ensemble: Nguyen Thuy Hoa (voice and clappers), Nguyen Manh Tien (*dan day* lute), Nguyen Van Mui (drum). Recorded August 2002.

Track 27. Extract of "Phu Ty Ba," performed by Le Ba Cao (voice and moon lute) and Giam (percussion). Recorded June 1997.

Track 28. "Ly Qua Cau" and "Ly My Hung," performed by Cao Mon (voice and percussion), Dang Cong Hung (moon lute and percussion), Le Tu Cuong (flute), Nguyen Ngoc Thu (percussion). Recorded July 1997.

Songs for the Spirits

Encountering Mediumship

The Phu Giay Festival, 1995

This book explores the music of Vietnamese mediumship. It attempts to convey the aesthetics of mediumship music, *chau van*, and its ritual role. *Chau van* is performed throughout spirit possession rituals, *len dong*, in which a medium is possessed by a succession of spirits.[1] It is music of and for ritual. *Chau van* songs evoke the spirit world and create a sonic environment for possession; they invite the spirits to descend to the human world and describe their formidable power and beauty; they recall the historic deeds of spirits, vividly bringing the past into the present.

I first encountered *chau van* at the Phu Giay festival in spring 1995. At the time, I was in Vietnam studying the chamber music genre *ca tru*. I had heard about mediumship as one *ca tru* piece incorporates some *chau van* songs, but I had yet to witness *len dong* or hear *chau van*. Musicians in Hanoi told me that one of the best places to experience mediumship music was at Phu Giay, a temple complex near the city of Nam Dinh about one hundred kilometers south of Hanoi, which is the site of a famous religious festival held annually in the third lunar month. So on a rainy day in March 1995, I hired a motorbike and headed south down Highway 1, the main road that connects Hanoi to Ho Chi Minh City, toward Nam Dinh.

The motorbike journey was an experience in itself. Persistent drizzle is a feature of spring in northern Vietnam, and the roads were covered with a treacherous film of wet mud. The large fume-billowing trucks that hurtled past at alarming speeds, seemingly with little regard to any other traffic, were an even greater hazard. After once sliding off my bike into the mud from trying to avoid a large hole in the road, I eventually arrived in the city of Nam Dinh and asked directions to Phu Giay from there. I made it to Phu Giay in the late afternoon to find the festival already in full swing.

The Phu Giay site is situated in and around two neighboring hamlets, Van Cat and Tien Huong, about fifteen kilometers from Nam Dinh. It consists of a connected network of spirit temples (*den/phu*), pagodas (*chua*) and communal village houses (*dinh*), and is famous for being home to the mausoleum (*lang*) of the goddess Lieu Hanh. For the festival, normal agrarian life is suspended as religious devotees flock to worship and honor Lieu Hanh and other famous spirits. Streams of festivalgoers take over the hamlets and they process to temples on the network of muddy, winding footpaths and small roads. The hamlets become a hive of commercial activity with stalls lining the thoroughfares selling a wide range of ritual goods, from incense sticks to bootleg cassette tapes of *chau van,* from votive paper offerings to canned drinks. I joined the throng, following the flow of pilgrims up an escarpment on the outskirts of the festival site to the Temple of the Mother of the Mountains and Forests (Den Mau Thuong Ngan). The temple itself was crammed full of people. The center of attention inside was a woman, a medium, dressed in a glittering green dress and ornamented headdress. She was dancing in front of the altar, brandishing two ropes lit on fire in each hand. The altar was a blaze of color. Its lower tiers beneath the brightly painted effigies of three mother goddesses were stacked with an array of offerings: incense, money, flowers, fruit, and canned drinks of Coca-Cola and beer. To the right of the altar against the wall sat two musicians, a man and a woman, both of whom were singing. The man was accompanying himself on the *dan nguyet,* the moon lute. The woman was playing a small set of percussion—a small drum, a bamboo slab, and two small cymbals—with wooden beaters. She played a repetitive groove with heavy accents, and the medium was dancing vigorously to the strong rhythm. I found out years later that because of the infectious dance rhythms, *chau van* has sometimes been called the "rock music of Vietnam" (*nhac roc Viet Nam*). *Chau van* is a vibrant, earthy music with popular appeal. At the Temple of the Mother of the Mountains and Forests, the energy of the crowd was heightened by the band's soaring vocal melodies and heavy, impulsive percussion rhythms. The music and worshippers generated overwhelming enthusiasm and excitement.

Most of the festivalgoers were women, from girls in their teens, wearing jeans and T-shirts, through to elderly women, many of whom wore head scarves and had black-enameled teeth in the traditional style. The crowds around the medium were watching her intently. Some devotees were whispering prayers and kowtowing with incense. After a few minutes, the medium stopped dancing and gave the lit ropes to one of the four assistants sitting around her, who extinguished the flames. A young devotee moved forward from the crowd with her hands clasped in a prayer position. The medium threw a red scarf over the woman's head and balanced a large metal plate stacked with burning incense sticks, sprigs of betel nut, and bank notes on top of it. After waving incense over the metal plate, the medium tossed some old coins, scrutinized how they fell, and then removed the plate and scarf. This procedure was repeated for several other eager festivalgoers, and then the medium sat in front of the central altar. This rite, I later found out, is an "asking rite" (*le khat*) called *doi bat huong*, which literally means "placing bowls of incense on the head." Its purpose is to prepare for initiation into mediumship. If both coins fall on heads within three throws, this indicates that the spirits accept that a devotee is destined to become a medium.

After the asking rite, the medium sat down cross-legged in front of the altar and gave out money and fruit to the crowd. In return, devotees approached the medium to speak to her and to make offerings. After about ten minutes, the medium herself had a red scarf placed over her head by one of the four assistants who sat around her. Her head shook and turned. She raised her arms above her head with six fingers outstretched, a signal that I found out indicated the "number" of the spirit. She then let out an ebullient cry and threw the scarf off her head. The assistants removed the outer layer of her clothes and dressed her in another female costume and headdress, this time colored blue. The ritual continued for over an hour, with each change of clothes followed by a different sequence of ritual actions and dances. Throughout the ritual, the band filled the temple with a continuous flow of music.

The first time I witnessed *len dong*, I knew little about mediumship or the spirits being incarnated, but the ritual atmosphere—the lively music and dance, the colorful ritual dress, the devotion and enthusiasm of the worshippers—was captivating. During my three-day visit to Phu Giay, I saw many *len dong*. Spirit possession was taking place in virtually all the temples I entered, throughout the day and night. The festival also featured numerous large-scale outdoor events. The climax was a huge procession, or *ruoc*, between two of the main festival sites, and other activities were organized in temple yards; these activities included "human chess" (*co nhan*), "dragon dancing" (*mua rong*), and "forming words" (*keo chu*). In this last activity, hundreds of people arranged themselves to form the shapes of Sino-Vietnamese characters.

By recounting my first trip to Phu Giay, I do not mean to present myself as a heroic figure who discovers an obscure ritual found only in remote pockets of rural Vietnam. In rural and urban areas, *len dong* is a popular and long-established way of "serving the spirits" (*hau thanh*), of enacting devotion through the embodied presence of spirits. Spirit possession relies on the miraculous response of the spirits and is sometimes described by devotees as "mysterious" or "mystical" (*huyen bi*), but ritual practice is embedded in everyday concerns. I have begun with Phu Giay in part because the festival was an extremely significant event for me personally. The effervescence of musical and ritual activity drew me into the world of mediumship and led to me returning to Vietnam to study *chau van* and mediumship. Witnessing *len dong* at Phu Giay changed my perception of Vietnamese music, as I had not previously experienced such an intense and excited response to musical performance. As Philip Bohlman's comments in his introductory text on world music, first encounters are "often personal, even intimate experiences, frequently engendering a sudden awareness of local knowledge," and they may "profoundly change what we perceive music to be and how we understand its functions and meanings in the lives of human beings" (2002:1–2). When I first went to a *len dong,* I experienced such a change as I became aware of the importance of musical performance as part of local ritual practice.

The 1995 Phu Giay festival was a significant event for other reasons, quite apart from the impact it had on me. Phu Giay is considered by many mediums to be the most sacred site in Vietnam because of its connections with the goddess Lieu Hanh, and, although I did not realize it at the time, the 1995 festival was a historic moment. This was the first year—after many years of prohibition—that the festival was officially permitted to take place. As well as being my first encounter with *len dong,* it was probably also the first time that many young devotees had been to the festival. When I visited Phu Giay again in 1997 and 1998, I became acquainted with the guardian of one of the main temples. He emphasized that the 1995 festival was a momentous occasion because it was the first time the Ministry of Culture and Information had granted permission for the festival to be held. For three years, from 1995 to 1997, it had been given the status of an "experiment," a trial period before full official endorsement was given in 1998. At least since the 1970s, the festival has been officially prohibited and condemned as superstitious, feudal, and depraved. The 1976 propaganda book *Here! The Real Essence of the Phu Giay Festival* (*Day! Thuc Chat 'Hoi Phu Giay'*) attacks the festival, arguing that it is rife with "many poisons in need of eradication" (Ha Nam Ninh Cultural Service 1976:27). In derisory, anecdotal prose, the book gives examples of how mediums exploit rituals to "sell the spirits" (*buon than ban thanh*) to prey on the ignorance and gullibility of ignorant, uneducated people for financial gain. Despite official condemnation, some mediums covertly disregarded the ban: Phu Giay residents told me that even during the height of the antisuperstition campaign a few small-scale *len dong* were held at night under the cover of darkness, in small temples away from the most prominent festival sites. However, many of the main festivities could not take place. The mass events, such as the procession and the games of "human chess," which ironically were deemed to be less superstitious than spirit possession, could not be organized without an administrative committee under the auspices of the local government.

On Religious and Musical Resurgence

The decision by the Ministry of Culture and Information to restore the Phu Giay festival is a prominent example of the cultural and religious change that has recently swept across Vietnam. In 1986, the Vietnamese Communist Party implemented a reform or renovation policy, known as *doi moi*. Following in the wake of similar reforms in China in the early 1980s, the liberalization of the socialist command economy, which was struggling badly in the late 1970s and early 1980s, was the main priority of *doi moi*. Alongside economic reform, however, Vietnam's cultural landscape has also undergone a process of transformation. In tandem with the introduction of the market economy and increasing openness to international influence and trade, there has been a resurgence of religiosity and prerevolutionary cultural activities in late socialist Vietnam.

The Vietnamese authorities have found it difficult to respond to the groundswell of religious activity. While the outpouring of religiosity stems from the adjustment and liberalization of state polices, the Party has continued its efforts to shape cultural and religious affairs. Contradictions and tensions continue to exist between official policies and practices at the local level, and these were very much in evidence at Phu Giay. The Party's policy to eliminate "backward" and "superstitious" aspects of the festival was, at least nominally, still in evidence during the three "experimental" years from 1995 to 1997. During these years, banners urging people to "eradicate superstition" (*xoa bo me tin di doan*) were prominently placed at the festival site, despite the fact that *len dong* rituals, which were one of the main targets of the antisuperstition campaign, were taking place in virtually every temple. The seemingly incongruous reiteration of antisuperstition slogans at the festival was part of the Party's continuing attempt to moderate the activities of mediums and other festivalgoers. However, in the reform era the antisuperstition policy has not been vigorously enforced, and it has gradually been overshadowed by a rising tide of cultural nationalism. The preservation and exaltation of "culture" (*van hoa*) as a means of bolstering "nation identity" (*ban sac dan toc*) has become a pervasive institutionalized mantra. The Phu Giay festival, for instance, once derided as a hotbed where corruption and superstition flourished, has been described by the folklore scholar Thang Ngoc Pho (1992:62) as "a rich, profound and unique folk culture activity . . . [that] contributes to the abundance of national culture." Such arguments praising the cultural value of Phu Giay have effected a transition from "superstition" to "culture," and this change was publicly declared at the festival after the three-year experiment. At the 1998 festival, the antisuperstition banners were replaced with cultural nationalist slogans like "promote and develop the cultural character of the nation" (*phat huy va phat trien ban sac van hoa dan toc*), thus signaling an important shift in the government's approach to culture and religion.

The resurgence of ritual activity has not gone unnoticed by commentators from within and outside Vietnam. The publication in Vietnam of numerous books, popular introductory works, and newspaper and magazine articles on religious philosophies, festivals, and customs since the early 1990s has responded to, and fueled, national and local interest in culture and religion. Scholarly work on mediumship has been led by researchers at the Folk Culture Institute (Vien Van Hoa Dan Gian) in Hanoi, under the direction of the head of the institute, Ngo Duc Thinh. Since the early 1990s, the institute has held conferences relating to the spirits incarnated during *len dong* and published several volumes on mediumship (Ngo Duc Thinh 1992; 1996a; 1996b; 2004). Given that institutions are part of the state apparatus, the work of the Folk Culture Institute has been influential in changing official attitudes toward mediumship. In the early 1990s, researchers at the institute worked hard to overcome opposition from censorious officials in the Ministry of Culture and Information. They argued that *len dong* and *chau van* should be respected and were legitimate topics for study because they were "phenomena of the collective folk culture" (*hien tuong van hoa dan gian tong the*) and "religious-cultural activities of the community" (*sinh hoat tin nguong-van hoa cong dong*) (Ngo Duc Thinh 1992; 1996a). These statements are carefully worded to promote a view of mediumship as culture. The religious dimension of mediumship is not denied entirely, but religious beliefs are linked to culture and are accorded cultural value because of their ancient folk roots. In an evolutionary schema, the religious system of mediumship—commonly referred to as the Mother Religion (Dao Mau) or the Four Palace Religion (Dao Tu Phu)—is said to have evolved from "primitive religious beliefs" (*tin nguong nguyen thuy*) (Ngo Duc Thinh 1996a: 312). The view of mediumship as a survival of ancient folk beliefs has been marshaled in support of arguments that indigenous cultural values and practices, which are increasingly perceived by cultural nationalists as being eroded by the forces of globalization and growing international influences, need to be preserved.

This book is the first ethnomusicological study of *len dong* and *chau van*. It is also the first in-depth study by a non-Vietnamese scholar of mediumship in Vietnam since Maurice Durand's 1959 book *Technique et Panthéon des Médiums Viêtnamiens*.[2] The foreign anthropologists who conducted fieldwork in the early years of the reform era have paid attention to various ritual practices, but discussion of mediumship is notably absent. This omission is mainly due to the difficulties of gaining access to the world of mediumship. In the early years of the *doi moi* period, when Vietnamese folklorists were starting to document mediumship, *len dong* rituals were still off-limits for scholars from outside Vietnam. Because of the political sensitivity of mediumship, it was not possible for foreign researchers to attend *len dong* in the early 1990s (pers. comm., Shaun Malarney 1998). By the mid-1990s, however, when I began field research on mediumship, restrictions on foreign researchers were becoming less rigid and I was able to attend *len dong* and spend time with mediums and ritual musicians. This general increase in access did not mean that difficulties did not arise. My attempts to obtain a research visa through an institute in Hanoi prior to going to Vietnam in 1996 were met with the suggestion that I was not permitted to research mediumship and I would have to change my topic. Undeterred, I took the option of enrolling as a language student at the Center for Research of International Culture at the Vietnam National University. This gave me the opportunity to further my language skills while remaining free to pursue my research interests independently, without direct institutional support or intervention.

Anthropological research on the intensification and resurgence of ritual and religious practices other than mediumship has investigated the changing dynamics between government policies and local practices. This includes accounts of rituals including weddings, funerary rites, and communal house rites in northern villages (Malarney 2002, 2003; Endres 2001; Kleinen 1999), Buddhism in urban Hanoi (Soucy 1999), and religious pilgrimage and female spirit worship in southern Vietnam (Taylor 2004). This body of research illuminates aspects of cultural and ritual transformation during the colonial, socialist, and late socialist eras. It documents the impact of war and revolutionary communist ideology on ritual life and attempts to unravel the complex social, economic, and political factors that have led to the revival, reconfiguration, and restructuring of prerevolutionary practices. The histories of different ritual practices exhibit some broad similarities, but the pattern of revival is not uniform. As Vietnamese strive for and adapt to economic and cultural development, some prerevolutionary rituals are left redundant, while others are being revived or reinvented to suit new aims and purposes.

Like religious practices, music and the other arts are being invested with renewed interest and vitality. The high demand for bands to perform at *len dong* has led to a *chau van* boom, and other musical traditions, such as *ca tru*, imperial court music (*nhac cung dinh*), and *quan ho* folk song, are gaining more national and international attention. The state-run music troupes specializing in water puppetry (*mua roi nuoc*) and the music-theater forms *cheo, tuong,* and *cai luong* have suffered declining audiences over many years, yet they are attempting to find new ways to promote and market their performances to domestic as well as tourist audiences. State-employed musicians, who can barely survive on their small state salaries, often diversify so they can carry out freelance work. Such work includes performing at *len dong:* some musicians from music-theater troupes can be found in the ranks of *chau van* bands.

Little ethnomusicological research has been done in Vietnam, so knowledge of contemporary Vietnamese music culture in the wider world is limited. In general, Vietnamese music is known primarily through the work of Vietnamese musicians and scholars living overseas (e.g., Tran Van Khe 1962, 1975; Pham Duy 1975; Nguyen Thuyet Phong 1998; Le Tuan Hung 1998). Nguyen Thuyet Phong has done much to raise awareness of Vietnamese music in America, and he founded *Nhac Viet: The Journal of Vietnamese Music,* which was published from 1992 to 1997. The small amount of research on Vietnamese music by non-Vietnamese scholars includes Adelaida Reyes's book on music and the Vietnamese refugee experience (1999), Miranda Arana's thesis on neotraditional music and the conservatoire system (1999), and Jason Gibbs's writing on popular music (2004). In Vietnam, musicologists have documented various aspects of Vietnamese music culture, yet there is little writing on *chau van,* mainly because it was not seen as a legitimate topic for research until recently.[3] In the reform era, however, the work done by researchers at the Folk Culture Institute has been supplemented by two other books on *chau van:* one that consists of transcriptions and analysis of songs (Thanh Ha 1996), and a second that focuses on the history of *chau van* in Ha Nam and Nam Dinh provinces south of Hanoi (Bui Dinh Thao and Nguyen Quang Hai 1996).

On Fieldwork and Representation: The Documentary
A Westerner Loves Our Music

> In principle, a foreigner is always a spy. Even a socialist . . . or even you.
> We live in constant suspicion . . . There is no mutual trust.
>
> —Ly, thirty-seven-year-old employee, Vietnam 1982, in *Surname Viet Given
> Name Nam* (Trinh T. Minh-Ha 1989)

In Trinh T. Minh-Ha's provocative film *Surname Viet Given Name Nam*, women from northern, central, and southern Vietnam speak of their hardships and struggles and the climate of suspicion in the aftermath of war. Although much has changed in Vietnam since the early 1980s, the endemic suspicion of which Ly speaks did not evaporate overnight. Shaun Malarney, one of the first American anthropologists to go to Vietnam in the early 1990s, was suspected by officials of spying for the American government. Just a few years before Malarney's field research in the Thinh Liet commune, just south of Hanoi, anyone talking to a foreigner would have faced police interrogation, and there were reports of "young people throwing rocks at foreigners" (Malarney 2002:xiv).

When I started to do field research in Vietnam in the mid-1990s, it was hard to imagine such hostility. In general, ritual participants were extremely generous and welcoming, talked openly about mediumship, and invited me to rituals. Nonetheless, my presence was not always welcomed. Some mediums were wary of my interest in *len dong* and would not invite me to rituals or talk about their activities, on the grounds that my presence would stir up problems with the local authorities. Rituals were conducted with an air of secrecy, as if they were an illegal underground activity. When I was invited to attend rituals, I was often quickly ushered into the confines of the temple to ensure my presence was covert, and any contact with the local authorities or police was usually avoided. Not least because of the political sensitivities of mediumship, the personal relationships I developed with mediums and musicians were crucial. It was only after months of studying *chau van* and spending time drinking tea, smoking, chatting, and visiting the temples of mediums that feelings of mutual trust were forged. In an attempt to ensure that my presence did not create problems for my hosts, I tried to be as unobtrusive as possible and was not accompanied by an "assistant" from a research institution. I wanted to engage with local activity and avoid becoming ensnared in official bureaucracy. Apart from on a few occasions when official letters of introduction from the Folk Culture Institute were necessary for longer trips in rural areas, I avoided the long bureaucratic procedures required when dealing with state-run cultural bureaus and organizations. Hanoi, where I was based, has a thriving mediumship scene, and once I had established acquaintances and friendships with prominent musicians and mediums, I found that I was most often welcomed into their circles. I attended numerous *len dong* in Hanoi and the surrounding area, and I also made frequent trips to provinces in northern Vietnam, such as Ha Tay, Ha Nam, Nam Dinh, and Ha Bac. These trips enabled me to compare mediumship practices in rural and urban areas and to visit famous temples and festivals in the countryside. Mediumship practices are more prevalent in northern Vietnam than in the rest of the country, and this book focuses on the main *chau van* tradition from the north.[4]

Trinh T. Minh-Ha's films and writing are a powerful critique of representation, spectatorship, and meaning. Her work takes anthropological discourse to task, laying bare its fascination with the Other, marginality, and authenticity, and demonstrating how it is grounded in a "totalizing quest for meaning" and an "all-owning spectatorship" (Trinh T. Minh-Ha 1991; 1992). Trinh T. Minh-Ha's critique engages with the poststructuralist reappraisal of fieldwork methodology and ethnographic representation, which has problematized the writing of culture. This reappraisal has raised difficult questions relating to authority and cultural translation, the authorial voice and self-reflexivity, subjectivity and intersubjectivity, and the ethics, politics, and power dynamics of field research (e.g., Clifford and Marcus 1986; Fabian 1990; Barz and Cooley 1997). Anxious theorizing about cultural difference and the representation of the Other has decentered the omnipotent, authorial voice of scholars from the West writing about distant places and cultures. Reflexivity has gone some way toward addressing important methodological and ethical issues, yet the notion of "giving voice" to the Other is problematic because it may cover up or reinforce, rather than disrupt, entrenched power asymmetries.[5]

Throughout the long process of researching, writing, and rewriting this book, which has spanned a decade, I have grappled with how to translate fieldwork experience into written form. My aim is to evoke the lived experience of ritual participants—mediums, musicians, and disciples—through a narrative ethnography that "invites the reader to share, imaginatively, in the experiences that are represented" (Titon 1997:96). It is not a text through which a totalizing view of the meaning of mediumship can be comprehended. Rather, it is a partial account based on my own limited experiences of "being there"—for a period of more than two years over six separate visits in 1994, 1995, 1996–97, 1998, 2002, and 2004–05—and I repeatedly return to fieldwork experience. By making clear how understandings arose from specific performance events, music making, and discussions and interactions, I have tried to bring to the fore the intersubjective, experiential moments on which reflections and interpretations are grounded. The DVD accompanying this book, which features video and musical examples, encourages a sharing of musical and ritual experience. The Ritual Songscapes section of the DVD consists of video clips of two rituals. The progression of possession is outlined in a table form, though the reader may explore and compare the embedded video extracts in a nonlinear way.

Although I emphasize intersubjectivity, dialogue, and reciprocity in this study, this does not dissolve issues of power and authority. It is often assumed that it is the sole prerogative of the Western researcher to represent the Other or alternatively to *give* the Other the means to self-represent. During field research, it became clear that I was not the only person invested with the authority to represent. Writings on mediumship and *chau van* by Vietnamese scholars, journalists, and cultural officials, as well as recordings by musicians released on cassettes, CDs, and the increasingly popular VCDs (video compact discs), have undoubtedly had a greater impact on domestic perceptions and attitudes toward *len dong* than my own research. The majority of ritual participants do not publish articles and books, yet mediumship itself is not immune from interpretations by Vietnamese commentators and ritual participants as, for example, a "symbol" (*bieu tuong*) of Vietnameseness, national identity, folk culture, and history. The enactment of mediumship is increasingly taking on an aura of representation, as evidenced by the considerable numbers of mediums who now video their rituals for domestic viewing. Most of these videos consist of raw footage of *len dong*, though some local video companies are now editing and "packaging" ritual performances as a commodity.

Self-reflective writing on fieldwork and ethnography has for the most part addressed how "we" represent "the Other." I would like to turn this formulation on its head by considering Vietnamese representations of "my" field research. My interest in Vietnamese music and culture was the focus of a few articles in the national press and in programs on the Voice of Vietnam Radio (Dai Tieng Noi Viet Nam) and Vietnamese Television (VTV), as well as, of course, being a topic of discussion among those with whom I worked. This was a salutary reminder that my research was being observed and recorded. Here I will discuss two video representations of my research. The first relates to a video recording organized by a temple medium at Phu Giay and the second to a thirty-five-minute documentary made about my research by VTV called *A Westerner Loves Our Music* (*Nguoi Tay Me Nhac Ta*).

During my visit to Phu Giay in July 1998, I stayed with a temple medium, Duc, who presided over one of the main temples, Phu Tien Huong. On the second afternoon of my stay I returned to Phu Tien Huong, after a day of meeting mediums and musicians in the village, to find that Duc had arranged for a local video company to film me performing *chau van*. The cameraman was ready to start, and I was hastily given a moon lute and asked to sing. I was exhausted and somewhat anxious that my performances would disappoint, but I dutifully performed several *chau van* songs for the camera. My teacher Pham Van Ty, who helped me arrange the trip, accompanied me on percussion, and one of Duc's sons played the bamboo flute, or *sao*. Before the performance, Duc said some words of introduction. He started by stating that Phu Giay was "the root" of the Mother Religion, was a place where everyone could come and worship the mother goddesses, and was a center for *chau van* and "national culture" (*van hoa dan toc*). *Chau van*, Duc continued, had spread to many countries in the world, and, because of its international renown, Ty and myself had come to conduct research at Phu Giay. He concluded, "Barley has studied *chau van* and knows some songs. So today, I have requested the artist Ty and Barley to 'offer literature' (*dang van*) in front of the altar of the Mother spirits. We thank you in advance for your efforts regarding *chau van*, and your singing today will let other people here know your admiration for the Mothers, Phu Giay, and *chau van*." My presence is therefore recorded as evidence of the international renown of Phu Giay and as a celebration and confirmation of its rich cultural heritage. The next day, the finished edited tape was delivered, and Duc's family and friends huddled into his reception room, in his living quarters behind the temple, to watch it.

The aesthetics of the video were, for me, much more interesting than hearing again my performances. The video was complete with titles, and numerous shots of the temple were added before and during the performance as cutaway scenes. The editors used all sorts of effects—split- and multiscreen and animation effects—on the footage of the temple architecture and of the pond and water lilies in the temple yard. These effects were presumably added to make the images more visually appealing. For me, the images had an almost psychedelic, otherworldly quality, yet the viewers of the video in Duc's reception room approved of the visual effects: Duc's wife said they made the temple look more magnificent and beautiful.

The professionally made VTV documentary, though it has a much more elaborate and complex narrative than the Phu Giay video, shares a fascination with the novelty of a foreigner learning traditional music. One of the questions the documentary tries to answer is, Why is this Westerner—who is described at one point as "the student with white skin, blue eyes and a hooked nose"— interested in Vietnamese music? From the outset, the voiceover portrays my interest in Vietnamese music as a fated quest for the "soul" (*hon*) of traditional music and, by extension, the soul of the Vietnamese people and nation.

The filming was done over seven days in May and June 1998. This short period of filming militated against showing the "natural" unfolding of research in progress. The scenes of "fieldwork" in the documentary—which included me learning *chau van;* performing *ca tru;* paying respects to one of my old *ca tru* teachers, Chu Van Du, who died after my first visit in 1994; and riding my old Russian-made Minsk motorbike out to the countryside to visit mediums and musicians—aimed to reconstruct the kinds of activities I had been involved in. The filming was done in locations in and outside Hanoi where I had spent much time, and the scenes featured some of the people I had worked with since my first visit to Vietnam in 1994. On my return to London in July 1998, Kim Huong asked me to shoot some scenes there. The video footage in London—which was shot by a filmmaker friend, Laurent Van Lancker—was used at the beginning and end of the documentary to give a sense of my passage from the UK to Vietnam and back again. I also sent Kim Huong an electronic music track that I produced with the London-based band Fructose. The track mixed a part I played on the three-stringed lute used in *ca tru*—the *dan day*—with electronic sounds and "drum 'n' bass" rhythms.[6] Kim Huong used the track as incidental music during the film and for the final credits. After the filming was done, I had no further input in the editing or postproduction of the documentary.

The director, Kim Huong, was well versed in approaches to ethnographic filmmaking. Before making the film, we discussed the use of voiceover and filming techniques, such as the sequence shot and issues including reflexivity and dialogue (see Baily 1989 for further discussion of ethnographic film styles). Kim Huong was keen to give me a "voice" to describe my motivations, aims, and methods. So I was interviewed in Vietnamese at the VTV studios, and extracts of the interview (with the questions edited out) were used throughout the documentary. Just as the quotes of mediums and musicians in this study are edited, interpreted, and reflected upon, so are my own comments in the documentary. Kim Huong uses my remarks, along with her own voiceover narration, to construct a narrative. Although I had discussed with Kim Huong more experimental documentary techniques that play with linear narrative, and foreground dialogue and the sensuous, evocative potential of the moving image, *A Westerner Loves Our Music* follows a fairly conventional narrative framed by my remarks and Kim Huong's voiceover. Importantly, there are only a few points in the documentary where musicians and others are given a chance to comment.

A *Westerner Loves Our Music* is fascinating for the way in which it mediates several agendas. As Felicia Hughes-Freeland has remarked in relation to Indonesian cultural documentation, "it is necessary . . . to know who is wielding the camera, on whose authority and to what end" (1992:244). The filmmakers were an elite group of Hanoians, mostly unfamiliar with mediumship, and although the director, editor, and cameraman had some measure of control over what was included, they were ultimately subject to the authority of the Ministry of Culture and Information and the censors at VTV, who vet all television productions.

In the documentary I am sometimes cast in the classic mold of observer and data collector through scenes where I am seen filming performances and editing recordings in a high-tech music studio. In the interview I did not discuss observing or data gathering. Instead, I emphasized practice and participation. This was something that the documentary-makers were keen to convey, as they saw this as a distinctive feature of my fieldwork method that was not common for Vietnamese researchers. The voice states explicitly: "He [BN] thinks that to understand what is interesting, beautiful, and soulful about *ca tru* you must directly participate." This statement is followed by shots of me playing the *dan day* lute with the *ca tru* singer Thuy Hoa and the drummer Nguyen Van Mui, and later I am also shown chatting with, and learning from, two *chau van* musicians, Dang Cong Hung and Le Ba Cao, who are profiled in Chapter 3. In a scene of a practical lesson with Dang Cong Hung, he explains one of the main *chau van* rhythms, the "two-beat rhythm" (*nhip doi*): "The last strikes of the cymbal are the most important. Wherever you go you must return for these two strikes, so that it fits the rhythmic pattern. That is a principle you must grasp to play *chau van*. If you do not grasp this, then you don't understand the rhythm and you will fall outside of the beat." Hung is later shown demonstrating a song, "Phu Dau", with me accompanying him on percussion with the two-beat rhythm. After Hung's rendition, I play the moon lute and sing the same piece. In the scene with Le Ba Cao, he discusses the relationship between *ca tru* and *chau van* and performs a *chau van* song called "Phu Ty Ba," which is closely related to the *ca tru* piece "Ty Ba Hanh."

Apart from the comments by Hung and Cao, other people featured in the film are not shown speaking about their ritual activities. This was partly because of censorship. Kim Huong knew that scenes of spirit possession would not be permitted by the VTV censors, and she had to be very careful about how the ritual context was mentioned. Although I am shown going to a temple and filming a *len dong*, all shots of the possessed medium are edited out.

The disparity between the state-approved narrative of the documentary and my interaction with followers of mediumship was much in evidence in one scene in which I am seen meeting a medium, Doan, and drinking tea in her house. While the camera was rolling I asked Doan about whether spirit possession was "superstitious" and therefore should be prohibited, or whether it was based on legitimate "folk beliefs." In the documentary, this live conversation is dubbed over the following voiceover:

> He [BN] has met Doan, who lives in Thuong Thin, many times . . . She follows the religious beliefs of the Four Palaces, a belief system of the Vietnamese people that has existed for a long time. Some of the spirits revered as part of this belief system were normal people who did good work for the people and the nation, and after they died they were venerated as spirits . . . On these trips Barley Norton furthers his understanding of the "soul" of the Vietnamese people and the role of *chau van* in "folk culture."

The voiceover's description of the Four Palace Religion makes no mention of mediums or spirit possession. Instead, it is depicted as an age-old belief system, and spirits are depicted as national heroes. This description reiterates the legitimating discourse of Vietnamese folklore scholars. That *len dong* and the Four Palace Religion are mentioned at all, however, is evidence of the liberalization of official policy on mediumship.

Although Kim Huong could not include scenes of spirit possession in the documentary, to give an impression of the ritual she included footage of folklorized reenactments of *len dong* performed on the stage by professional theater performers. Such folklorized versions of *len dong*, which were first devised and performed in the early 1990s, indicate a significant change to government policy, as all references to mediumship were previously banned. The footage of folklorized *len dong* used in the documentary is taken from a tour by Vietnamese performers to the UK in April 1998. The tour featured performances of *ca tru* by the Ca Tru Thai Ha Ensemble and *chau van* by Pham Van Ty with the *cheo* artist Van Quyen performing the role of the "medium." The tour was organized by the UK-based arts organization Asian Music Circuit (AMC), and I worked on it as the concert programmer and interpreter.

Toward the end of the documentary, a clip is included of an interview with the then vice minister of culture and information, Nguyen Trung Kien, who was present at the AMC concert held at the Purcell Room in London. He expressed his support for the event by remarking, "Many of the audience told me afterwards that it was an extremely precious occasion and that it helped them understand more about the Vietnamese nation and people." In this cultural nationalist framework, the primary purpose of traditional music is to promote national identity. In the final words of the voiceover at the end of the documentary, I am also implicated in the development of Vietnamese culture:

> Is there anything strange about this story about a Westerner? Yes. The strange thing is that unintentionally or not, through his research of Vietnamese national and traditional music, Barley Norton has helped us with something we ought to do, that is to "see" Vietnamese culture and to develop our national identity.

In her theorizing on "Third Cinema," Trinh T. Minh-Ha writes: "The moment the insider steps out from the inside, she is no longer a mere insider (and vice versa). She necessarily looks in from the outside while also looking out from the inside" (1991:73). Filming an outsider taking tentative steps to the inside, the VTV documentarymakers were looking in from the outside and reassessing the inside. Although they knew little of mediumship before making the film, they were of the opinion that more respect should be paid to folk music and religious traditions. This respectful view of tradition among the cultural elite in urban areas has been influential in the rethinking of state policy in the reform era. The double turning back where I ponder Vietnamese representations of my research could be interpreted as yet another form of what Trinh T. Minh-Ha calls "all-owning spectatorship." Yet my motive for discussing *A Westerner Loves Our Music* is not to reclaim authority over representation, but rather to problematize this fieldwork study and to critically acknowledge the unpredictable consequences of a Westerner experiencing "our" music.

Music and Mediums in Modern Vietnam

This book discusses the multilayered historical processes that have shaped and been shaped by ritual and music. It emphasizes how ideologies of modernity, which resurfaced in different guises time and again in Vietnamese discourse in the twentieth century, have interacted with *len dong* and *chau van*. Narratives of modernity are plural, mythical, and contested (Comaroff and Comaroff 1993), and in this work modernity is understood, following Taylor (2001), as an "imagined condition" or "subjective reality" in relation to which Vietnamese have, at different times and in different ways, objectified themselves. The history of mediumship tells us much about broader processes of social, cultural, and political change. It provides a fascinating insight into the social tensions and crises of identity that have arisen in modern Vietnam, not least because of the frequency with which mediumship practices have been viewed as incommensurable with modern ideals and values.

Chapter 1, "Mediumship, Modernity, and Cultural Identity," provides the backdrop for the rest of the book by tracing the history of *len dong* and *chau van* from prerevolutionary times, through the rise of communism and the long periods of war since the 1940s, to the current reform era. The persistent attacks on mediumship in different historical periods are indicative of its perceived threat to centralized, rationalized systems of power, and its resurgence can be seen in part as a response to the social, economic, and cultural contradictions and uncertainties that have arisen with the introduction of the market economy and globalization.

Alongside ritual practices, music and the other performing arts have been subjected to processes of modernization, perhaps most dramatically during the communist-led cultural revolution. Chapter 1 outlines the transformation of musical forms and traditional teaching methods in northern Vietnam since the mid-twentieth century. Revolutionary socialist ideology has had a profound impact on musical expression and pedagogical methods. The aim of forging a modern, socialist music culture, which would contribute to the project of nation building and the war effort, led to the creation of "revolutionary" versions of traditional genres and a neotraditional music genre called "modern national music" (*nhac dan toc hien dai*). The analyses of "revolutionary *chau van*" and neotraditional compositions that incorporate traces of *chau van* melodies in Chapter 1 serve as case studies that illustrate the communist-inspired appropriations and adaptations of traditional music.

At the heart of this study are an investigation of the phenomenon of spirit possession and the multifaceted relationship between musical and ritual performance. The importance of music as a primary medium through which spirit possession is experienced has been examined by ethnomusicologists in various ritual contexts in other parts of the world (e.g., Roseman 1991; Friedson 1996; Emoff 2002). I share with this research a concern with musical poetics and experience as part of distinctive, ritualized modes of behavior and ways of being in the world. I am also interested in the performative processes of musical creativity and "musical interaction" (Brinner 1995). Hence this book explores the ritual role of *chau van* from several perspectives: it examines the significance of sound for possession, the interrelationships between the *chau van* musical system and ritual practice, the interaction between musicians and mediums, and the creativity of music performance.

An appreciation of the experience of spirit possession and the religious system of mediumship is crucial for understanding the role of musical performance in ritual practice. Informed by phenomenological approaches to being and embodiment, Chapter 2, "Experiencing Spirit Possession," considers the bodily changes reported by possessees. Sensory experiences of possession are conceptualized in terms of "somatic modes of attention" (Csordas 2002). Possession during *len dong* is understood as an "aware" (*tinh tao*) state involving distinctive modes of bodily engagement with the spirits and ways of relating to other ritual participants. Chapter 2 also examines why and how individuals become mediums and the identities of spirits incarnated during *len dong*.

The second chapter provides the necessary background for the elaboration on music and ritual that follows. Chapter 3, "Songs for the Spirits," lays out the particularities of ritual music through a detailed examination of the incarnation of four spirits at two rituals. The video extracts from these two rituals included on the DVD facilitate analysis of the musical interaction within *chau van* bands and between band members and mediums, and the aesthetic choices made in the course of performance. Chapter 3 delineates the distinctive song sequences—or "songscapes"—performed for incarnated spirits and the correlation between songs and ritual actions. I have coined the term *songscape* to evoke the idea that bands create a unique, multipart sonic entity for each spirit. A songscape manifests the incarnation of a spirit in sound; it reflects the identity and ritual actions of the embodied spirit.

Having established how songscapes are created, Chapter 4, "The Musical Construction of the Spirits," investigates the transformative power of *chau van*. It highlights the multiple effects of *chau van* performance through the different stages of possession and how the presence of spirits is manifested in song. I propose that the musical evocation of the identities of spirits is central to *chau van*'s ritual role and reflect upon the ways in which the musical articulation of divine identities relates to dominant conceptions of ethnicity, place, and gender.

Musical performance during *len dong* is a creative process, and performance practices are continually evolving. Within the conventions of the *chau van* musical system, ritual musicians respond to and affect the flow of rituals. Not only do they make decisions about which songs to perform at different stages of possession, they also freely arrange the poems dedicated to the spirits to different songs so that sung text matches ritual action. To narrate ritual progression in song, musicians must be highly skilled at setting poems to different melodies. *Chau van* songs, which are commonly referred to as "ways" (*loi*), have a fluid quality. Songs are realized differently in each performance, but each rendition must conform to the underlying melodic shape of the song, "the way." This aspect of musical performance was brought home to me through my own attempts to learn *chau van*. In a scene from *A Westerner Loves Our Music*, in which I am seen having a lesson with Dang Cong Hung, he explains the challenges of learning *chau van*:

> Our traditional music has a particular characteristic that is difficult because, all the old musicians, when they play and sing something and then do it again, it is completely different the second time. So it is very difficult to teach and to study. You can only teach the "backbone" (*xuong song*), that is, the main part; small details you can't teach.

The flexibility inherent in performances of traditional music, described by Hung, is taken up in the fifth chapter, "Musical Creativity and Change." Through analysis of multiple versions of songs, Chapter 5 examines the melodic identity of "ways" and the processes of musical creativity involved in their realization. It considers Hung's notion of "backbone"—which is a type of "implicit melody" (Perlman 2004)—as an aspect of the metaphorical thinking musicians employ to guide their performances. In addition to the creative processes involved in the performance of songs, creativity and innovation are also evident at the level of changes to the *chau van* repertoire and performance practice. Following the detailed analysis of vocal melodies, Chapter 5 addresses the processes of musical change that are influencing *chau van* tradition within the context of broader social, cultural, and political change.

Issues of gender are developed in the sixth chapter, "Engendering Mediumship," which situates the musical construction of gender and transgendering possession within discourse on gender relations and sexuality in Vietnamese society. Drawing on theories of gender performativity, I argue that mediumship is a site in which gender identities are performed, contested, and negotiated. By demonstrating the ways in which ritual practices affect mediums' identities in their everyday lives, I hope to show the importance of mediumship for understanding gender roles in Vietnamese society. The chapter concludes with a discussion of how mediumship, and in particular the sexual identity of male mediums, figures in emergent public debate about homosexuality.

The seventh chapter, "Ritual and Folklorization in Late Socialist Vietnam," considers the resurgence of mediumship in relation to the market economy and the folklorization of *len dong* in the reform era. The *len dong* boom in many ways signals a return to prerevolutionary ritual practices, but rituals have become more opulent as levels of prosperity have increased and the creation of folklorized versions of *len dong* promotes a secular view of spirit possession as national culture, as a form of theatrical entertainment for Vietnamese and foreign audiences. Chapter 7 outlines the economic aspects of ritualizing and the re-presentation of mediumship as folklore, which has led to a questioning and blurring of the boundaries between "theater" and "ritual," between theatrical and spiritual performance. I contend that mediumship has maintained its popular appeal and social relevance in late socialist Vietnam because it is a flexible religious system that enables contemporary concerns, anxieties, and aspirations to be expressed and mediated, while at the same time maintaining a sense of connection and continuity with the past.

The Epilogue concludes with an account of a "thanking ritual" (*le ta*), which was held by a medium, Doan, on my behalf to thank the spirits for overseeing my studies. This ritual was the last I attended before leaving the field. As this book is devoted to describing and reflecting upon spirit possession, it seems appropriate that it should close with discussion of a ritual that expressed gratitude to the spirits.

1

Mediumship, Modernity, and Cultural Identity

This chapter provides a historical perspective on mediumship and its music from the colonial period through the cultural revolution to the reform era. The history of mediumship is marked by resilience, despite continued criticism in the name of modernity and progress. Modernity, as "an imaginary construction of the present in terms of the mythic past" (Comaroff and Comaroff 1993:xiv), has often been defined in opposition to "tradition" and "ritual," and this is also the case in Vietnam. In colonial and postcolonial times, ideologies of modernity, whether colonial, nationalist, or socialist, have been employed as the primary justification for the condemnation of mediums' activities and ritual music. The various forms of religious resurgence that have swept across Vietnam as well as other parts of Asia in recent years have overturned the Weberian assumption that modernization inevitably leads to secularization (Keyes, Kendall, and Hardacre 1994). Since the implementation of the Renovation policy (*doi moi*) in 1986, mediumship has gained a measure of legitimacy as it has become increasingly wedded to the construction of Vietnamese cultural identity and the continuing project of nation building. No longer antithetical to the modern or in need of reform, "tradition" is now being used to bolster national identity, which many cultural nationalists consider to be threatened by the forces of globalization.

The history of spirit practices and ritual music is a barometer of social, cultural, and political change in modern Vietnam. Throughout its history, mediumship has been a contested site in which ideas about cultural identity and gender relations, among other things, have been asserted, negotiated, and transformed. The fact that mediumship has repeatedly been subject to hegemonic forms of control is a measure of its potency as a cultural force. This chapter outlines the strategies employed to discipline and prohibit mediumship and the multiple ways in which these strategies have affected ritual practices. It is observed that official policy, while ultimately unsuccessful in entirely eliminating *len dong* rituals from Vietnamese cultural life, has interacted with the views and practices of adepts of mediumship and has, since the late 1980s, been reinterpreted in the light of a nationalist and culturalist discourse that legitimates mediumship as "folk culture."

In the context of the Vietnamese Communist Party's attempts to comprehensively overhaul and modify Vietnamese musical practices, *chau van* as performed during *len dong* rituals was prohibited, but decontextualized traces of *chau van* lingered in Party-approved public culture. To conform to socialist ideology, *chau van* was refashioned as revolutionary song, and its traces were incorporated into neotraditional compositions. The discussion of the political transformation of music in this chapter is oriented around *chau van* and is not meant to be comprehensive. Nonetheless, it does give an impression of how musical practices have been influenced by the cultural revolution. Following an analysis of neotraditional music, I consider the reasons why composers in Vietnam, as in other parts of the communist world, strove to combine Western forms and harmonies with indigenous material. Drawing on Peter Manuel's discussion of modernity and musical structure (Manuel 2002), I also assess the extent to which the form and structure of neotraditional compositions is congruent with the social structures of revolutionary communist society.

Mediumship and Music in Prerevolutionary Vietnam

Spirit possession, and its suppression, has a long history in Vietnam. Influenced by evolutionary models, the French anthropologist Maurice Durand argues that mediumship is a survival of a primitive, archaic form of shamanism (1959). More recently, contemporary Vietnamese folklorists have also sought ancient origins for spirit worship. The prominence of female spirits in the pantheon encourages a reading of female spirit possession as a vestige of the matriarchal system, which some claim existed prior to Confucian influence and was never fully eradicated (Ngo Duc Thinh 1996a). The goddess Lieu Hanh, one of the Four Immortals (Tu Bat Tu), who resides at the top of the pantheon as the First Mother, is thought to have been worshipped at least since the sixteenth century. The goddess has remained a popular focus of devotion, and her tomb at Phu Giay is a site of mass pilgrimage. Doan

Thi Diem's novel about Lieu Hanh written in the 1730s, *The Story of the Van Cat Goddess,* forms the basis for many oral legends about Lieu Hanh. Olga Dror's careful reading of this novel argues that the author used Lieu Hanh's story to articulate her own aspirations for women's development and emancipation (Dror 2002:76).

The positioning of local female spirit possession in opposition to centralized Confucian patriarchy is a recurrent theme in the history of mediumship. Regulatory systems emanating from the courts, the sixteenth-century Le code and the nineteenth-century Gia Long code, outlawed the practices of Taoist priests and mediums involving possession and magic. In the reign of King Gia Long (1802–20), severe punishment was prescribed for those involved in mediumship, including *chau van* musicians. Quoting a chronicle from Gia Long's time, Dong Vinh notes, "According to Dai Nam Thuc Luc Chinh Bien (Veracious Chronicles of Vietnam): 'Sorcerers, liturgical singers (*cung van*) and mediumship shall be punished with 100 whiplashes and 6 months of forced labor. Women-mediums, if caught red-handed, shall be subjected to a 100–whiplash punishment and be condemned to pound rice for the state for 6 months'" (1999:77). While little is known about how widely such punishments were enforced, they do not seem to have had much effect on stemming the popularity of mediumship. Do Thien has suggested that there was a rise in female traders' involvement in spirit possession in the late nineteenth century (2003:91). Confucian literati associated female mediums with sexual wantonness and saw the prevalence of mediumship as "a symptom of the decay and dissolution of Confucian hegemony," at a time when the French colonial authorities had weakened Vietnamese dynastic power (Do Thien 2003:98).

Issues of power and control were at the forefront of early French colonial investigations into local religious practices. After watching a male medium being possessed by the historical hero General Tran Hung Dao in a temple in the city of Cao Bang in 1904, E. Diguet, a colonel in the colonial infantry, immediately forbade such practices (Diguet 1906:223). Assessing the threat posed to the social and political order, Diguet concludes: "It is wise from a political as well as a moral and civilized point of view" to forbid mediums' activities (1906:224). The policy of outright prohibition as professed by Diguet was not the only mechanism of colonial control. As Philip Taylor notes, some early colonial occupiers, such as Du Hailly and P. C. Richard, thought that local spirit beliefs might be utilized to sustain their rule. However, attempts to co-opt the spirits in support of French authority met with little success (Taylor 2004:32).

When reading early French accounts of local religious activity, it is hard not to be struck by the derogatory view of the colonialists. In typical fashion, Diguet wrote of the "scandalous" and "savage" scenes of "exorcism" he witnessed at Cao Bang. He described a male medium piercing his cheeks with a sharp iron rod as "revolting barbarity" and as a debasement of Taoist religion (Diguet 1906:223). Paul Giran's overview of "Vietnamese Magic and Religion," while more scholarly than Diguet's account, saw the "incoherent" and "vast" spirit pantheon as evidence of the "primitive confusion of Vietnamese thought" (Giran 1912:7–19). Strongly influenced by evolutionary theory and Durkheimian ideas about collective consciousness, Giran was concerned with identifying the stages of development of "primitive" religious beliefs and showing how these related to collective morals and psychology.

Accounts of mediumship in the first half of the twentieth century make a distinction between male mediums (*ong dong, thanh dong,* or *thay phap*), who belonged to the "cult" of General Tran Hung Dao, and female mediums (*ba dong, ba cot,* or *dong cot*), who worshipped the spirits of the Three Palaces (Tam Phu), with each "palace" headed by a mother spirit (Dumoutier 1908; Phan Ke Binh 1987 [1913/1914]; Giran 1912; Durand 1959). The group of male mediums was known for healing rituals involving expelling evil spirits and acts of self-immolation, such as cheek and tongue piercing and fire walking. The absence of spectacular acts of exorcism in female mediumship rituals led Giran to assert that the cult of the Three Palaces had gradually moved away from "magic," although he thought it still had lots of "magic reminiscences," such as curing through drinking water mixed with incense ash (*nuoc thai*) (Giran 1912:293).

Giran reports antagonism between female mediums and male "sorcerers," who, when possessed by General Tran Hung Dao, challenged the authority of the "assembly of spirits" (1912:292). In Giran's view, the cult of the general had a superior moral doctrine and higher status than the Three Palace cult, although the use of "magic" by sorcerers had a detrimental effect on its more honorable aims. Despite the inferior position Giran accords to the cult of the Three Palaces and its female adepts (whom he severely chastises for lacking social responsibility), he singles it out as "an original production of the religious thought of the Vietnamese," as opposed to being a Chinese import (1912:438). The fascination of French anthropologists with identifying what was indigenous and exterior continued with Leopold Cadière, who famously claimed that the "true religion of the Vietnamese is the cult of the spirits" (1992 [1955]).

The separation of spirit possession into two relatively distinct male and female "cults" seems to have existed at least until the 1950s, when Maurice

Durand conducted his research (1959). However, in contemporary Vietnam no such distinction exists, and the exorcism rites associated with the incarnation of the general are no longer practiced. Today, General Tran Hung Dao is incarnated by both male mediums (*ong dong*) and female mediums (*ba dong*) during *len dong*.[1] The general has therefore essentially been incorporated into the Three Palace (also known as the Four Palace) pantheon (see Pham Quynh Phuong 2006).

Criticism of mediumship in the colonial era was not just limited to the reports of French colonial occupiers. Some Vietnamese nationalist intellectuals influenced by modernist ideals also voiced their disapproval of the "backward" and "irrational" practices of their countrymen. In his work on Vietnamese customs, one such modernist intellectual, Phan Ke Binh, ridiculed both male and female mediums as "idiots" who profited from others' misfortune (1987 [1913/1914]:295–301). For Phan Ke Binh, "superstitious" and "nonsensical" practices were a source of national shame.

In the 1930s and 1940s, an upsurge in spirit worship practices among women in rural areas across the country gave rise to further criticism from male urban-based intellectuals who saw spirit beliefs as contrary to the advance of modernity (Taylor 2004). Such critiques saw the countryside as "a breeding ground for all manner of superstitions" because of the "comparatively low level of education of its population," and they recycled gendered arguments about ignorant, immoral women and their "susceptibility to trickery" (Taylor 2004:34–35). While mediumship no doubt appealed to women in the countryside and from across the social spectrum, many mediums in the north were wealthy urban women of relatively high social standing who could afford the substantial cost of holding rituals (Long Chuong 1942; Durand 1959:11).[2] Indeed, critiques by Vietnamese modernist intellectuals homed in on the threat that powerful female mediums posed to their husbands' authority. For instance, in a series of articles that appeared in the weekly *Phong Hoa* (Customs) magazine in 1935, Trong Lang asserts both his own Westernized superiority and his disgust at the demeanor and behavior of female mediums and their weak, henpecked husbands (Do Thien 2003:99–100).

Two satirical novels by Long Chuong (1990 [1942]) and Nhat Lang (1952) provide further insight into modernist attitudes toward mediumship at the close of the colonial era. Both novels describe mediumship in terms that anticipate many of the tenets of the Vietnamese Communist Party's antisuperstition campaign. Belief in the spirits is attributed to a lack of education and a desire to make money through "selling the spirits" (*buon than ban thanh*). Superstitious practices are said to harm the progress and development of the nation (Nhat Lang 1952:4).

Long Chuong's novel, *Serving the Spirits* (*Hau Thanh*), provides a fascinating, if derisory, view of mediumship among the upper echelons of Hanoian society in the 1930s. The central protagonist is a wealthy woman called Mrs. Han Sinh, who becomes immersed in the world of mediumship because of unhappiness in her life. According to Long Chuong's portrayal, this world is full of jealous, scheming, narrow-minded people, who prey on Mrs. Han Sinh's irrational devotion to the spirits to trick her into giving them money. Once initiated, Mrs. Han Sinh spends all her time with a close circle of religious devotees. Instead of looking after domestic affairs and caring for her husband, she goes away for weeks on end visiting temples and busying herself with errands such as shopping for ritual offerings and costumes. Although Mrs. Han Sinh initially hides her ritual activities from her husband, he finds out and has to suffer the "humiliation" of being married to a "fickle" medium. Mr. Han Sinh is portrayed as being extremely tolerant of his wife's ritualizing, partly because of his modern belief in "the freedom of the individual," but in the end, husband and wife are irreconcilable. Their marriage breaks down because of Mrs. Han Sinh's ritualizing and because of an "indiscretion" by Mr. Han Sinh, which resulted in the birth of an illegitimate child. Toward the end of the novel, Mrs. Han Sinh leaves her husband and remarries a *chau van* musician called Ky Sin, who performed at all her rituals. Mrs. Han Sinh was charmed and infatuated by Ky Sin's "crystal clear" voice and his ability to flatter her in song. But at the end of the novel he is described as a no-good opium addict. The story of Mrs. Han Sinh's downfall is meant as a cautionary tale, one that details the disastrous effects that superstition can have on family life and society.

Throughout Long Chuong's novel, the attraction of religion for weak-minded, emotionally volatile, and deceitful women is contrasted with the modern, educated values of the male characters. For the author Nhat Lang, whose wife was a medium, this issue was close to home. Despite his incredulity and opposition, Nhat Lang, just like the fictional Mr. Han Sinh, had to "endure the humiliation" and go along with his wife's wishes (Nhat Lang 1952:59).

The title of Nhat Lang's novel, *Dong Bong*, has two meanings. *Dong Bong* is one of the terms used to refer to mediumship rituals, and it also ironically connotes the "fickle" or "temperamental" character commonly associated with mediums. The novel is subtitled "A Fictional Report" (*Phong Su Tieu Thuyet*), yet it draws on some of the author's actual experiences. In one extract, Nhat Lang records a dialogue between himself and his possessed wife. In the exchange, his wife, speaking as the spirit, strongly reprimands him for his lack of belief. Although superficially Nhat Lang acquiesces and tries to convince his possessed wife of his devotion, he ruefully remarks: "My wife, under the protection of the spirit's shadow, continued to transmit orders. I knew full well it was a ruse to obtain my submission" (1952:60).

Like religious practices, musical expression was also reassessed in relation to modern values and forms in the late colonial period. Vietnamese musicians and other artists experimented with combining "modern" Western artistic forms and concepts with Vietnamese traditions and themes. *Cai luong* (reformed opera) and *cai cach* or *tan nhac* (renovated or new music) were the most prominent examples of new syncretic genres (Le Tuan Hung 1998; Arana 1999; Tu Ngoc et al. 2000; Gibbs 2004). *Cai luong* was, from its inception in the late 1910s, a highly eclectic genre drawing on Vietnamese, Chinese, French, and other foreign sources. The most overt musical combination of "West" and "East" in *cai luong* was the use of two separate music ensembles. One ensemble was made up of Vietnamese instruments and played repertoire borrowed and adapted from traditional genres, primarily *tai tu* chamber music. The other consisted of Western instruments and performed newly composed incidental music. Western popular song, harmony, and phrasing also had a strong influence on Vietnamese songwriters, who composed new music or *cai cach*. These *cai cach* songs often had a romantic or sentimental character and were later condemned by communist cadres as "yellow music" (*nhac vang*). The emergence of *cai cach* and *cai luong* was partially the result of sustained French–Vietnamese contact and the growing popularization of European music, theater, and arts. Vietnamese musicians and artists devised new cultural forms that, while often influenced by Western models, also strived to be distinctly Vietnamese.

Alongside the creation of new music genres, there were also attempts to renovate traditional music-theater genres such as *cheo* and *tuong* by devising new contemporary characters and storylines (Arana 1999; Tu Ngoc et al. 2000). While there is very little information on *chau van* in written sources on Vietnamese music from the late colonial period, it does not seem to have been subject to a conscious modernizing agenda. Based on oral accounts of elderly musicians in the 1990s who learned *chau van* prior to the August Revolution of 1945, it would seem that performance practices in the 1940s and 1950s were not radically different from today's. This is not to say that mediumship music has been preserved and frozen in time; it has undergone gradual processes of change, as will be discussed in Chapter 5. But today's *chau van* does not bear any obvious hallmarks of radical renovation, and contemporary musicians have maintained a conservative attitude toward fundamental aspects of musical style.

The Antisuperstition Campaign

The condemnation of mediumship as superstition was part of a number of related campaigns promoted by the Vietnamese Communist Party, which sought to reform "backward customs and habits" in order to achieve a thorough "cultural and ideological revolution" (see, for example, Vietnam Government 1962). Such a revolution, it was argued, was necessary for progress and the creation of a "new society" (*xa hoi moi*) based on socialist principles.

According to the living memory of elderly *chau van* musicians and mediums, it was not until the late 1950s and early 1960s that mediumship was severely condemned and prohibited. Certainly, by the late 1950s, the highest echelons of the Party saw mediumship as a "bad tradition" that needed to be eradicated, as the following extract from a speech made by Ho Chi Minh on October 30, 1958, demonstrates:

> If old traditions are to be restored, then only restore good things; bad things must be gradually eliminated . . . Last year, *dong bong* [i.e., *len dong*] and "the procession of spirits" (*ruoc xach than thanh*) were revived. If that kind of restoration is carried out in the countryside, many places will forget production and continue to drum and sing willy-nilly. Some communes spend millions of *dong* buying clothes, hats and shoes. Is this kind of restoration of old traditions right? Good traditions we must restore and develop, bad ones must be got rid of. (Ho Chi Minh 1976 [1958]:83)

Although Ho Chi Minh does not explicitly mention superstition in his speech, the term was used in speeches by Party ideologues in the 1940s and 1950s and in early propaganda literature (e.g., Lao Cai Cultural and Information Service 1964). A distinction between "superstition" (*me tin di doan*) and legitimate "religious beliefs" (*tin nguong*) was central to the antisuperstition campaign:

> It is necessary to distinguish between religious beliefs and superstition. Going to the pagoda and the ancestor altar belong to the freedom of religious beliefs; fortune telling, fate prediction, phrenological fortune telling, calling up the souls of dead ancestors, *len dong*, divination with sticks, casting spells, worshipping ghosts, exorcising and chasing away evil spirits, "carrying incense on the head," burning paper effigies, miraculous healing etc. are superstitions. Freedom of religious beliefs is guaranteed in law, whereas the state strictly bans superstition.[3]

Although examples of superstitious practices as opposed to religious beliefs are given in the above extract, the basis for this distinction is elusive, as both involve supernatural entities. But as Shaun Malarney has discussed, the use of the term *tin nguong* "brought with it a strong sense of prestige and legitimacy, while superstitions implied stigma" (2002:106).

The practitioners of superstitious rituals were portrayed in the campaign as liars and swindlers who did not even themselves believe in the supernatural. Those "exploited" by such practitioners were portrayed as infantile and uneducated: ignorant people who cowered in a world full of miracles and mystery. The slogan "selling the spirits" was employed to brand mediums and spirit priests as fraudsters who manipulated others for financial gain. In accordance with the virtues of thriftiness and industriousness, the campaign argued that the money and time spent on superstition was extravagant, wasteful, and decreased production.

Belief in the spirits' capacity to cure illness and to alleviate misfortune was ridiculed in the propaganda because it was seen to have "no basis in reality" and was "completely unscientific" (Truth Publishing House 1985:19). As Malarney notes, "One of the prime strategies used to undermine ideas about spirits was to demonstrate that claims of supernatural causality could not be empirically verified" (2002:82). The following anecdote taken from an antisuperstition document is typical of the campaign's attempts to illustrate the ineffectiveness and nonexistence of spirits:

> Mrs T. had a child . . . [who] was more than two years old but could not yet stand and walk. Many people encouraged her to take the child to the hospital for a doctor to cure the problem. But Mrs T. refused everybody's sincere advice and instead listened to her mother whose head was full of superstition. She went . . . to find a "good fortune teller" and beg the "spirits" to show how to cure the illness (!). The old fortune teller said she could not live on the land her house was build on and that if she wanted the child to be cured then she must pray for several months and move house. After several months of rituals, Mrs T. spent and wasted more than 8,000 *dong*. She had lost her house but not the illness because the child still had to be carried! (Truth Publishing House 1982:36)

The campaign against superstition had the effect of greatly diminishing the number of *len dong* that took place, but it did not eliminate them entirely. Many mediums still continued to hold small-scale *len dong* in secret. These secret rituals were referred to as *hau vung*, "secretly serving [the spirits]." So that rituals would be less noticeable to the authorities, they were arranged in remote places or late at night. As one medium remarked when I asked her about her activities before the 1980s, "In reality *len dong* was banned, but if you went to mountainous regions far away then you could still hold *len dong.* If you gave the police money it was easy. It was only in Hanoi that it was strictly prohibited." In order for rituals to remain secret, even in cities like Hanoi, the length of *len dong* was reduced and fewer people were invited to attend. *Chau van* was still sometimes played at clandestine rituals, but sometimes a full band was not present because of fears that the music would be heard by the authorities.

Mediums and musicians caught at *len dong* were usually punished. This usually involved confiscation of votive objects and ritual clothes, and in some cases arrests were made. One musician from Hanoi said he was twice held at the police station in the early 1980s, the first time for five days and the second for twenty days, for performing at *len dong.* Despite these periods of detention, he was undeterred and continued to perform at rituals. This attitude demonstrates how even the most stringent measures failed to prevent *chau van* performance entirely.

Although the antisuperstition campaign did not completely eradicate *len dong* rituals, it has had lasting effects on mediums' activities and how they think about what they do. Many mediums I spoke to about the antisuperstition campaign discussed "superstition" in such a way that it did not include *len dong.* This was achieved through two strategies. First, some mediums adopted some of the arguments of the antisuperstition campaign. For instance, they distanced themselves from the most "negative" (*tieu cuc*) aspects of superstition mentioned in Party propaganda, such as "selling the spirits" and some types of ritual healing and fortune-telling. Second, mediums tried to legitimate their activities by classifying them as religious beliefs rather than superstition and by aligning mediumship with Buddhism and ancestor worship.

The following remarks made by a medium, called Doan, in May 1998 illustrate aspects of these two strategies:

> Doan: The government should ban social evils. It has banned superstitions such as "phrenological fortune-telling" (*doan tuong*) and horoscopes, and it has banned people whose fortune-telling creates disruption in society.
>
> BN: But you also tell fortunes, don't you?
>
> Doan: But I don't tell fortunes through horoscopes or phrenology. I only bow in front of Buddha and the spirits in order for people to pray and make offerings. For example, if somebody is in impoverished circumstances or has problems, then the spirits advise them so that their heart's wishes are fulfilled, so they have belief and confidence . . . I just follow and respect my [deceased] parents, Buddha

and the spirits . . . If somebody's child is ill they come and pray, and ask me to implore the spirits to see if the child has a "problem in the blood" (*mau huyet so sinh*) or an "illness of the other world" (*benh am*) . . . [If it is an illness of the other world], I advise and help them, but if it is in the blood then they should go to the hospital . . . If superstition was my profession, I would prophesy for whoever came and they would have to give me several million *dong,* or I would force them to carry out some rituals. That is a social evil. People who sincerely pray to the spirits and light incense might donate 500 or 1000 *dong,* it is up to them, but I don't force them to do anything.

In the above extract, Doan takes on board many of the policies of the anti-superstition policy, such as being thrifty, using modern medicine, and not swindling or taking advantage of people. She even accepts that superstition can have negative effects on society and agrees with Party criticisms of some forms of fortune-telling. The only points at which Doan deviates from the Party line are when she refers to the spirits' power to cure illnesses and to her ability, as a medium, to channel the advice of the spirits for others. Rather than seeing *len dong* as superstitious, Doan considers spirit worship to be a religious belief that is closely related to paying respects to her ancestors and Buddhism.

Some mediums went even further in their acceptance of the arguments of the antisuperstition campaign. One male medium, Thang, who was himself a Party member, maintained that the spirits had no effect on everyday life and that people who believed in the spirits' power to cure illness were "uncultured"/"uneducated" (*vo van hoa*). This view is hard to reconcile with his activities as a medium, especially as I witnessed him giving "incense water" to a disciple when possessed by the Third Lady during *len dong,* an act that many ritual participants claim can help cure illnesses. When I questioned him about the incense water, he replied that it made some disciples "feel more relaxed" but denied it could cure illness. Thang did not, I think, make such remarks because he felt that was what he ought to say to a "foreigner" but because he really had no belief in, as Malarney has put it, "spiritual causality in corporeal life." Thang's views represent the most extreme example of how some mediums have adopted many of the tenets of the antisuperstition policy.

Recent research on ritual life in Vietnam has documented the major impact of communist ritual reform, while at the same time pointing to the limits of state control over ritual practices and the meanings ascribed to them (Malarney 2002; Endres 2001). As with other areas of ritual life, the state did not achieve absolute control over mediumship practices; the antisuperstition campaign did not succeed in its aim of eliminating mediumship entirely, as some mediums continued to hold secret rituals. Similarly, musical practices were not completely controlled by the Party, even though the antisuperstition campaign profoundly disrupted and curtailed *chau van* performances. Despite the limits of state control, however, the antisuperstition campaign continues to shape some mediums' activities and conceptions of *len dong*.

Music and the Cultural Revolution

The ideological and cultural revolution also extended to music and the other arts. One of the Vietnamese Communist Party's earliest statements on culture, the Cultural Thesis of 1943, prescribed that Vietnamese culture needed to be "reformed" so that it had a "national, scientific and populist character." According to the three main principles of the Cultural Thesis, culture had to be national in order to embody an independent Vietnamese identity free from colonial "enslavement"; scientific so that it could progress and not be constrained by feudal and backward characteristics; and populist because art must serve the masses and not be the preserve of the ruling classes (Truong Chinh 1985). While the Cultural Thesis was driven by communist fervor in the buildup to the August Revolution of 1945, its nationalist sentiment resonated with some of the views of non-Communist nationalists in the 1920s and 1930s.

Following the Cultural Thesis, there was a great deal of debate among intellectuals and Party leaders about the cultural direction of the nation (Ninh 2002; Pelley 2002). The ideological basis for the cultural revolution gradually evolved, from the 1940s onward. How to modify the form and content of the arts—including literature, art, theater, and music—was hotly contested in the period immediately following the August Revolution. At this time, cultural debates were conducted in a relatively open and frank atmosphere, which enabled intellectuals to express their views about the role of art in society and voice dissent about restrictions on artistic freedom (Ninh 2002). The Party tightened its grip on cultural expression after the Second National Congress of Culture in 1948. It was around this time that some important decisions were made about which artistic forms should be given state support and which ones should be prohibited. For example, there were differing opinions about the merits and pitfalls of the three main music-theater genres, *tuong*, *cheo*, and *cai luong*. All of these genres were eventually afforded state support and modified to incorporate socialist themes, but *tuong* was criticized in the late 1940s for its "feudal" character, and *cai luong* was banned for a period in the early 1950s because of its emphasis on sentimental romantic plays (Ninh 2002:100). *Cheo* was generally more favored by communist revolutionaries because of its credentials as a popular folk art and its potential as a vehicle for mass propaganda.

Emerging victorious from the Franco-Vietnamese war in 1954, the socialist government pushed toward the socialist transformation of all areas of cultural life. The hegemonic Party position, outlined by Ho Chi Minh and Party ideologues such as Le Duan, Truong Chinh, Pham Van Dong, and Luu Huu Phuoc, was that the arts should serve the ideological interests of the Party, the nation, the socialist revolution, and the fight for the unification of the country (Ho Chi Minh et al. 1976). In order to "use culture" in this way, the government sought to coordinate and control all cultural expression through nationalizing and professionalizing the material bases of artistic activity and cultural production, from publication presses and newspapers to music and theater troupes. The Ministry of Culture, founded in 1955, worked toward establishing a complex network of cultural institutions, which radiated from Hanoi and the provincial capitals, to the district, commune, and village levels. In the musical sphere, the forerunner of the Hanoi Music Conservatoire, the Vietnam National Music School, was opened in 1956, and music troupes, clubs, unions, and associations were established throughout the north. Music performance was primarily centered in national and regional *cheo, tuong, cai luong* and "song and dance" (*ca mua*) troupes.

Many of these troupes incorporated modified versions of "folk song" (*dan ca*) into their programs, but, with the exception of the Quan Ho Folk Song Troupe (Doan Dan Ca Quan Ho) established in Bac Ninh province in 1969 (Le 2002), amateur folksingers were not systematically organized into professional troupes. Traditional music genres that were not incorporated into the new network of music institutions were discouraged or banned because of alleged associations with "corrupt," "feudal," or "superstitious" practices. These included the chamber music genre *ca tru,* imperial court music (*nhac cung dinh*), and many forms of ritual music like *chau van,* funeral music (*nhac dam ma*), and ceremonial music (*bat am*). While some of these genres, notably *chau van,* continued to be performed and transmitted in secret, public performances were largely curtailed.

Through the professionalized network of institutions and the prohibition of some genres, the government aimed to forge a new music culture rich in "socialist content and national character" (*noi dung xa hoi chu nghia va tinh chat dan toc*), a slogan indebted to Stalin's dictum of "national in form" and "socialist in content." The challenge for cultural cadres was to create new music forms that conformed to socialist ideology and celebrated national heritage. Truong Chinh, the general secretary to the Party, advised musicians to exploit and modify the nation's heritage according to the following principles: "1. Use old forms to propagate new content. 2. Transform and improve old forms. 3. Create new forms drawing upon fundamental features of traditional music" (Ha Huy Giap 1972:17). Such ideological reforms of music gave rise to a new genre of neotraditional music and modifications to traditional genres. To illustrate how musicians practically realized these ideological aims, the next sections discuss how the "fundamental features" of *chau van* were incorporated into neotraditional music and how songs were modified and transformed "to propagate new content."

While distinctive historical circumstances shaped the way the Vietnamese cultural revolution unfolded, the political transformation of music in Vietnam has much in common with other communist states. The idea of improving the national heritage, of putting "new wine into old bottles" (*binh cu ruou moi*) and creating new neotraditional forms, is a familiar feature of socialist musical reform from China (Stock 1996; Jones 1999; Rees 2000) to Bulgaria (Rice 1994; Buchanan 1995), from Cuba (Hagedorn 2001) to Uzbekistan (Levin 1996). The strong similarities in the techniques of ideological control and the revolutionary musical styles and forms in different communist states are not surprising given the global ambitions of the communist movement and the extensive networks of cultural exchange that were fostered between socialist states. Maoist-Leninist-derived policies on the role of "culture" in society were propagated and applied widely throughout the communist world, albeit with some national variations. To strengthen and develop cultural links, musicians and other artists were given state support to travel within the communist world and to perform, study, and research. Influenced by cultural exchange, many of these artists were the lifeblood of the state-run institutions in their home countries.

Revolutionary Chau Van

Revolutionary *chau van* was devised in order to transform *chau van* from a "superstitious product" to a "cultural product" so that it could take its place on the "revolutionary stage" and help promote "socialism." It was first devised by the Nam Dinh Cheo Troupe in the late 1950s and early 1960s. In addition to performing *cheo* musical theater, the troupe devised programs that celebrated other types of local folk music. *Chau van* was particularly favored, as Nam Dinh province and the neighboring Ha Nam province are famous for the genre. The Phu Giay festival is held in Ha Nam province, and recently scholars have even claimed that the province is the "cradle" of *chau van* (Bui Dinh Thao and Nguyen Quang Hai 1996:8).

The moon-lute player Nguyen The Tuyen was a key figure in the creation of revolutionary *chau van*. From an early age he learned *chau van* from his father, and before joining the Nam Dinh Cheo Troupe in 1959, he regularly performed at rituals. As the prohibition of *len dong* became more rigorously enforced, Tuyen stopped performing at *len dong* and started work on adapting *chau van* so that it was suitable for the new socialist society. As Tuyen explained when I met him in December 2004, the state authorities did not accept *chau van* because they thought it propagated bad, superstitious individualistic thinking that was contrary to the aims of collectivization, socialism, and the war effort. Tuyen's aim was to "improve" *chau van* so that it "served the people." He wanted to use song to raise the morale of the workers and soldiers and to support their efforts "to save the country and fight the Americans" (*chong My cuu nuoc*).

The best-known singer of revolutionary *chau van* is the *cheo* artist Kim Lien. Although Kim Lien had no previous experience of singing traditional *chau van*, she worked with Tuyen to devise revolutionary *chau van*. Led by Kim Lien and Tuyen, the Nam Dinh Cheo Troupe first gained notoriety when they won a gold medal for the item "Nam Dinh, My Hometown" (Nam Dinh Que Toi) at a national festival held in Hanoi in 1962. Following this initial success, the troupe performed revolutionary *chau van* throughout northern Vietnam, and Kim Lien's voice was frequently heard on the Voice of Vietnam radio. She also performed revolutionary song abroad when she visited France in 1968–69 at the height of the war.

One of the main ways in which *chau van* was adapted to become revolutionary was through the use of new song texts that erased any reference to mediumship. In place of traditional song texts that describe and praise the character and deeds of the spirits, poems with revolutionary, socialist, and patriotic themes were used. As Kim Lien commented, these new poems "praised Uncle Ho, the Party, the army, the people and the workers" (pers. comm., December 2004). For example, poems like Dao Nguyen's "Deep Feelings for the Homeland" (Tham Tinh Que Huong) and Chu Van's "Nam Dinh, My Hometown" (Nam Dinh Que Toi) expressed a patriotic love of the nation and the people. Others, such as Chu Van's poem "The Moon Remembers Uncle Ho" (Vang Trang Nho Bac) and Kim Ma's "Presenting Lotus Flowers to Uncle Ho" (Mua Sen Dang Bac) revere President Ho Chi Minh and the armed struggle for socialism. The poem "The Moon Remembers Uncle Ho" illustrates the patriotism and revolutionary fervor evident in many of the new song texts:

> Looking at the moon I remember the smiling face of Uncle Ho. Seeing the clouds reminds me of his gray hair.
> The wind is like his young hands stroking the beard of the revered and loved Uncle Ho.
> The young moon comes out early, in the afternoon.
> The moon has waited for the night so many times.
> Do not be sad, moon!
> Moon, people are busy on the military training ground.
> Visit the compassionate soldiers,
> Visit the villages of the homeland.
> Where the people are, the moon will follow.
> Follow the footsteps of Uncle Ho and write a people's poem,
> A happy poem full of the sentiments of Uncle Ho.

"The Moon Remembers Uncle Ho" evokes Ho Chi Minh's memory, as it was written by Chu Van in the 1980s, but revolutionary *chau van* also played an active propaganda role in the 1960s and 1970s during the "American War." The song "Welcoming Vietnam's Great Victory," for example, was broadcast to the nation on the Voice of Vietnam in June 1975 shortly after the "fall"/"liberation" of Saigon. A version of this song performed by Kim Lien and accompanied by Nguyen The Tuyen and Pham Van Ty can be heard on the DVD (Track 1). The following extract of the song text of "Welcoming Vietnam's Great Victory," which celebrates the communist military victory, is a vivid demonstration of the use of revolutionary *chau van* as propaganda at a momentous point in Vietnam's recent history:

> The magnificent ancient capital, Saigon, resounds with the sound of the city's glorious new name, Ho Chi Minh.
> Suddenly in a historical night, a fifty-five-day campaign brings back the bright light to the capital.
> After thirty years the whale has now displaced the wolf and cleared the borders of barbed wire.
> The rising tide of hundreds of thousands of brave troops have made the tower fall under the light of the stars.

Revolutionary *chau van* did not just consist of changes to the song texts used; the music and musical system were also transformed in order to suit wartime conditions and the new revolutionary socialist aesthetic. Kim Lien described this transformation in the following terms:

> Traditional *chau van* is wordy, drawn-out, and sluggish, so it was not suitable for real life in society. We [Nguyen The Tuyen and Kim Lien] "improved" *chau van*, made it suitable for the "machinery" of the state. At the time, the war was escalating, and everyone was entering the army . . . How should we sing as people went to the battlefield? We couldn't "drawl" (*e a*) . . . we had to serve the reality of everyone going to war . . . Song had to transmit the life and abrupt rhythm of the time . . . (pers. comm., December 2004)

In the above extract, Kim Lien reiterates the commonly held view that much Vietnamese song is melancholic and sad. Such song was therefore deemed inappropriate in times of war. To reflect "real life," changes had to be made to the *chau van* repertoire and performance practice. These changes can be summarized as follows:

(1) REPERTOIRE

Revolutionary *chau van* suites include only a small number of the main *chau van* songs. The *chau van* repertoire consists of over forty songs, but just seven songs—"Bi," "Doc," "Con Giay Lech," "Cheo Do," "Nhip Mot," "Xa Thuong," and "Phu Binh"—regularly feature in revolutionary suites. "Nam Dinh, My Hometown," for instance, consists of a suite of four songs, "Bi," "Doc," "Con Giay Lech," and "Xa Thuong" (Track 2). By using such a limited number of songs, revolutionary *chau van* focuses on a few outstanding features that identify the genre, rather than on its subtleties. Only one song, for instance, is taken from each of the four main groups of songs, that is, the "Doc," "Con," "Phu," and "Xa" melody groups (see Chapter 3 for further details of the *chau van* repertoire). The choice of songs, as well as the way they are performed, aims to bring out the "lyricism," "confidence," "liveliness," and "happiness" of the music (Bui Dinh Thao and Nguyen Quang Hai 1996:198). In keeping with the revolutionary spirit, the palette of *chau van* songs is constrained and interpreted in a one-sided manner so as to bring out positive and happy elements, whereas more ambiguous or "negative" aspects are reinterpreted or excluded. For instance, "sad" songs such as "Phu Dau" and "Con Oan" are never included in the revolutionary *chau van* repertoire, and "Phu Binh," which is traditionally performed for mandarin spirits and is associated with the strictness of feudal authority, is reworked to convey the "confidence" and "success" of the revolution.

(2) STRUCTURE OF REVOLUTIONARY CHAU VAN SUITES

Revolutionary *chau van* suites ignore the conventions of *chau van* songscapes because they are disconnected from spirit possession. The construction of suites is driven by purely musical factors, rather than by ritual practice. This is evident in two main ways. First, revolutionary suites aim to encapsulate the "essence" and "diversity" of *chau van* in a short song sequence, so songs that would never be performed in the same songscape during *len dong* are abruptly juxtaposed. For example, in the context of *len dong,* the songs "Con Giay Lech," "Xa Thuong," and "Phu Binh" have quite different associations and aesthetics and are performed for different spirits, but in revolutionary *chau van,* these songs are linked together and musical and aesthetic differences are elided. Second, structural patterns that build to a climax are favored. "Nam Dinh, My Hometown," for instance, begins with the unmetered "Bi" melody and gradually increases in tempo during the "Doc," "Con," and "Xa" melodies. As the "Xa" melodies are among the most "lively" *chau van* melodies, they are often used as a rousing finale to suites. Also, revolutionary *chau van* suites typically end with a dramatic ritardando, a sign of "musical closure" that is not employed in *len dong.*

(3) TEMPO AND VOCAL FORCES

Revolutionary *chau van* suites are usually performed very fast and are sung by a female singer or by a group of female singers in unison. This contrasts with *chau van* songs during *len dong,* which are usually sung at a more moderate tempo by a solo male voice. The differential between the tempi of songs is also decreased during revolutionary *chau van* suites, which has the effect of diminishing the expressive range. According to Nguyen The Tuyen and current members of the Nam Dinh Cheo Troupe, the fast tempos of revolutionary *chau van* songs and the use of female voices helped portray the "bustling happiness" of the socialist revolution.

In general, revolutionary *chau van* songs do not exhibit changes such as the harmonization of melodies or the transformation of melodic lines to fit the diatonic scale. One exception is the suite for Kim Ma's poem "Presenting Lotus Flowers to Uncle Ho." In a recording made by the Voice of Vietnam in February 1972, some of the songs in the suite have instrumental accompaniments influenced by tonal harmony. For example, at the end of the piece there is a modified version of a "Xa" melody, which has a quasitonal instrumental accompaniment that is unrelated to the conventional instrumentation of *chau van* songs. The suite also includes the following spoken narration, which sounds like a kind of propaganda "advert" inserted into the song sequence:

When Uncle Ho says go, then go.
When he says victory, there is victory.
The nation's people united, the whole country with one heart.
Independence, reunification and success is certain.

Revolutionary *chau van* was devised on a relatively small scale. Apart from the Nam Dinh Cheo Troupe, the Vietnam Cheo Theater in Hanoi occasionally performed and recorded revolutionary *chau van,* but it was not regularly performed by state-run troupes throughout northern Vietnam. Nonetheless, through broadcasts on the Voice of Vietnam radio during the 1960s and 1970s, revolutionary *chau van* played an important role in promoting socialist propaganda during the war. Kim Lien was proud of the contribution she had made to the war effort: "People said the voice of Kim Lien contributed to the great work of fighting the Americans" (pers. comm., December 2004).

Throughout the 1980s, the Nam Dinh Cheo Troupe continued to devise revolutionary *chau van* suites, and members of the troupe still occasionally perform them at local venues and national festivals. However, there have been few additions to the revolutionary *chau van* repertoire since the 1980s. An exception is Pham Van Ty's piece "For the Fighters at the Frontier" (Gui Anh Chien Sy Bien Thuy) (Track 3), which won a gold medal at a national festival in 1998. The piece uses a poem, written by Pham Van Ty himself, that is set to a suite of three songs, "Phu Noi," "Xa Thuong," and "Cac Ban Tien." The poem pays homage to the great hardships endured by soldiers and the sacrifices they made to bring peace to Vietnam. Like Tuyen's suites, "For the Fighters at the Frontier" juxtaposes melodies that would not be performed consecutively during *len dong.* However, informed by his extensive experience as a *chau van* musician, Ty wanted to use "authentic" songs, and he performs them in the same way as he would during a mediumship ritual.

Despite occasional innovations, performances, and radio broadcasts, revolutionary *chau van* has lost much of its relevance in late socialist Vietnam, and it has not had a significant long-term impact. *Len dong* rituals have not incorporated revolutionary *chau van* precisely because it makes no reference to spirit possession. The songs performed during rituals have therefore not changed in accordance with the political and ideological climate. Most contemporary *chau van* musicians do not perform revolutionary *chau van,* and it is not included on recent commercial recordings by, for example, the artists Pham Van Ty, Xuan Hinh, and Ta Duc Thang on the Ho Guom and Dihavina record labels. This points to the limits of state control over musical practices, despite the Vietnamese authorities severely curtailing the music performance at rituals and the strenuous attempts by the Party to create a new musical aesthetic that embodied socialism. The use of *chau van* as a tool for communist propaganda should therefore be understood as being restricted to particular state-controlled contexts, rather than as a strategy that succeeded in controlling and eliminating all musical activities related to *chau van* at the local level.

Chau Van and Neotraditional Music

The Hanoi Music Conservatoire (Nhac Vien Ha Noi) has been instrumental in the creation and development of "modern national music" (*nhac dan toc hien dai*), which Miranda Arana (1999) has glossed as neotraditional music. In accordance with official policy to "reform" and "improve" traditional music, the conservatoire's Department of Traditional Instruments has been the main center for the development and teaching of the genre. Following the lead of the Hanoi Music Conservatoire, neotraditional music has been widely propagated through regional Schools of Culture and Arts (Truong Van Hoa Nghe Thuat), and after the reunification of the country in 1975, it was taught at the conservatoires in Ho Chi Minh City and Hue. It has also been disseminated through the media, primarily through radio broadcasts and, in recent years, television broadcasts, tapes, and CDs.

As Arana (1999) has discussed in her detailed account of modern national music, numerous Vietnamese terms have been used to refer to the national folk music phenomenon, including *nhac dan toc hien dai* (modern national music), *nhac dan toc cai bien* (reformed national music), *nhac dan toc kieu moi* (national/ethnic music in a new/Western style), and *nhac co truyen Viet Nam* (traditional Vietnamese music). This profusion of terminology reflects the multiple ideological tenets of nationalist musical developments and gives an indication of their heterogeneous nature and complex evolution. Neotraditional music encompasses numerous different types of pieces, styles, and ensembles that have evolved over time.

Le Tuan Hung divides modern national music into "three main categories of works": reformed traditional music (*nhac cai bien*), typically instrumental arrangements of folk songs; political songs arranged for traditional instruments (*ca khuc chinh tri soan cho khi nhac*); and modern national compositions (*sang tac dan toc hien dai*) (1998:98). In addition to these three main categories, modern national music also includes arrangements for traditional instruments of non-Vietnamese pieces, such as Russian folk tunes, and Western classical pieces and well-known movie themes. The ensembles used to perform modern national music are equally varied, ranging from large-scale national orchestras to smaller chamber ensembles. Many of these ensembles combine traditional and modified traditional instruments, and since the 1980s, pop-style bands consisting of modified traditional and Western instruments have also emerged (Arana 1999:52–53).

Neotraditional composers and performers use traditional music genres as a source of inspiration and musical material. The person largely responsible for incorporating *chau van* into neotraditional music is Dang Xuan Khai. Born in 1936, Xuan Khai became familiar with these melodies because his grandfather was a *chau van* musician. He started to play string instruments at a young age, and in 1949, at the age of thirteen, he played the mandolin and guitar in a music group from his native Bac Ninh province, which performed for the army during the war against the French. At the end of the Franco-Vietnamese war in 1954, he became a member of a "youth vanguard" (*thanh nien xung phong*). The main purpose of this vanguard was to entertain the troops who were assigned to building and construction projects. When the Hanoi Music Conservatoire opened, Xuan Khai enrolled in the Department of Traditional Music Instruments and was among the first cohort of students to graduate, in 1959. Encouraged by Vu Tuan Duc, the first director of the Department of Traditional Instruments, he also began composing. After graduation, Xuan Khai taught in the department and climbed through the ranks to become the vice director in 1968 and then director in 1975. He continued to teach the moon lute and compose until his retirement in 1996.

Xuan Khai has composed over two hundred pieces, the majority of which feature solos for his favorite traditional instruments: the moon lute (*dan nguyet*), the sixteen-string zither (*dan tranh*) and the monochord (*dan bau*). As the main tutor of the moon lute at the conservatoire for nearly thirty years, Xuan Khai was an important figure in the development of new pedagogical methods. The next section compares the method for teaching at the conservatoire with traditional methods of learning, with particular reference to a classic example of reformed traditional music known as the "Hat Van Solo" (Doc Tau Hat Van). The following section goes on to discuss how *chau van* "material" (*chat lieu*) was also integrated into one of Xuan Khai's compositions, "Que Ta" (Our Native Homeland). I have chosen to analyze "Que Ta" because it is the best-known composition influenced by *chau van* and holds a prominent place in the neotraditional canon.[4]

Scientific Pedagogy and the "Hat Van Solo"

One of the objectives of the Hanoi Music Conservatoire was to devise a methodical and scientific pedagogy to replace traditional ways of learning, which were perceived as lacking a coherent, progressive system. Performers of genres like *cheo, tuong, cai luong, ca tru,* and *chau van* traditionally learn music through a process of osmosis involving long periods of immersion followed by imitation and self-practice. Typically, immersion is achieved through "following" an experienced master musician, or *thay,* who is often a relative or family friend, when they rehearse and perform. Through sustained contact with a particular genre, the novice gradually memorizes the vocal melodies, song texts, and instrumental parts and learns to perform primarily through self-practice. In the traditional pedagogical system, experienced musicians guide learning by commenting upon and criticizing a student's playing and by demonstrating techniques or phrases. However, they do not teach in formal one-to-one lessons and do not usually give detailed verbal guidance or explanations.

The traditional "ethnopedagogy" of immersion and self-practice encourages variation and improvisation. As will be discussed in Chapter 5, musicians do not learn a fixed melody when learning melodies orally. Rather, they internalize the melodic framework or basic melody, which is realized with different variations and embellishments in each performance. Oral processes of music learning have largely been replaced in the conservatoires with Western-influenced models using Western notation. Tutors in the Department of Traditional Instruments were encouraged to write textbooks using Western music notation for particular instruments. The informal method of traditional learning was seen by reformers at the conservatoire as deficient, ineffective, and unscientific.

Xuan Khai's two textbooks for the moon lute illustrate the pedagogical approach used at the conservatoire, and similar textbooks were written for other traditional instruments. The first textbook, *Moon-Lute Text Book* (Sach Hoc Nguyet), published in 1983, is a compilation of exercises and pieces that had been used at the conservatoire since the late 1950s. The exercises progressively introduce instrumental techniques such as fret position shifts; changing the tuning between the strings; plucking techniques like tremolo (*ve*); and ornaments (*luyen lay*) like glissandi (*nhan*), vibrato (*rung*), and harmonics (*am boi*). Well-known pieces from different traditional genres, such as *quan ho* and central Vietnamese folk songs, *cheo, chau van,* and *cai luong,* are included after each technical exercise to enable students to practice the instrumental techniques. Two "solos" (*doc tau*), an arrangement by Phong Ky and a composition by Xuan Khai, which draw on the "flavor" of central Vietnamese music, are added as an appendix.

The second textbook (Xuan Khai 1994) is divided into three sections and builds on the "primary" (*so cap*) techniques introduced in the 1983 textbook. In a similar way to the 1983 textbook, the first section includes technical exercises and a selection of pieces from traditional genres and neotraditional compositions. The more technically advanced second section consists of arrangements of pieces from four different genres: *hat van, cheo,* imperial court music from Hue (referred to as "Hue music"), and *cai luong.* The final section includes new compositions by Xuan Khai, Phong Ky, Xuan Ba, and others. These neotraditional compositions are frequently performed by students as undergraduate exam pieces.

The "Hat Van Solo" (Doc Tau Hat Van), included in Xuan Khai's second textbook, consists of a suite or medley of the four main *chau van* melodies: "Doc," "Phu," "Con," and "Xa."[5] A version of the "Hat Van Solo" performed by Pham Van Ty can be heard on the DVD (Track 4). The solo consists of an introduction (0–17") followed by sections that draw on the *chau van* melodies, as follows: "Doc" (18"–1'16"), "Phu" (1'17"–1'42"), "Con" (1'43"–3'36"), and "Xa" (3'37"–end). The aesthetic of the "Hat Van Solo" has many similarities with revolutionary *chau van:* distinctions between different melodies within the "Doc," "Phu," "Con," and "Xa" groups are elided; the tempi of melodies are increased; and the structure is shaped by musical factors (e.g., the "Xa" melody is used as a rousing finale) rather than ritual practice. A major difference, however, is that revolutionary *chau van* suites are oriented around a vocal part, whereas the "Hat Van Solo" is purely instrumental and mostly draws on the instrumental phrases played between song verses.

Pham Van Ty's rendition of the "Hat Van Solo" conforms to the general shape of Xuan Khai's score, but he deviates substantially from the notation. Although Ty learned the piece while studying with Xuan Khai at the conservatoire, after he graduated, Ty became a professional *chau van* musician, and he has incorporated some of the instrumental phrases he performs during *len dong* into the "Hat Van Solo." However, even if Ty was not an experienced *chau van* musician, he would have been expected to deviate from the written score.

The transcription of traditional melodies into Western music notation has done much to fix particular versions of melodies as part of a standardized neotraditional canon. But Xuan Khai and other members of the Department of Traditional Instruments were acutely aware that playing melodies from notation was antithetical to traditional performance practice. Going against the presumption that the score should be rigidly adhered to in the manner of Western art music, the introduction to Xuan Khai's 1994 textbook urges students to treat the notation as a "melodic framework": "In this book, all the pieces, from folk songs and traditional music to new compositions, are notated as "melodic frameworks" (*long ban*). Students studying the moon lute must first learn to sing and study directly with an artist if they want to play interestingly and correctly" (Xuan Khai 1994:4). This statement aligns the Western scores of neotraditional music with the traditional techniques of elaborating upon and ornamenting a basic melodic outline. Xuan Khai was of the opinion that the main advantage of Western notation was that it speeded up the learning process. Yet he insisted that students must learn the techniques of ornamentation and variation orally from a "master" (*thay*); otherwise they would not be able to "release" (*thoat ra*) the "soul" (*tam hon*) of Vietnamese music (pers. comm., Xuan Khai, January 2005). For musicians like Xuan Khai, who had learned traditional music orally before studying and teaching at the conservatoire, it was natural to try and combine Western and traditional pedagogical approaches.

While Xuan Khai's teaching of neotraditional music demonstrates some elements of cultural continuity with traditional practices, the reform of traditional music did, in many respects, radically transform traditional musical forms, repertoire, and aesthetics. By following the neotraditional curriculum, as exemplified in Xuan Khai's textbooks, students are introduced to the "essence" of a diverse range of genres in the context of a progressive pedagogical method, rather than becoming specialists in a particular genre. In accordance with the nationalist aims of neotraditional music, the curriculum at the conservatoire incorporates famous pieces as representative examples of genres and regional styles, and it presents diversity within the frame of a single national tradition.

The Neotraditional Composition "Que Ta" (Our Homeland)

For Vietnamese, the idea of the *que*—meaning "native village" or "homeland"—is a powerful cultural imaginary that nostalgically evokes patriotic, utopian images of rural Vietnam (Rosenthal 2002). The *que* (or in compound form *que huong*) has long been a popular source of inspiration for Vietnamese artists. However, in the context of the cultural revolution and the "American War," the countryside was seen by revolutionaries as an ideological battleground. The violinist and ideologue Dao Trong Tu, for instance, lists numerous revolutionary songs inspired by "attachment to the Vietnamese homeland" (1984:126). And he argues that through such songs, "the Vietnamese countryside . . . raises its voice in the powerful chorus of the nation in struggle" (Dao Trong Tu 1984:129).

The "homeland" is a central theme of instrumental neotraditional compositions as well as revolutionary song. Indeed, the titles of many neotraditional compositions either directly or indirectly refer to the countryside or homeland. Other popular themes include praising the army and war heroes, and depicting the seasons, particularly the "new spring of socialism," which echoes Ho Chi Minh's slogan "Each spring is happier" (*Xuan nao vui hon*).

In "Que Ta," and some of his other compositions like "Tinh Que Huong" (Love for the Homeland) and "Cam Xuc Que Huong" (Sentiments for the Homeland), Xuan Khai gave voice to his patriotic feelings. Xuan Khai said he composed "Que Ta" to express his "sentiment" (*tinh cam*) and "pride" (*tu hao*) for his country and his native village following the "liberation" of south Vietnam in April 1975 (pers. comm., Xuan Khai, January 2005). He also related the military victory of the People's Army of Vietnam to the hard work of people living in the countryside. While composing the piece, he had in his mind glorious images of villagers in his native village happily working together in the agricultural collectives, and he wanted to congratulate them on their success in the fight for liberation.[6] In this way, love for the homeland and a sense of national pride are fused with the progress and victories of the communist state.

"Que Ta" is scored for solo moon lute with a dulcimer (*dan tam thap luc*) and percussion accompaniment. On the recording included on the DVD (Track 5), the set of percussion consists of a drum (*trong*), cymbals (*canh*), and clappers (*phach*). The overall structure of the piece is as follows: Introduction–A section–B section–cadenza–coda. This structure is typical for neotraditional compositions, which usually combine Western forms, such as binary (A–B) and ternary (A–B–A), with virtuosic, concerto-like cadenzas and codas. Another staple of the neotraditional canon, Thao Giang's "Ke Chuyen Ngay Mua," for instance, has the same structure as "Que Ta," except it includes a recapitulation of the A section after the cadenza (Arana 1999:86).

"Que Ta" begins with solo moon-lute phrases, which feature the tremolo technique and establish the pentatonic scale G–A–C–D–F. Between some phrases the dulcimer repeats, like an echo, the previous moon-lute phrase. The A section has one main motif, which primarily consists of strident fifths played in unison on the moon lute (top stave) and dulcimer (bottom stave; the dulcimer part is transposed a perfect fourth below actual pitch):

Figure 1.1. A motif

Midway through the A section there is an increase in tempo from moderato to allegretto. The change to the B section is marked by a change in tuning between the two strings of the moon lute from a fourth (D–G) to a fifth (D–A). The B section has two main motifs. These are labeled in Figure 1.2 and 1.3 as B1 and B2, respectively (moon lute, top stave; dulcimer, bottom stave; the dulcimer part is transposed a perfect fourth below actual pitch).

Figure 1.2. B1 motif

Figure 1.3. B2 motif

The main scale used in the B section is D–E–G–A–C, although pitches B and F are also included. The cadenza reestablishes the G as the tonal center, yet it employs the scale G–A–B–D–E–F, rather than the pentatonic scale of the introduction.

The motifs in section A and B are repeated and included in sequences but are not subject to extensive melodic development. In the latter part of the B section, the B motifs are combined with variations of bars 3 and 4 of the A motif. The cadenza and coda also combine musical elements from the A and B sections.

The piece is scored in duple time (2/4) throughout, although in the recording the introduction (marked *rubato*) and the cadenza do not rigidly follow the pulse. The percussion part is primarily based on the two-beat rhythm, one of the main *chau van* rhythms (see Chapter 3). For the most part, the dulcimer plays in unison with the moon lute or plays accompanying arpeggio figures.

The A and B sections are reminiscent of the "Doc" and "Con" melodies, respectively. The A motif, for instance, is somewhat similar to instrumental phrases (*luu khong*) of "Doc." But the references to *chau van* melodies in "Que Ta" are general rather than specific. Xuan Khai said he was inspired by the "Doc" and "Con" melodies when composing "Que Ta," but he did not transcribe and quote these melodies exactly.

For some aficionados of Western art music, the adoption of Western musical forms, figuration, and quasitonal harmonies in neotraditional compositions might sound crude and derivative. Pentatonic folk melodies are harmonized with quasi-triadic chord structures and arpeggio-like figures, yet the thirds in the "dominant" and "tonic" triads are often absent. Shifts in tonal center in neotraditional music often consist of a change in an anhemitonic pentatonic or heptatonic scale, but they are not full-fledged tonal modulations. In neotraditional compositions like "Que Ta," it is hard to hear the tension and release, and sense of progression, evident in the modulations and cadences of tonal harmony. The strong emphasis in "Que Ta" on the intervals of the fourth and the fifth (G–D, C–G, D–A) does little to ground the piece in a particular key. The coda of "Que Ta" essentially consists of repeated jumps from the "fifth" (D) to the "tonic" (G). This imitates the repeated perfect cadences that conventionally conclude classical symphonies, but the raised leading note, which enhances the sense of cadential resolution, is not included in the "Que Ta" coda.

From what logic does the fusion of Western conventions and folk melodies in neotraditional music arise? Why did folklore ensembles in Vietnam and throughout the communist world adopt structures and styles derived from Western art music? The hegemony of the "scientific" West, with its developed musical forms, tonal harmonies, notation system, and progressive teaching system, was certainly central to the socialist rhetoric of cultural modernity. Yet how appropriate were Western forms and aesthetics for the new socialist society in Vietnam? To explore these questions, it is necessary to consider the relationship between musical and social structures.

Musical Structure, Social Structure, and Modernity

Peter Manuel's study into the homologies between social structures and formal structures in music is based on the premise that there is "at least an indirect causal relationship" between song form, understood as closed arch forms like the thirty-two-bar AABA pattern and sonata form, and the "emergence of capitalist modernity and a coherent bourgeois aesthetic" (Manuel 2002:47). Manuel argues that song form, which makes use of "techniques of symmetry, recapitulation, and internal development to achieve dramatic climax and clear closure," is predominant in bourgeois capitalist societies (Manuel 2002:47). Song form contrasts markedly with "collective-variative" forms such as strophic song, open-ended additive structures and ostinato-based forms, which are characteristic of premodern, nonbourgeois societies. Unlike song form, premodern, collective-variative forms "lack a sense of dramatic progression and closure" and are "flexible entities whose length and internal structures are open-ended" (Manuel 2002:48). A sense of closure in collective-variative forms is determined by convention rather than formal structure.

Lyrically, collective-variative forms like strophic song are typically made up of short, semantically independent epigrams about stock historical and mythical characters, whereas song forms often portray scenes of romantic love between autonomous individuals free from social constraints (Manuel 2002:53–54). The former emphasizes precapitalist communal heroic values; the latter promotes a heightened sense of individualism or "ego-centeredness," which is associated with capitalist modernity.

Chau van, like many other traditional musics in Vietnam and elsewhere, is a classic example of a collective-variative form and neotraditional music displays many of the characteristics of song form. As will be discussed in detail in Chapters 3 and 4, *chau van* is strophic song form, which uses epigrammatic lyrics, and the sequences of songs performed during spirit possession, which I refer to as "songscapes," are open-ended additive structures. This contrasts with the closed, internally structured musical forms of neotraditional compositions and the teleological dramatic climaxes and closure of revolutionary *chau van* and the "Hat Van Solo." Vietnamese neotraditional compositions are usually instrumental and feature a virtuosic solo with ensemble accompaniment, which serves to heighten the role of the individual. This use of the solo–ensemble format might therefore be interpreted as a formal expression of ego-centeredness, which Manuel maintains is central to "bourgeois" music.

The transition from strophic song to neotraditional closed song form in which *chau van* becomes a soloistic, virtuosic trace symbolizing the native village, demonstrates the radical aesthetic shift inherent in the modernization of Vietnamese music. If one accepts the validity of the homologies between musical and social structure outlined by Manuel, the use of closed song form in neotraditional compositions would seem to stand directly opposed to the stridently noncapitalist socioeconomic context of revolutionary communism. The alignment of neotraditional music with bourgeois musical aesthetics is contrary to the ideology of collective socialism. How can, for instance, collectivized modes of production be reconciled with bourgeois aesthetics and musical structures that are inherently individualistic?

The main explanation for such apparent discontinuities between social economy and song form is that the architects of neotraditional music simply did not consider song form to be embedded in bourgeois aesthetics. Composers at the Hanoi Music Conservatoire followed the lead of their counterparts in Soviet Russia and China and aimed to compose new music that was modern, socialist, and nationalist. Although they consciously used song forms derived from Western compositional techniques, closed musical structures were associated with modernity and international communism, not bourgeois ideology. Despite attacks by Ho Chi Minh and the Ministry of Culture on "bourgeois culture" (Pelley 2002:121), the Western classical tradition was immune from such attacks. Instead, Western compositional forms and instrumental techniques were seen as providing composers with modern devices that could be Vietnamized through the use of traditional instrumentation and material. As Xuan Khai said in response to my question about his motivation for composing modern national music, "Vietnamese traditional music is extremely abundant and varied . . . but there is a lack of new compositions. To respond to the needs of the modern age, you must have new compositions, new content, new subjects. That was what inspired me" (pers. comm., Xuan Khai, January 2005).

Since its inception, Vietnamese neotraditional music has been performed at numerous concerts and broadcast on national radio and television, but it was not been wholeheartedly embraced by the "masses" it purportedly sought to serve. Despite considerable state support, it has failed to gain a truly national following. Some composers attribute the relative lack of popularity of neotraditional music to the fact that Vietnamese audiences are unused to listening to purely instrumental music, and they have tried to counter this difficulty by drawing on traditional songs in their works (pers. comm., Thao Giang, January 2005). Other contributing factors for the muted enthusiasm for neotraditional music may be the use of a relatively unfamiliar musical language and the formality of Western-style staged performances.

In late socialist Vietnam, the presence and influence of neotraditional music has decreased considerably. It is still frequently performed as entertainment for tourists, typically in expensive restaurants. But the response of Western tourists, who are often interested in discovering the "traditional" and the "authentic," has not been favorable to neotraditional music because it sounds too "Westernized" (Arana 1999:112). As Helen Rees has discussed in relation to tourist performances in China, foreign tourists tend to prefer "endangered," "authentic," and "ancient" music, rather than professional staged performances, which may come across as "sanitized folk" (Rees 2000:183).

Manuel's interest in pursuing the causal relations and correspondences between formal musical structure and socioeconomic context does not preclude him from also noting discontinuities. With the increasing dominance of global capitalism since the collapse of the Soviet Union and the communist bloc in Eastern Europe, song form is widespread, but it has not been as pervasive as a rigid homology theory would suggest. For example, traditional forms like strophic song persist outside the developed West, and in Western popular music culture the prominence of song form is currently rivaled by ostinato-based forms of Afro-American derived musics like hip-hop and R 'n' B. While some of these discontinuities are explained by Manuel as being a consequence of "the general undermining of many aspects of bourgeois ideology and aesthetics," he also acknowledges that numerous factors, such as cultural nationalism, nostalgia, and ethnicity and gender issues, can play a dominant role in conditioning musical aesthetics (Manuel 2002:57). But this, Manuel argues, does not invalidate homology theory: "Most music cultures are complex and heterogeneous, allowing modern and pre-modern forms to coexist side by side. Moreover, a sophisticated homology theory proposes not a vulgar one-to-one determinism, but a relatively loose iconicity, in which, for example, song form would constitute the most typical form, but not the sole form, of bourgeois society (or of a society dominated by bourgeois ideology)" (Manuel 2002:57).

Vietnamese music culture consists of many different strands and is far from uniform and homogenous. The dominant musical forms in revolutionary Vietnam were neotraditional and revolutionary, but popular song and traditional musics were still performed. As Vietnam has embraced capitalist free-market economics, albeit within the framework of communist political structures, there has been a resurgence of some traditional musics like *chau van*, which goes against the grain of a rigid homology theory. The decreased presence of revolutionary song and neotraditional music is understandable given the economic and social liberalization of the Renovation policy, but, at the same time, the use of song form is still prominent in popular-music culture. Popular songs, known as *ca khuc,* which have been written by Vietnamese songwriters since the 1930s, have gained greater currency in recent years. For instance, *ca khuc* composed by Trinh Cong Son, one of the most famous songwriters in Vietnam, have grown in popularity in the reform era after many years of relative neglect (see Schafer 2007).

In contemporary Vietnam, popular music culture is flourishing as a result of the more liberal cultural climate and increasing access to Internet technology, international media, and Western popular music. Following the karaoke craze in Vietnam in the mid-1990s, young popular musicians have found inspiration in diverse idioms including jazz, pop, rock, and rap: there is now a thriving rock scene in Hanoi led by the group Buc Tuong (The Wall); numerous video compact discs (VCDs) of rap- and R 'n' B-influenced music are being produced by singers and rappers based in Ho Chi Minh City; and artists such as Tran Manh Tuan, Quoc Trung, Ngoc Dai, and Le Minh Son have experimented with fusing Western-influenced jazz and pop with traditional Vietnamese musics.

In contemporary Vietnam, then, song form, which is the most typical form of much Vietnamese popular music, coexists with the collective-variative forms characteristic of many traditional genres. As will be discussed in the next section, cultural nationalism and anxiety about Vietnamese identity are important factors in the recent revival of "premodern" music forms.

Cultural Nationalism and Globalization in the Reform Era

Len dong rituals have been conducted with increasing openness since the late 1980s, even though the antisuperstition policy is still officially in place and mediumship continues to be criticized in the press. The seeming contradiction between the Party officially condemning superstitious activities while tacitly accepting the occurrence of *len dong* may be due to Party cadres no longer considering it feasible to vigorously suppress cultural activities such as *len dong* and *chau van* in light of the liberalization of *doi moi*. This suggestion assumes that the Party still considers *len dong* to be superstitious. However, the discourse of Vietnamese folklore scholars during the 1990s legitimates *len dong* in nationalist and culturalist terms. While this legitimating discourse would seem to contradict the antisuperstition policy, publication of the folklore scholars' research would not have been possible without the acceptance of the censors who regulate academic publications. Furthermore, I will argue that the discourse legitimating *len dong* draws on, and is given strength by, a nationalist Party agenda.

As mentioned in the Introduction, the research into *len dong* and *chau van* since the early 1990s by scholars at the Folk Culture Institute in Hanoi has characterized *len dong* and *chau van* as "folk culture" (Ngo Duc Thinh 1992; 1996a). This research emphasizes the historical importance of mediumship as a community activity and the heroic role of certain spirits, like the Second Prince and General Tran Hung Dao, in "building and defending the nation" when they lived as mortals on the earth. Scholars at the Folk Culture Institute have thus attempted to show how *len dong* and *chau van* have contributed to the cultural life and "soul" of the Vietnamese people and have downplayed "superstitious" elements such as fortune-telling and curing illness (Ngo Duc Thinh 1996a:317).

It is not just folk-culture researchers who have interpreted *len dong* and *chau van* in nationalist and culturalist terms: mediums often justified their activities by saying they were respectfully remembering historical figures who had done "good work" (*cong duc*) for the Vietnamese nation. For instance, when I asked Thuy, a medium who had done some fortune-telling in the past, whether she carried out fortune-telling during *len dong* she replied:

> No, [*len dong* is] solemn and serious, and based on the traditions of the dynasties of the past when the spirits did battle with the enemies. Today we review history to make people aware of: how the spirits fought the enemies with swords and spears; how the Ninth Lady Spirit danced with a fan as if cooling humanity; how the Third Holy Lady Spirit rowed a boat for Le Loi in order for him to cross the river and fight the enemies.[7] Through doing the "work of the honorable spirits" these stories are relived. (pers. comm., Thuy, May 1998)

Thuy's comments illustrate how mediums themselves interpret *len dong* as an activity that draws on the Vietnamese nation's heritage, rather than a superstitious activity involving fortune-telling.

Promoting the national merit of folk beliefs on which *len dong* is based chimes with a long-held policy of the Party. The development of a national Vietnamese culture imbued with the character of the Vietnamese people has been a pillar of the nation-building project. Ever since the Cultural Thesis, this policy has resurfaced again and again in slightly modified guises. In the reform era the development of culture "rich in national identity" (*dam da ban sac dan toc*) has been the favored nationalist slogan (Ministry of Culture and Information 1999). By representing mediumship as "national culture," which expresses the identity of the Vietnamese people, folklorists and some ritual adepts have aligned spirit possession with hegemonic discourse on culture. The effect of this alignment is that mediumship is increasingly being understood as a "cultural form," a kind of folk theater performance. The emergence of folklorized versions of mediumship in the early 1990s, which will be discussed in Chapter 7, further promotes a view of mediumship as cultural performance.

At the turn of the millennium, the issue of globalization entered the fray. As Vietnam has gradually become more integrated into the global economy, anxieties about the survival of "traditional culture" have increased. Globalization, understood negatively as an unstoppable "flood" of foreign culture, technology, and mass media, is seen by many cultural nationalists as a threat to indigenous cultural forms and values (Vietnamese Institute for Musicology 2004). At two music conferences in Hanoi in 2004 and 2005, the dangers that globalization poses to traditional music was hotly debated by music scholars. Fears that traditional music will disappear are being voiced with increasing urgency, and the preservation of cultural identity has moved center stage. Ways are now being sought to promote and invigorate genres that were previously prohibited. Vietnamese music institutes are responsible for much of this work. However, one of the ironies of cultural revival projects is that they are often embedded in the very processes of globalization that they attempt to resist, as many are dependent on financial investment from international organizations and, in some cases, tourism. For instance, in 2002 and 2005 the Ford Foundation funded *ca tru* teaching projects. In Hue, the preservation of court music has also been enhanced by tourist performances and by international assistance from France and UNESCO (To Ngoc Thanh et al. 2004).

In contrast to some other traditional genres, *chau van* is in no danger of disappearing. With the *len dong* boom in the reform era, there has been a corresponding rise in *chau van* performance. Vietnamese musicology and folklore researchers have been involved in recording and documenting ritual music. But the revival of *len dong* and *chau van* has largely taken place at the local level without state support. It is now time to turn to this local, ritual effervescence.

2

Experiencing Spirit Possession

The fascination with spirit possession in academia has spawned numerous theories that attempt to explain the phenomenon. Janice Boddy's review of the literature points out that "spirit possession research has been characterized by a fundamental tension between reductive, naturalizing, or rationalizing approaches on the one hand and contextualizing, more phenomenological approaches on the other" (1994:410). The approach taken here is contextual and phenomenological rather than reductive. Possession experiences are situated within the religious system of the spirit pantheon and are conceptualized in terms of embodiment, as a mode of bodily engagement with the spirits. Based on mediums' own accounts, the interactions between human and divine forces are understood as grounded in the body and bodily being-in-the-world.

Phenomenological approaches to spirit possession are diverse, but they share a concern with the complexity of lived experience. In the broadest sense, a phenomenological orientation "demands a turning back to the world of lived human experience and taking what people do and say seriously" (Kapferer 1991 [1983]: xix). Bruce Kapferer's study prioritizes the power and logic of the lived experience of Sinhalese exorcism and resists reductionist understandings of human action in terms of social functionalist or individual psychological theories.

Since Kapferer's study, anthropological and ethnomusicological studies of spirit possession have paid attention to lived experience, the body, and embodiment in quite different ways (e.g., Roseman 1991; Stoller 1995; Friedson 1996; Lambek 1998; Emoff 2002; Tanabe 2002). From the perspective of the anthropology of the senses, Paul Stoller has made one of the strongest calls for consideration of the "centrality of the sentient body" in spirit possession (1995:20). He draws on Paul Connerton's theories about collective memory and commemorative ritual and Michael Taussig's writing on mimesis and alterity to theorize how sensuous, embodied possession among the Songhay of Mali and Niger triggers cultural memory and is related to colonial encounters and political power. For Stoller, "spirit possession is an arena of sensuous mimetic production and reproduction, which makes it a stage for the production and reproduction of power" (1995:37).

Positioning the sentient body at the center of investigations into spirit possession is closely related to "radical empiricism," an approach espoused by Stoller, in which the experiences of the ethnographer and the interaction between "observer" and "observed" are brought to the fore in narrative ethnography (see also Jackson 1989). As in other related disciplines, there has been a strong shift toward experiential approaches in ethnomusicology (see Titon 1997), but Steven Friedson is one of the few ethnomusicologists who has adopted a form of radical empiricism, which he blends with Heidegger's philosophy of "being." Friedson's ethnographic inquiry is about Heideggerian "questioning" or investigating possibilities (1996:8). Understandings arise from "ethnography as a questioning" through intersubjectivity at the ontophenomenological level, rather through the "encounter of a perceiving subject (ethnographer) with the world of the 'other'" (Friedson 1996:3). Friedson's research on Tumbuka trancing and healing in Malawi proposes a "phenomenology of musical experience" in which "lived experience *is* a musical mode of being in the world" (1996:5; emphasis in original). For the Tumbuka, Friedson demonstrates that music is not merely an acoustical phenomenon that is the object of reflection. Instead, musical experience "penetrates directly into the realm of bodily existence" and "musical structure reveals itself as a mode of being-in-the-world that can be understood in formal terms, an important onto-phenomenological opening not available to all modes of being" (1996:168).

Part of Friedson's phenomenological mode of inquiry is his own experience of "dancing *vimbuza.*" By carrying out the dances of the class of *vimbuza* spirits in the intense atmosphere of the *thempli,* the healer's temple, Friedson experiences a change in conscious awareness that brings him closer to Tumbuka modes of being-in-the-world. Although on a few occasions, I actively participated in *len dong* by playing the moon lute for some songs, I was not initiated as a medium. For initiation to take place, a "master medium" (*thay dong* or *dong truong*) or "spirit priest" (*thay cung*) must diagnose an adept as destined to become a medium. Initiation is usually deemed to be necessary following some sort of affliction attributed to the spirits. None of the mediums and spirit priests I met suggested I should be initiated, and I felt it was inappropriate to push for an initiation ritual as a "fieldwork exercise" without a prognosis from a master medium. Perhaps the closest interaction I had with the spirits occurred during a "thanking ritual" (*le ta*) held by a medium on my behalf to thank the spirits for their assistance in my research (see Epilogue).

As I did not experience possession myself, I investigate the possibilities of possession through mediums' accounts of their experiences. One of the most striking aspects of mediums' reflections was the way they talked about their bodies in relation to the embodied presence of spirits. Mediums reported manifold somatic changes while possessed. Bodiliness is altered by the embodiment of spirits and the displacement or disembodiment of the quotidian self. Previous writing on *len dong* has paid little attention to possession experiences beyond brief references to mediums being in a "trance" or "hypnotized." Vietnamese mediums did not discuss possession in terms of mentalistic notions of consciousness or altered states of consciousness, but rather in terms of somatic change and bodily interaction with the spirits. So what is offered here is a questioning about spirit possession in terms of the body and embodiment. In this regard, medical anthropologist Thomas Csordas's theorizing on embodiment is useful. In a series of publications, Csordas has outlined what he refers to as a cultural phenomenology, which elaborates upon the paradigm of "embodiment as the existential ground of culture and self" (Csordas 1994, 1999, 2002). Csordas's aim in advancing a cultural phenomenology is to establish "a methodological standpoint for the analysis of culture and self from the standpoint of embodiment" (1999:151). Put a different way, the promise of the paradigm of embodiment is to show how "culture is grounded in the human body" (Csordas 1994:6).

The theoretical orientation of Csordas's cultural phenomenology is complex and wide-reaching. Embodiment as a methodological field is proposed as an alternative to the paradigm of textuality, which has dominated much cultural analysis. Within the context of this study, Csordas's paradigm of embodiment is pertinent because it opens up the possibility of appreciating mediums' experiences and the cultural manifestations of possession from the phenomenological standpoint of bodily engagement with the spirits. In his analysis of revelatory phenomena among Anglo-American Catholic Charismatic healers and Puerto Rican spiritist mediums, Csordas suggests the phrase "somatic modes of attention" to refer to the "culturally elaborated ways of attending to and with one's body in surroundings that include the embodied presence of others" (2002:244). In a related way, mediums have particular ways of attending to, and with, their bodies during *len dong;* they adopt culturally constituted modes of somatic attention for the presence of embodied spirits and for the interactions with ritual participants. Somatic modes of attention are articulated and experienced through ritual action, dance, gift exchange, and divine utterances.

Mediums' bodily experiences of possession take place in temples saturated with *chau van* songs. This chapter prepares for the in-depth examination of the ritual performance of *chau van* in Chapters 3 and 4 by outlining mediums' possession experiences and other key aspects of the ritual process, including initiation, fortune-telling, healing, and prophesy. We begin with an introduction to the religious framework of mediumship and the identities of spirits.

The Four Palace Religion and the Spirit Pantheon

Mediumship rituals hold a central place in a "system of religious beliefs" (*he thong tin nguong*) commonly referred to as the Four Palace Religion (Dao Tu Phu). The religious system is based upon the stories and characters of a large pantheon of "spirits" (*than* or *thanh*). Vietnamese scholars characterize the Four Palace Religion, which is also known as the Mother Religion (Dao Mau), as a syncretic popular religion that blends indigenous beliefs with imported, foreign elements drawn from the institutional religions of Buddhism, Taoism, and Confucianism (see Ngo Duc Thinh 1996a, 2004; Nguyen Thi Hien 2002). This research, and the earlier work of French scholars (Durand 1959; Simon and Simon-Barouh 1973), devotes much attention to the classification of the "assembly of spirits" (*chu vi*) or spirit pantheon. Scholarly classifications of spirit pantheons can give the impression of a fixed, timeless taxonomy to which all adepts adhere. But the spirit pantheon of the Four Palace Religion is constantly changing and exhibits considerable regional diversity. It is therefore not surprising that the pantheons outlined by scholars differ. Attempts to outline a definitive classification are complicated by regional variation and by the fact that adepts have different conceptions of the pantheon depending on their personal histories and backgrounds. Spirit worship thrives as a localized activity, which has not been subject to central systematization and control, and the flexibility of spirit worship permits the incorporation of regional spirits, some of which are worshipped only in specific areas or by certain mediums. Also, not all the spirits venerated by followers of the Four Palace Religion are incarnated during *len dong.*

Despite differences in the scholarly and folk classifications of the pantheon, all share a common core consisting of a hierarchy of groups or ranks of spirits in the following order: mother spirits (*mau*), mandarins (*quan*), ladies (*chau*), princes (*ong hoang*), princesses (*co*), and young princes (*cau*). Within each rank, spirits are numbered as "first," "second," "third," and so on, with the exception of some regional spirits, which are not always named with an ordinal number. Mediums incarnate the spirits in the order of the pantheon hierarchy. Sometimes as few as three spirits are incarnated, but usually between fifteen and twenty-five spirits from the pantheon possess the medium consecutively over a period of several hours. The pantheon outlined in the Appendix lists the spirits incarnated at the numerous rituals I went to during the course of my field research. Its purpose is to provide a point of reference for the spirits mentioned during the course of this book; it should not be read as a comprehensive classification of all the spirits worshipped by followers of the Four Palace Religion. Apart from the six spirit ranks already mentioned, the Appendix lists one other rank of spirits, the "Tran family spirits," consisting of General Tran Hung Dao, the military leader who lived in the thirteenth century, and four of his children. As noted in Chapter 1, in the colonial era the general was the focus of a separate "cult" of male mediums, but he is now incarnated alongside other spirits during *len dong*.

Some classifications include the female bodhisattva Quan Am, who is sometimes referred to as the Goddess of Mercy, and the Taoist Jade Emperor, Ngoc Hoang, at the top of the pantheon, and animal spirits—five tigers and a snake—at the bottom, after the rank of young princes. Statues of Quan Am and Ngoc Hoang are found in temples, and mediums worship and make offerings to these deities, but they are not incarnated during *len dong*.[1] Colorful paintings of the snakes and tigers adorn many temples, and some mediums are possessed by these spirits, although this did not happen at any of the rituals I attended.[2] The other main differences in the pantheons documented by scholars lie in the precise number of spirits in each rank.

The hierarchy of the spirit ranks delineates their relative level of seniority and prestige. Spirits within each rank share some general characteristics but have distinctive personalities, histories, and attributes. The mothers at the top of the pantheon are the most powerful deities. In part because of their high status, mother spirits do not perform ritual actions in the same way as other spirits: they only "descend" (*giang*) for a few seconds while the scarf is placed over the medium's head before "returning" (*ve*) to the other world. General Tran Hung Dao and the mandarins are the most prestigious male spirits and are the first to be fully incarnated during *len dong*. As "warrior-scholar"

Figure 2.1. Temple altar with effigies of the First, Second and Third mother goddesses

(*van vo*) spirits, they are known for their prowess in the art of war and their mastery of the affairs of state. Some of the ladies are avatars or attendants of the mother spirits, and many are also thought to belong to different "ethnic minority" groups, such as the Tay (Tenth Lady), Nung (Sixth Lady), Man (Second Lady), Muong (Third Lady), and Dao (First Lady). When possessed by ethnic spirits, mediums wear colorful clothes that borrow eclectically from the traditional costumes of minority groups, who mainly live in the highland regions in Vietnam. Like the mandarins, the princes are warriors and scholars, but they are younger, more irreverent, and less reserved than their higher-ranking counterparts. The princesses are graceful unmarried maidens who are known for their beauty as much as their miraculous powers. Some of the princesses, like the ladies, are ascribed an ethnic-minority origin and identity. The lowest-ranking spirits, the young princes, are playful and naughty children who tease and joke.

Information about the miraculous deeds and characters of spirits has been transmitted orally in *chau van* poems and folk tales. These stories and poems use rich, poetic language and combine legend and history in a way that is difficult to disentangle. Deities are either considered to be "celestial spirits" (*thien than*) of divine origin who descended to the earth to help and guide mortals or "human spirits" (*nhan than*), historical personages who were deified after their death.

The term *Four Palace Religion* refers to the four "palaces" (*phu*) or domains to which many of the spirits are ascribed in the "yin spirit world" (*coi am*). These four palaces, which are associated with different colors, can be represented as follows:

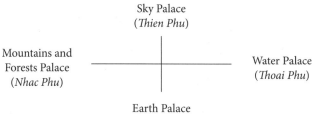

Sky Palace
(*Thien Phu*)

Mountains and
Forests Palace
(*Nhac Phu*)

Water Palace
(*Thoai Phu*)

Earth Palace
(*Dia Phu*)

Figure 2.2. The four palaces

The color code of the four palaces determines the color of the spirits' clothes and other ritual paraphernalia. Literature from the colonial period often makes reference to three, rather than four, palaces, and the fourth palace of the mountains and forests is thought to have been added at a later historical stage. Vietnamese folklore scholars have interpreted the development of the religious cosmology in evolutionary terms. They have argued that the cosmology of three palaces evolved from a "primitive" duality of yin and yang, to three and then four palaces, but they offer little historical evidence for this interpretation (Ngo Duc Thinh 1996a).

The palaces relate to the place of spirits in the "yang human world" (*duong tran*) as well as the celestial domain. Spirits are associated with particular places through having originated from, lived in, or visited particular villages and towns. Their activities in the human world connect them to places in Vietnam, and they are accredited with powers to oversee and govern particular regions. The spirits' governance maps out the physical and human terrain of the country, its parameters, and the ethnicity of its populace. The mountainous border regions in the north are "surveyed" (*giam sat*) and "guarded" (*tran giu*) by powerful warriors like the Second Mandarin and Seventh Prince, and ethnic minority spirits in the lady rank like the Tenth Lady. The perception that these regions require protection is connected to the long history of conflict with Vietnam's neighbor to the north, China. The most recent incursions by Chinese forces along the northern border in the late 1970s resulted in fierce battles and heavy casualties on both sides, and these conflicts are very much in living memory. One *chau van* musician, who had fought in the army against the Chinese, thought that the spirits of the Four Palace pantheon helped protect Vietnam's borders; he saw *len dong* as a symbol of the vitality and strength of the Vietnamese people, qualities that made age-old enemies like China fearful.

Ritual enactment and tales of ancient battles against the Chinese prior to colonialism resonate with modern conflicts, but recent wars involving the French and Americans are not referred to in song texts or the actions and words of spirits. The spirits' histories predate the twentieth-century nationalist and communist struggles for independence and reunification. However, during my visit to Vietnam in 2004–5, I heard reports that the revolutionary communist leader, Ho Chi Minh, was being incarnated during *len dong*. Although I never saw such a practice myself, mediums possessed by Uncle Ho apparently dressed humbly in his signature Maoist suit and sandals. In mediumship circles, the reaction to the existence of such a practice ranged from incredulity and derision to thoughts that Uncle Ho could, with the passage of time, be incorporated into the pantheon. Ho Chi Minh is already a figure of worship in village communal houses as a tutelary spirit, a "living god" (*than song*) (Malarney 2002:201). It is possible, therefore, that the manifestation of this "living god" in the ritual arena of *len dong* could become more common in the future.

Geographical associations imbedded in the religious system are maintained and reinforced through the numerous temples and mausoleums scattered throughout the country. In a religious cosmology that exhibits correspondences between the human and spirit worlds, popular sites of pilgrimage and worship relate to the spirits' celestial palaces. For example, the temples dedicated to the spirits of the Mountains and Forests Palace are located in mountainous regions in northern and central Vietnam, and the holy sites of Water Palace spirits are usually close to famous rivers or waterfalls. Many of these temples have been recently restored and officially recognized as "historical-cultural vestiges" (*di tich lich su van hoa*), according to the policy pursued by the Ministry of Culture since 1984. While this policy has ensured that temples and other sacred buildings like pagodas (*chua*) and village communal houses (*dinh*) have been renovated and maintained, it has also resulted in sacred places being reassigned under the auspices of the state.[3] Local branches of the Ministry of Culture have promoted the cultural-heritage value of sacred sites and sought to control the kinds of religious practice that take place in them, for instance by prohibiting *len dong*.

The folk expression Dao Mau, or "Mother Religion," highlights the importance of the mother spirits at the top of the pantheon. Although mediums sometimes used the term Mother Religion, its increasing prominence is due in large part to recent publications by researchers at the Folk Culture Institute (Ngo Duc Thinh 1996a; 1996b; 2004). The preference for the term Mother Religion, rather than Four Palace Religion, in these publications is bound up with cultural nationalism and evolutionary theories about the development of indigenous beliefs. Ngo Duc Thinh suggests the Mother Religion evolved from indigenous, primeval beliefs in goddesses of nature connected with the earth, with water, and with rice cultivation and that the worship of goddesses is indicative of the high respect for women in "primitive" Vietnamese society, prior to Confucian influence. Furthermore, female spirits are celebrated as cultural heroines and linked to narratives about the important role women have played in "building and protecting the country" throughout Vietnamese history (Ngo Duc Thinh 1996a:14). The nationalist view of Vietnamese history as resistance to foreign aggression is also evident in references to the historical contribution of male spirits, most notably General Tran Hung Dao and some mandarin spirits. But female spirits, headed by the mothers, are prioritized as the primordial source or point of origin of spirit worship and mediumship.

Research on the Mother Religion is part of a broader wave of interest among Vietnamese folklore scholars on female deities (e.g., Nguyen Minh San 1996). In an overview of this research, Philip Taylor identifies the various ways in which female deities have recently been portrayed as bearers of "the nation's tradition and of its cultural integrity," in a process he refers to as "mothering the nation" (Taylor 2004:50). Female deities are being promoted by urban intellectuals as symbols of the nation and indigenous cultural identity at a time when the rapid change and globalization in the *doi moi* era has been perceived as a threat to cultural sovereignty and social cohesion. The romanticization of rural traditions as survivals of indigenous culture also gives weight to folklorists' calls for the preservation and revitalization of traditional culture, which is purported to be threatened by the forces of globalization. Recent evolutionary interpretations of the Mother Religion are a facet of impending cultural crisis and the promotion of national identity in the reform era.

A Question of Identity

Philip Taylor's book on spirit worship in southern Vietnam elaborates upon a distinction between "warrior–scholar–official spirits," who are male historical personages with specific identities, and female spirits or goddesses, who have less fixed, more fluid identities. The former are closely associated with state power and have been honored by the socialist state "as models of heroic citizenry and symbols of the revolutionary resistance spirit" (Taylor 2004:215). The latter have a more indeterminate identity and ambiguous cultural status because goddesses often have a less identifiable human biography. Despite the recent attempts by Vietnamese folklorists to interpret female spirits as cultural heroines in a similar way to male historical personages, Taylor argues that the indeterminacy and polyvalence of goddesses like the Lady of the Realm has "allowed them to become loci of diffused meanings and disparate usages and to speak to a geographically extensive following" (Taylor 2004:287). Compared with goddesses, warrior–scholar–official spirits in the south have more restricted popularity and are attributed less magical responsiveness. This symbolic interpretation usefully outlines the polyvalent and ambiguous quality of religious symbols and the patterns of their appeal and perceived efficacy. Regarding the Four Palace pantheon, which Taylor does not consider, a similar distinction can be made between male warrior–scholar spirits and female goddesses, but the differences in the specificity of male and female identities are not as marked as in spirit worship in the south.

General Tran Hung Dao is one of the most prominent historical figures revered as a symbol of military resistance to foreign aggression, and his identity is largely fixed by official historical accounts (e.g., Trinh Quang Khanh 2000). Other male spirits are also known for their contribution to defending and building the nation: the Fifth Mandarin is renowned for vanquished Chinese invaders on the Do Tranh river in Hai Hung province, and stories about the Third, Seventh, and Tenth princes refer to their prominent positions in the feudal courts. However, precise historical details and dates are often ambiguous, and the multiple stories about the spirits are sometimes contradictory. A brief discussion of "the five great mandarins" (*ngu vi vuong quan*) will serve to illustrate the ambiguities in the histories and identities of male spirits. The Third and Fifth mandarins are the most renowned of the group, and tales about them relate to Vietnamese prehistory. The Third Mandarin is reputed to have been a military general for the founding fathers of Vietnam, the Hung kings, prior to the millennium of Chinese rule (111 B.C.–938 A.D.). *Chau van* song texts refer to him as "the son of the water king of Dong Dinh lake" and tell of his descent to numerous lakes, waterfalls, and rivers throughout Vietnam. Tales about the Fifth Mandarin recount that he is the son of the legendary dragon king, Long Vuong. He is reputed to have seduced a mandarin's daughter in Ninh Giang province and to have became manifest as a snake. As a snake spirit he created a storm on the Do Tranh river to defeat enemy invaders. In the northern provinces of Quang Ninh and Lang Son, the Fifth Mandarin is alternatively revered as one of Tran Hung Dao sons (Ngo Duc Thinh 1996a). The First, Second, and Fourth mandarins are less frequently incarnated at *len dong*, and their human biographies are less specific. They are spirits of celestial origin: the First and Fourth mandarins descended to earth to rescue the people from evil forces, and the Second Mandarin is known primarily as a guardian of the mountains and forests.

If the human biographies of male spirits are not always clearly defined, the mortal lives of most goddesses are similarly indefinite. The princesses, for instance, are famed for their connections with the natural features of the Four Palaces and their miraculous powers, yet little detail is known about their activities as mortals. Although male spirits are also associated with the Four Palaces, the natural world is anthropomorphized most strongly in the female form. This anthropomorphizing is evident in the honorific titles commonly used for female spirits, such as "the Third Princess of the Water" (Co Bo Thoai) and "the Little Princess of the Mountains" (Co Be Thuong). The ritual actions of the goddesses confirm associations with the natural world, and song texts depict wondrous scenes of goddesses in harmony with nature. In ritual action and song, ladies and princesses joyfully stroll through abundant orchards in the hills or row along rivers and streams, far and wide, visiting sacred sites. The goddesses of the Four Palace pantheon have a geographically extensive following, and numerous ethnic minority spirits from the border regions in the lady and princess ranks have attracted large numbers of devotees. But famous male spirits like the Third and Fifth mandarins and the Third, Seventh, and Tenth princes enjoy similar levels of popularity as renowned regional goddesses.

The only goddesses about whom detailed biographical information has been transmitted in oral tales and literary sources are the mothers. The Third Mother, who is also considered to be an incarnation of the First Mother, has the most detailed and documented biography. The various stories about the Third Mother, Lieu Hanh—in song texts, oral legends, and Doan Thi Diem's novel *The Story of the Goddess of Van Cat* (*Van Cat Than Nu Truyen*), written in the 1730s—merge popular Vietnamese legends with religious ingredients borrowed from Taoism and the spiritual qualities of the Cham goddess Po Nagar (see Vu Ngoc Khanh and Pham Van Ty 1990; Nguyen The Anh 1995; Dror 2002). Accounts of Lieu Hanh's life tell of a short, fragile human existence. Born into a family of a mandarin in 1557, she was renowned in her youth for her radiant beauty and exceptional talents at music and poetry.

She married and gave birth to two sons before dying suddenly at the age of twenty-one and returning to the heavens. Because of the deep compassion she had developed for mortals while on earth, the Jade Emperor permitted her to return to earth two years after her death. On her return, she made her immortal identity known and traveled widely performing miraculous deeds to help the people. As well as spreading prosperity and happiness, Lieu Hanh is reputed to have unleashed an epidemic in revenge for the destruction of her retreat at Pho Cat during the reign of Le Huyen Tong (1663–71). After her act of vengeance, the temple was restored and she was acknowledged by the court as a powerful deity.

Lieu Hanh is the preeminent mother spirit and is arguably the most celebrated deity in the pantheon. In balance with the "mother" Lieu Hanh, the highest-ranking male spirit, General Tran Hung Dao, is popularly referred to as the "father." The cosmological balance between mother and father is formulated as the centerpiece of the religious calendar in the aphorism "August is the father's death anniversary, March is the mother's death anniversary" (*Thang tam gio cha, thang ba gio me*). The large festivals in honor of Lieu Hanh and Tran Hung Dao, at Phu Giay and Kiep Bac during the third and eighth lunar months, respectively, are two high points of ritual activity.

Comparison of the identities of goddess Lieu Hanh and General Tran Hung Dao, and their relationship to the state, confirms some of the points made by Taylor in his analysis of spirit worship in the south. Lieu Hanh's potential during her human life was largely unrealized because of her premature death; her fame is based on her miraculous feats when she returned to earth after her death, rather than on her lifetime accomplishments. Her cultural status is therefore more ambiguous compared with the general's, as his lifetime achievements are represented as the pinnacle of human endeavor. Therefore, it is difficult for Lieu Hanh to be tied to state projects and historic nation-building deeds. General Tran Hung Dao's more specific identity as a famous historical figure, on the other hand, has meant that he has been officially recognized and promoted by the state, and commemoration of the general has intensified in the reform era. However, the ritual embodiment of the general during *len dong* was prohibited by the Party and continues to contravene officially condoned modes of ritualization and veneration. When I went to the Kiep Bac festival in Hai Duong province in 1996, spirit possession was strictly forbidden in the main temple. While I was looking around the temple, a group of worshippers started to dance vigorously in front of the general's statue as if they were being spontaneously possessed. Upon seeing the dancing, one of the festival officials stepped in; he forcefully told them to stop and dispersed the group. Despite these restrictions, the authorities were unable to stem the tide: General Tran Hung Dao was being incarnated in the temples I visited on the fringes of Kiep Bac. Acts of self-mutilation, such as self-strangulation, flame eating, and tongue and cheek piercing, which were associated with incarnations of the general by male mediums in the colonial era, seem to have been effectively curtailed by the antisuperstition policy. Certainly, none of the mediums at Kiep Bac were engaging in such acts, although I heard rumors that acts of self-mutilation are still practiced by some mediums.

Despite state control concerning the appropriate way to honor and respect national heroes, the general has maintained his reputation for spiritual responsiveness and continues to be incarnated during *len dong*. State sanctions may have curtailed certain practices, but they have not made the general inaccessible to mediums. Through inclusion in the Four Palace spirit pantheon and incarnation at rituals, the general has retained relevance as a spiritual agent. This is in contrast to the official rehabilitation and endorsement in southern Vietnam of male spirits such as Viceroy Le Van Duyet and Marshal Nguyen Huynh Duc, which has had the effect of decreasing their popularity and perceived magical responsiveness (Taylor 2004:219).

Although the life histories and identities of the goddess Lieu Hanh and General Tran Hung Dao are characterized by different degrees of specificity, this is not replicated across the Four Palace pantheon as a whole. In general, the goddesses and male warrior-scholar spirits incarnated during *len dong* have similarly indeterminate and fluid identities, and their usages and spiritual efficacy have not been strongly circumscribed by official narratives that concentrate on their historical contribution to the nation. The qualities and attributes of male spirits are therefore not substantially more fixed or constrained than the goddesses. Spirits strongly embody culturally defined gendered characteristics, yet both male and female deities in the Four Palace pantheon are called upon by adepts to address a diverse range of issues affecting their lives.

"Coming Out" as a Medium

"Coming out as a medium" (*ra dong* or *trinh dong*) is a life-transforming event that is usually prompted by a crisis or affliction. The period prior to initiation can be physically and emotionally turbulent, and initiation is prescribed as a resolution or cure. Becoming a medium is understood as being part of a person's fate, as an inevitable occurrence. The language of initiation is specific to mediumship. Initiates are said to have the "destined aptitude" or "spirit root" (*can* or *can so*) for mediumship.[4] Those who possess a "heavy destiny and a high aptitude" (*can cao so nang*) cannot deny the will of the spirits and are compelled to become mediums. Compulsion and submission are prominent features of mediumship. Mediums are servants or "soldiers" (*linh*) who obey the spirits' "orders" (*truyen lenh*); they are "chosen" (*cham dong*), "seized"/"forced" (*bat*), "tormented" (*hanh*), and "punished" (*phat*) by spirits; they are "children" (*con*) who "serve" (*hau*) the spirits; they are "chairs" (*ghe*) mounted by the spirits. Many mediums develop special relationships with one or more spirits. An initiate who is "chosen" for mediumship by a particular spirit is said to have a "destined aptitude" for that spirit. A medium with the "destined aptitude of the Third Mandarin" (*can Quan De Tam*), for instance, has been touched by the mandarin's spiritual powers and has a strong affinity with his character and attributes.

Adepts consult spirit priests or master mediums to determine the etiology of afflictions. They typically seek such consultations when other health care resources, such as Western biomedicine and Chinese or Vietnamese herbal medicine, have not improved the situation or when these alternatives are not available for financial or other reasons. In such cases, afflictions may be attributed to spontaneous involuntary possession by "evil spirits" (*ma quy*) or to punishment by the benevolent spirits (*than/thanh*) of the Four Palaces. Unexplainable misfortune or bad luck, rather than illness, may also be diagnosed as having a divine cause. The proof of the diagnoses of ritual specialists depends on whether there is a successful resolution of difficulties after initiation; I did not come across any mediums who thought their problems had not, at least to some extent, been alleviated after initiation.

While there are common themes in mediums' narratives about their calling and initiation, the manifestation of afflictions relates to the social circumstances and life histories of individuals. To explore the range of reasons why individuals become mediums, in the following discussion, I draw on in-depth interviews with seven mediums, five female (Xuan, Hoa, Doan, Lai, Binh) and two male (Quyet and Nguyen), which I conducted in 1997 and 1998.

The afflictions suffered by these seven mediums were diverse. They ranged from problems with fertility and the death of a newborn baby, to "madness" (*dien*) and complaints relating to the "nervous system" (*than kinh*), to illness and debilitating states including lethargy to long periods of severe immobility. Doan had problems with conceiving children; two of Binh's children died shortly after birth for no explainable reason; Hoa was tormented by the spirits to such an extent that she said she "died for three and a half hours"; Xuan suffered tiredness, headaches, and illness of the "heart and mind" (*tam tinh*), which could not be cured by medicine; Nguyen was tired and weak and was then involuntarily possessed by evil spirits, which made him lose control of his body and thrash around; Lai and Quyet were so ill that they could not move and were bedridden for months. Dreams featured in Binh and Lai's descriptions of being "seized" by spirits. In Lai's dream she was bitten by mandarins, who appeared as snakes, and she found that she could not walk the next day. In Binh's dream she was visited by the spirits, who taught her how to perform ritual dances. Lai also mentioned that "knotted hair" is another common manifestation of punishment by the spirits.[5]

All seven mediums said their afflictions were alleviated through initiation. After becoming mediums, Doan and Binh gave birth to healthy children; Hoa said she "had to 'come out' so that I could live again" after her "death"; Xuan's illness was eased through ritualizing; Nguyen controlled his involuntary possession by evil spirits; Quyet recovered from "madness" and his "heart became peaceful"; and Lai could walk again and became prosperous, healthy, and relaxed.

Explanations of personal crises and spirit possession have often been sought in terms of psychoanalytic models (see Obeyesekere 1977; Lewis 1989 [1971]:160–84). However, psychoanalytic interpretations are problematic, because they tend to assert unconscious motivations for religious practice that are not acknowledged by adepts themselves. The cross-cultural imposition of Western psychoanalytic categories, such as "sexual repression," "aggressive drive," and "hysteria," also often fails to take into account the social and cultural meanings of local practices (see Atkinson 1992:309–13; Stoller 1995:18–19).

In Vietnam, little research has been conducted on the way illness is experienced from a sociocultural point of view. Tine Gammeltoft's pioneering study of women's health and family planning in a Vietnamese rural community is a notable exception (1999). Drawing on the work of the medical anthropologist Arthur Kleinman, Gammeltoft discusses the ways in which illness is constructed within "local moral worlds." She argues that Vietnamese women express distress through "somatic expressions," through physical ailments like headaches, dizziness, and weakness, and that these somatic expressions are one of the main ways in which women can actively change and affect their social surroundings (Gammeltoft 1999:235–36). It is noteworthy that mediums described afflictions of "madness" or problems with "the nervous system" as abnormal bodily behavior resulting in the breakdown of close social relationships. Doan said she wandered around in a dream, went begging at the market, and failed to look after her children; Xuan talked too much and was rarely at home; and Quyet was excessively active one minute and bedridden the next, and when spontaneously possessed by evil spirits he lost control of his body. Madness is conceptualized in the discourse of mediums as an abnormal bodily state rather than as a "mental illness," and its cause is related to spirits rather than an individual's psychology.

Madness is usually associated with crises that lead to initiation. In Lai's words: "If you avoid [coming out as a medium], then you will suffer 'madness' and be punished by the spirits." Unusually, Doan suffered a bout of "madness" for several months after the birth of her second child, a few years after she was initiated. According to Doan she was involuntarily possessed by the Ninth Princess, and the princess made her go far from her family to visit the famous Bac Le temple in northeast Vietnam. Her abnormal behavior and neglect of her children subsided only when she established her own private temple next to her home and began to tell fortunes. Doan said she had a "destined aptitude for the Ninth Princess" (*can co Chin*) and that the princess had bestowed upon her fortune-telling powers. She rationalized her "madness" as an affliction caused by the spirits and as part of the process of becoming a fortune-telling medium.

Initiation: "Opening the Palaces"

Once it is established that a person has a destined aptitude for mediumship, an initiation ritual is arranged.[6] The initiation ritual is known as "opening the palaces" (*mo phu*), because it gives initiates access to the spirits of the Four Palaces. To "open" the palaces, the initiate is assisted by an experienced master medium. At the start of the ritual, the master medium is possessed by several spirits in succession while the initiate watches. She then invites the initiate to kneel in front of the altar to carry out an "asking rite" (*le khat*), which is also known as "placing bowls of incense on the head" (*doi bat huong*). The purpose of the asking rite is to gain the acceptance and approval of the spirits for the initiation. A red cloth is draped over the initiate's head, and a large tray, containing incense sticks and other votive objects and "spirit petitions" (*so*) written in Chinese or Sino-Vietnamese characters, is balanced on top of the red cloth. The experienced medium consults the spirits by throwing two old coins, in a procedure known as "asking yin and yang" (*hoi am duong*). If both coins land on heads or tails, then the spirits' response is favorable and unfavorable, respectively. If one coin falls on heads and the other tails, then the spirits are undecided. If both coins do not land on heads after three throws, the initiate is not accepted by the spirits and the coins have to thrown again on another occasion. This procedure is not only carried out during formal initiation rituals; mediums also carry out the asking rite for devotees at other times of worship and at religious festivals to get an indication of whether they have a destiny for mediumship.

On successful completion of the "asking yin and yang" procedure, the initiate comes before the altar to be possessed. On the two occasions I attended initiation ceremonies, the initiates seemed overwhelmed by the occasion and looked hesitant and unconfident when carrying out ritual actions. They were helped through their first rituals by the master medium and ritual assistants, who whispered advice to the initiates and occasionally guided their movements. Although it was clear that both initiates had much to learn before they could "serve the spirits beautifully" (*hau bong dep*), their initiations were successful, and I did not hear of any "failed" initiations.

The initiation process is concluded with a "thanking ritual" (*le ta/ta phu*), which is usually held one hundred days after "opening the palaces." The thanking ritual is held by the newly initiated medium, without the assistance of a master medium, to express gratitude to the spirits. Thanking rituals may also be held at other times outside of the context of initiation when an occasion arises to give thanks to the spirits.

Fortune-Telling and Healing

In her folklore study of mediumship, Nguyen Thi Hien notes, "In the Viet conception of health, there are two kinds of disease—yang (*duong*) and yin (*am*)" (2002:20). When afflictions are thought to stem from the "yin spirit world" (*coi am*), as opposed to the "yang human world" (*duong tran*), they require treatment and resolution through ritual performance and worship. The embodied presence of spirits enables mediums to tackle difficulties rooted in the yin spirit world. Mediums overcome difficulties through initiation, but mediums vary in the extent to which they carry out acts of healing and prophecy for other ritual participants. Some have an aptitude for fortune-telling and healing, whereas others do not.

Some ritual acts associated with curing or prophecy take place during *len dong*. Two of the most common are the giving of "incense water" (*nuoc thai*) and a rite known as *cat tien duyen* (lit. "cutting off from the love fate of a previous life"). Mediums give out incense water consisting of a little incense ash mixed with water, usually when possessed by the Third Princess. The *cat tien duyen* rite involves separating "yin" and "yang" offerings. The disciple kneels in front of the altar with a scarf draped over her head, and a large tray of votive objects is placed on top of the scarf. Votive objects typically include spirit petitions, paper shoes, fans, rice, and salt. The medium divides these objects in half. The yin offerings are burned for the spirit world, and the yang are retained in the human world. This separation makes a break with the difficulties in love in a previous life. As one medium explained:

> The separation of votive objects enables the "yin people" (*nguoi am*) [i.e., the deceased] and people in this world to enjoy blessed gifts. The yin will return to the yin and the yang will return to the yang; then the living will be able to love whom they wish and get married. After the *cat tien duyen* rite, the yin no longer haunts the living.

Mediums' prophecy and healing arise from divine embodiment. Some spirits are reputed to have fortune-telling and healing powers and bestow these powers on devotees. Only those mediums who can call on the powers of the spirits at will are able to heal and prophesy while not possessed. There has been a surge in popularity for fortune-telling and healing in the reform period, and renowned mediums are inundated with visitors seeking consultations.

Fortune-telling and healing sessions are typically held in temples. Mediums use numerous esoteric techniques, such as "face reading" (*tuong mat*), palmistry, astrology and divination by casting sticks, and examining chicken's feet or spliced betel nut. The topics raised at the fortune-telling sessions I witnessed were mainly about health, work, and love. Often with no prior knowledge of the client, mediums respond to questions and speak about the client's present situation and future. The language of fortune-telling is infused with proverbs, religious terminology, and aphorisms. At one session, a twenty-five-year-old woman, called Phuong, was told she would have obstacles in her work and love life. Regarding work, Phuong was told that she worked on the land but had aspirations to do something different. Regarding love, she was advised that she would marry the third or fourth person she loved and that she already knew her husband. Phuong's husband-to-be was from her home village and was a large, handsome man. To achieve a happy marriage, Phuong was urged by the medium to perform the *cat tien duyen* rite. The prescription of religious activity, such as a rite or initiation into mediumship, is a common feature of fortune-telling sessions.

At healing consultations, the illness is discussed with the client, and after hearing about, and perhaps also examining, the physical symptoms, the medium diagnoses whether the complaint is a "yin illness" (*benh am*) or whether it is a disease appropriate for other forms of medical treatment. Mediums work within a plural system of health care and emphasize that their diagnoses are complementary to, rather than a replacement for, forms of Western biomedicine and Chinese and Vietnamese herbal remedies. People usually approach mediums after Western biomedicine or herbal medicine has proved ineffective or when the cost of doctor and hospital appointments is prohibitive. As one healing medium remarked:

> For example, if somebody has a chest pain I will "look at" their heart-soul ... If the cause of the illness is due to their fate ... or if the illness is due to evil spirits, then it can be cured by an "invocation" (*khan*) to the spirits ... I tell [people] to go to the hospital first, but I will also "call out" (*keu*) to help them use the "spirits' medicine" (*thuoc thanh*).

Invocations muttered in front of the spirit altar are central to the healing sessions. These include stating the name and address of the client, the name of the temple, the date, the client's complaint, and the names of spirits who are implored for assistance. Petitions written to the spirits in Chinese or old Sino-Vietnamese characters seal the invocations as text. After the invocation, petitions are burned and the ashes are mixed with water and, like incense water, may be drunk as a remedy.

Embodied Language: The Words of the Spirits

Mediums become the vehicle of spirits when possessed and "the words of the spirits" (*loi thanh*) are "transmitted" (*truyen*) through them. The utterances of spirits vary from just a few standard phrases, which exhibit a high degree of redundancy, through to more extended statements and dialogue with disciples. The focal point of the verbal interactions between embodied spirits and ritual participants is the exchange of offerings and blessed gifts. Divine utterances confirm the authority of the spirits and establish the mutual dependency between the human and spirit worlds. Disciples are encouraged to worship deities with statements like "worship the four palaces" (*tho bon phu*), "with 'one heart' do Buddha's work, with a true heart do the work of the spirits" (*nhat tam viec phat, thuc tam viec thanh*), and "organize the work of the spirits above, endure the earthly work below" (*tren thi lo viec thanh, duoi thi ganh viec tran*). In return, the spirits transmit words of protection and assistance to their devotees. When disciples approach the medium with offerings, it is conventional to "plead for blessed gifts" (*xin cho loc*), to implore the spirits to "protect" (*phu ho*) their "family lineage" (*ho*). Hearing the disciples' pleas, the spirits "praise" (*ban khen*) and "pity" (*thuong*) their devotees and their lineages, they "witness the hearts" (*chung tam*) of mortals.

An example of a general pronouncement by the Third Mandarin can be heard in Video Extract 12 on the DVD. Just before the termination of possession, the medium, Hang, declares: "I, the mandarin, witness the heart of the master of the temple; I witness the heart of the spirit priest; I witness the hearts of all the 'chairs' [devotees] in the cosmos; I witness everyone's hearts" (*Quan chung tam cho thu nhang; chung tam cho phap su; chung tam cho cac ghe vu tru; chung tam cho bach gia tram ho*). With these words, the mandarin asserts his awareness of the thoughts and feelings of ritual participants and grants them spiritual protection.

Mediums who fortune-tell and heal are often the most loquacious when possessed. They expand upon the stock phrases and sometimes transmit specific advice about the health and future of individuals when they approach embodied deities with offerings. Divine engagement with disciples is a vital part of religious practice, as it brings deities close to the everyday lives of their followers. The words of the spirits, along with other aspects of ritual performance, are a tangible manifestation of divine power. The verbal interactions between the spirits and ritual participants are discussed further in Chapter 6 with reference to an "end of year" ritual.

Aware Possession and Obsession

Mediums recognize two distinct possession states. During *len dong*, possessees were adamant they were aware of everything going on around them: they were "alert" or "aware" (*tinh* or *tinh tao*). This form of controlled "aware possession" contrasts with an undesirable possession state characterized by a loss of awareness and bodily control, which was described as being "*me.*" This state is associated with involuntary possession prior to initiation by evil spirits or by displeased spirits of the Four Palace pantheon.

Out-of-control states prior to initiation have been variously described in the literature on spirit possession as "crisis," "possession crisis," "fit," or "trance." In his discussion of the terminology used to describe possession states prior to and after initiation, Gilbert Rouget differentiates between possession and obsession: "The difference between obsession and possession lies in the fact that obsession calls for either initiation—thereby becoming possession—or exorcism, whereas possession, which can only occur after initiation . . . never in any case leads to exorcism" (1985 [1980]:46). This distinction draws on the meanings of the term obsession in the Renaissance. Although in the Christian context of Renaissance Europe, obsession was used to describe involuntary tormenting by the devil—a "prepossession" state of being besieged, but not possessed, by the devil—Rouget extends its usage to include the forms of possession that call for initiation or exorcism.[7] Obsession, Rouget argues, is preferable to terms like unhappy or inauthentic possession (1985 [1980]:45).

I gloss *me* as "obsession" because it evokes the Vietnamese meanings of the term. The two main literal meanings of *me* are (1) to be infatuated with love for somebody or very keen about something; (2) to be unconscious or insensible.[8] *Me* possession involves being tormented or infatuated by spirits. This kind of possession is similar to being "unconscious," in that it is characterized by a complete lack of awareness, but it does not imply immobility. When mediums are *me* they are often thrown into an agitated bodily state, which may involve violent activity.[9] Obsession resonates with the meaning of *me* as an infatuated, involuntary possession state, while avoiding an inappropriate use of "unconscious." In the Vietnamese context, the notion of obsession is similar to Rouget's definition because it refers to a possession state that usually leads to initiation. However, for Vietnamese mediums obsession does not lead to exorcism, and in rare cases obsession may also occur after initiation.

Previous research written in English and French has asserted that *len dong* involves trance.[10] Folklore scholars writing in Vietnamese have also attempted to find a term for trance. The book *Hat Van* states: "Mediums must hypnotize themselves to create a 'state of trance' (*trang thai ngay ngat*)" (Ngo Duc Thinh 1992:43). *Ngay ngat* has two meanings: (1) to be thrilled, enraptured, or thrown into ecstasy; (2) intoxicating or heady. When I discussed *ngay ngat* with Ngo Duc Thinh, he confirmed the term was a scholarly attempt to find an equivalent for the notion of trance, and he suggested that those mediums who did not enter a state of trance were not truly possessed by spirits but just wanted to "perform" (*bieu dien*) (pers. comm., June 1998). However, mediums themselves did not use the term *ngay ngat*. For instance, when I asked a medium called Van whether she entered "a state of trance" (*trang thai ngay ngat*), she ignored the phrase and did not use it in her own description of her possession experiences.

Studies of mediumship and shamanism have often coupled possession and trance together, as if one cannot exist without the other. However, scholars have inappropriately applied the notions of trance and ecstasy to some ritual contexts. In her reevaluation of scholarship on Siberian shamanistic societies, Roberte Hamayon argues that the notion of trance is "irrelevant" (1995:20). She makes the point that the notion of trance does not concur with Siberian shamans' understandings of their ritual activities, and she challenges its usefulness as an analytical concept.

Despite such reevaluations, the notion of trance shows little sign of being abandoned by scholars. Judith Becker, for instance, makes a strong case for retaining trance as "a cover term for a set of events that more or less resemble each other" (2004:44). Becker is acutely aware of the variability of languaged reports of trance experiences and the difficulties of applying the term cross-culturally. Nonetheless, she considers trance to have "defining characteristics." For Becker, trance is "a bodily event characterized by strong motion, intense focus, the loss of the strong sense of self, usually enveloped by amnesia and a cessation of the inner languaging" (2004:43). This definition focuses on the emotional body, but Becker ultimately aims to bridge the gulf between humanist and scientific approaches to embodied experience.

In her attempt to understand how varied first-person reports of trancers relate to the neurophysiology of trance consciousness, Becker draws on the theories of the neuroscientist Antonio Damasio concerning core consciousness and extended consciousness. Core consciousness or "core self" is short-term and about the sensation of immediate events, whereas extended consciousness is much longer-term. Extended consciousness or autobiographical self is "linked to our personal history, our lifelong memories and our social sense of who we are" (Becker 2004:139). Becker hypothesizes that trance consciousness involves temporary loss or displacement of the autobiographical self, so trancers experience a modified, alternate extended consciousness. At the same time, trancers are able to maintain an immediate awareness of their environment and continue interacting appropriately with the things and people around them because of the continued presence of core consciousness. In Becker's words, "Damasio's theory of the distinction between core consciousness and autobiographical consciousness better allows me to imagine the neurophysiology of trance as the substitution of a trance persona during trancing, a circumscribed, alternate autobiographical trancing self who enacts a prescribed role within a stable, sacred narrative" (Becker 2004:146).

Becker's application of Damasio's theories to trance experiences is conjectural, and further research is required to establish whether diverse, culturally bound trance experiences can be equated to an alternate extended consciousness. Nonetheless, her suggestions are stimulating and provocative. In the ritual context of *len dong,* could it be that mediums experience a form of modified extended consciousness in which their autobiographical self is displaced, while retaining their core consciousness and hence their immediate awareness of their body and environment? While this is an intriguing possibility, without neuroscientific investigation of mediums' experiences of aware possession (which, needless to say, would raise numerous practical and ethical problems), it remains just a possibility. The thorny issue also remains about how obsession might relate to core and extended consciousness. Leaving aside for now the issue of Damasio's theory of two-leveled consciousness, let us turn to mediums' descriptions of the embodied state of aware possession as a sensuous, bodily experience.

Experiencing Possession: The Body and Embodiment

Csordas makes a methodological distinction between "'the body' as a biological, material entity and 'embodiment' as an indeterminate methodological field defined by perceptual experience and mode of presence and engagement in the world" (1994:12). The importance of this distinction lies in moving away from the study of the body as an object in relation to culture toward a consideration of the body "as the subject of culture, or in other words as the existential ground of culture" (Csordas 2002:58).[11] In Csordas's cultural phenomenology, the body is the intersubjective ground of experience and embodiment is a paradigm concerned with how "culture and experience . . . can be understood from the standpoint of bodily being-in-the-world" (1999:143).

The way Vietnamese mediums described their experiences encourages a consideration of possession from the methodological standpoint of embodiment. In a direct way, the body is the source or ground of possession and ritual action. Embodied possession is rooted in mediums' conceptions of bodiliness.

Verbal reports of aware possession elaborate on somatic changes centered in the "heart" (*tam*) and "heart-soul" (*tam linh/tam hon*). The following discussion of the bodily experience of possession refers to descriptions by six mediums about how they felt when they incarnated spirits. Five of these mediums—Doan, Binh, Lai, Hoa, and Xuan—have already been introduced earlier in this chapter, and the sixth is a female medium called Van.

In aware possession, spirits "enter" (*nhap*) the "body" (*than/xac than*). Doan and Xuan reported that the spirits entered their head as well as their bodies, whereas Binh said the spirits entered her heart. When the spirits enter, the possessee experiences feelings like "heavy shoulders and head" (Doan and Xuan), "lightness" (Binh), and "hotness" and "dreaminess" (Lai). While possessed, Van had two "roles" (*vai*) in her head, her brain felt "limitless"(*menh mang*), and her mind "flew away" (*phieu dieu*).[12] Xuan said her mind was "elated" (*sang khoai*), as if the spirit was "flying and gliding" (*bay bay luon luon*).

The heart is involved with possession in multifaceted ways. Binh said that when the spirits entered her heart, she had "premonitions" (*linh cam*). Mediums often pointed out the heart as the locus of interaction with the spirits: a "true heart" (*thuc tam*) is necessary in order for premonitions to occur (Van); the spirits enter the "innermost feelings of the heart" (*tam tu*) (Xuan). Doan said that the "miraculous response" (*linh ung*) of the spirits is felt in the heart, that the spirits "inscribe the heart" (*de tam*), and that the utterances of the spirits are transmitted through the heart.

The heart is the primary site of possession because it feels the presence of spirits and responds to them. There is a dialectical relationship between the heart and spiritual forces: mediums "have heart" (*co tam*) for the spirits and are devoted with "one heart" (*nhat tam*) to worship, and in return the spirits "witness the hearts" (*chung tam*) of their followers. The heart is also present as the first part of the compound words for "soul," *tam linh* or *tam hon,* and I have emphasized the connection between the heart and soul by rendering these words as *heart-soul.*[13] Like the heart, the heart-soul is affected by being possessed by spirits. During possession, Van's heart-soul "floated up" to the top of the sky, and Doan said her heart-soul felt "different than normal."

A distinction between the heart (and heart-soul) as the seat of emotion and the mind as the seat of cognition was not significant for mediums. Xuan remarked that her heart "thinks" (*nghi*) about the spirits, suggesting that the heart is a locus of cognition as well as emotion, and conversely she said her mind was "elated" during possession. Other compound words like *tam tri* (lit. "heart-intellect") also imply a merging of heart and mind. This is confirmed by Tine Gammeltoft's research in rural Vietnam. She found that in everyday life, "talking about brains seems to be another way of talking about hearts, and intellectual capacities are also social/emotional categories" (Gammeltoft 1999:211).

The intertwining of heart and mind in Vietnamese discourse has similarities with Chinese ideas about emotion. As Thomas Ots explains: "In traditional Chinese medicine, the mind is placed within the heart (*xin*). The heart is understood as the supreme viscera because it is perceived as the seat of cognition and of virtue (*de*). The heart-mind is the grounding space for all aspects of bodily as well as social well-being" (Ots 1994:118–19). In his study of *qigong* exercises and techniques of health preservation, Ots refers to the "the Chinese 'heart-mind controls emotion' model," in which excessive emotions are understood as disruptive utterings of the body that hurt the heart and heart-mind. He traces the conception that emotions hurt the calm physical body to classical Taoist thought.

Given that Taoism has had some influence in Vietnam, Vietnamese conceptions of emotion may also relate to Taoist thought. Notably, scholars have traced Taoist elements in the Four Palace religion. But the connection between heart and mind is not just restricted to China and Vietnam. In Malaysia, Temiar people say they "think in the heart" and "the heart soul is the locus of thought, feeling and awareness" (Roseman 1991:30).

In addition to the heart, the stomach or gut (*bung/long/ruot/da*) features as the seat of emotions and feelings in many Vietnamese expressions. For example, the compound words "to fall in love" (*phai long*), "to hurt someone's feelings" (*mech long*), and "good-natured" (*tot bung*) all refer to the stomach. Gammeltoft also notes that in everyday expressions, thoughts as well as emotions are metaphorically placed in the stomach. Just as it is possible for the heart to "think," one can also "think in the stomach" (*nghi trong bung*) (Gammeltoft 1999:210). In the context of mediumship, spirits were not said to enter the stomach as they did the heart. However, mediums did use some expressions in which the heart and guts are interchangeable: *thuc long* (lit. "true gut") and *mot long* (lit. "one gut") were used synonymously with *thuc tam* (lit. "true heart") and *nhat tam* (lit. "one heart"), respectively. Also, female mediums are known for being "hot-gutted" (*nong long/nong ruot*), which means they are hot-tempered and often feel uneasy or impatient.

When asked to objectify their bodily experiences, mediums did so in slightly different ways, but all felt the sensory presence of spirits through bodily changes. When a spirit is incarnated, various parts of the body—the heart, heart-soul, head, and shoulders—are affected. According to mediums, the primary nexus between human and spirit is the heart: the presence of spirits is felt in the heart; premonitions and magical responses come from the heart; the spirits "speak through" the heart. To experience the heightened emotion arousal of possession, it is necessary to adopt a particular somatic mode of attention, to borrow Csordas's phrase. The somatic mode of aware possession becomes manifest through having a true heart and concentrating with one heart on the spirits, and in return the spirits witness the hearts of ritual participants. Embodied possession is a way of being-in-the-world that affords interaction between humans and the divine, and that being is inherently musical, as will be elaborated in the next chapter.

3

Songs for the Spirits

A possession ritual is an architecture of time . . . composed
of various phases connected with different kinds of music.

—Rouget 1985 [1980]:32–33

The sequences of songs or "songscapes" performed by *chau van*
bands create a continually changing sonic environment in which spirits are
immersed and their presence is articulated.[1] Songscapes have a temporal
as well as a spatial dimension (song-scape: time-space): they structure the
flow of ritual time and acoustically mark out the space in which rituals are
carried out. By establishing an "atmosphere" (*khong khi*) within the temple,
songscapes also aid the active participation of all who attend rituals.

Through a system that links songs to ritual action, different songs are performed at each stage of possession. A songscape lasts as long as a particular
possession and is best thought of as a single unit consisting of many different parts. Each spirit has its own distinctive body of song texts, but only a
few songs are performed for one particular spirit. Although most songs are
performed for more than one spirit, only certain songs or groups of songs are
permitted for certain ranks of spirits (the mandarins, ladies, princes, and so
on). For example, most of the "Phu" group of melodies are performed only
for prestigious male spirits, usually the mandarins and occasionally princes.
The overall structure of songscapes is therefore distinctive to the identity and
actions of spirits.

In this chapter, I discuss the *chau van* musical system and the creation of
songscapes. *Len dong* are performative in the sense that they are multime-
dia events incorporating sound, movement, visual elements, taste, and smell
(Tambiah 1985). The approach I take relates musical performance to other
aspects of ritual practice and experience. A performance-oriented analysis
of *chau van* is necessary because of the intimate connections between songs

and ritual action. As will become clear, the interaction between the medium and the band is of central importance. When the medium carries out certain actions, such as kowtowing to the altar, waving incense, drinking rice wine, or dancing, the songs performed embody the ritual action. *Chau van* bands sonically articulate ritual acts; they make bodily movement manifest in sound.

By exploring how musical performance and aesthetics are entwined with other modes of ritual activity and the character of spirits, the analysis of songscapes in this chapter is concerned with what Regula Qureshi has called "music–context interaction" (1995 [1986]:140). Following earlier attempts to integrate performance theory into ethnomusicology and to investigate the "ethnography of performance" (McLeod and Herndon 1980), Qureshi's study of Qawwali in India and Pakistan sought to establish a synthesis between musical and contextual analysis of the performance occasion. Her analyses of Qawwali events focus on the "interplay between music and audience behavior" and demonstrate how musicians change their performances in order to increase the ecstatic arousal of the audience (Qureshi 1995 [1986]:143). Qawwali musicians appraise the state of arousal of the audience by observing their gestures. They then intensify the audience's arousal by repeating, recombining, and inserting musical phrases. The dynamics of musical performance at Qawwali events and *len dong* differ, in that *chau van* musicians primarily respond to the actions of the medium, rather than the "audience," and do not usually modify musical phrases or the basic structure of songs in the course of performance. Most of the interaction between mediums and musicians occurs at the "macro level" of song changes and tempo rather than "micro level" of individual music phrases.

As the main thrust of Qureshi's analysis is to demonstrate "how the context of performance affects the music being performed" (1995 [1986]:231), she does not concentrate on the interaction between the musicians themselves. This chapter not only includes discussion of the interrelationships between ritual action and songscapes, but also examines the different roles band members perform and how song changes are carried out by bands. To this end, I will draw on Benjamin Brinner's study of "making music" in Javanese gamelan performances and his theory of musical interaction (1995). Although Brinner's study concentrates on the dynamics of performance between musicians, the analytical framework of musical interaction he outlines is sufficiently broad to include performers whose main role is not music making. The interaction between the medium and the band during *len dong* is therefore included—along with interaction within the band—under the rubric "musical interaction."

The bulk of this chapter focuses on the performance dynamics during incarnations of four spirits at two different rituals. Thirty video extracts from the two rituals are included in the "Songscapes for the Spirits" section of the DVD accompanying this book. By watching the video extracts, the reader is able to directly experience the rituals and listen to the "songs for the spirits" discussed. First, some background on bands and the *chau van* repertoire.

Chau Van Bands

Historical and contemporary oral accounts suggest that male "spirit priests" (*thay cung*) were responsible for performing *chau van* in prerevolutionary Vietnam (Dumoutier 1908:243). This is not always the case today. However, spirit priests who are not proficient at *chau van* still play an important role, through reciting prayers and incanting "spirit petitions" (*so*) before and sometimes during possession. As accomplished ritual specialists who usually have knowledge of Sino-Vietnamese characters, spirit priests are skilled in a broad range of spirit invocations and forms of "worship" (*cung*). In addition to being called upon for spirit worship, they officiate at numerous rites, including funerals and commemoration ceremonies for family ancestors in order to resolve conflicts and ensure harmonious relations between the human and spirit worlds (Malarney 2002:97). Outside of specific ritual occasions, people consult spirit priests for divinations about the future or about their family and love lives, and seek advice for illness that may be attributable to the spirits or involuntary possession. It is also customary for initiates to consult a spirit priest before becoming a medium.

The *chau van* musicians I met during fieldwork had quite diverse backgrounds. Elderly musicians were more likely to be spirit priests, a profession they usually inherited from previous generations of their family, whereas only a few younger musicians had acquired the broad knowledge of invocations and prayers necessary to act as spirit priests. The recent resurgence in ritual activity, and the concomitant increase in demand for *chau van* performers, has attracted many musicians previously trained in other genres to learn mediumship music. Many bands, especially in Hanoi and other urban areas, are made up of professional musicians who are also employed in state-run music troupes, typically *cheo* and *cai luong* troupes, or musicians diversifying from other ritual musics like funeral music (*nhac dam ma*). In the reform era, the salaries of state employees have not kept up with the pace of economic development and are barely sufficient to cover basic living expenses. Many musicians employed by state-run troupes have had to seek freelance work to supplement their incomes, and performing at rituals provides one of the few opportunities for them to do so.

The fee bands receive for performing at *len dong* depends on the medium's circumstances. In 2004, Hanoi-based bands would expect to receive an "advance" (*tien coc*) of anything between 30 and 150 U.S. dollars. Throughout *len dong*, the medium also gives the band "reward money" (*tien thuong*) and other gifts—such as fruit, cigarettes, cans of soft drink, and beer—in appreciation of their performance. The money and gifts are usually shared equally among the members of the band, which serves to confirm the largely unhierarchical composition of bands. Taking into account the advance and reward money, band members in Hanoi typically receive the equivalent of about 30 U.S. dollars in cash. The fees for musicians in rural areas is usually significantly less, but *len dong* is still lucrative when compared with state salaries, which are usually less than 100 U.S. dollars per month.

Apart from spirit priests and professional musicians, the other main route to *chau van* is through mediumship itself. Some ritual participants, including mediums, their relatives, and disciples, become attracted to *chau van* as a consequence of their enthusiasm for spirit worship. People who learn music in this way typically do so through a process of osmosis, with little or no formal training.

The overwhelming majority of *chau van* musicians are male. When I asked my teacher Pham Van Ty why this was the case, he referred to the tradition of spirit priests. Ty suggested that because only men were educated to read and write Sino-Vietnamese characters in colonial times, women could not become spirit priests and perform *chau van*. Although many contemporary *chau van* musicians are not spirit priests, the tradition of men performing mediumship music has continued. However, I did come across some women who sang in bands. Most of these women had come to *chau van* through being mediums or were introduced to it by their husbands who performed ritual music. But female singers were not generally favored. Many mediums told me they preferred male singers because they were able to "flatter" (*ninh*) the spirits more effectively than female singers. Female mediums also seemed to like the male–female dynamic between musicians and mediums, a dynamic that has long been satirized in sexualized terms by critics (Long Chuong 1990 [1942]). Female moon-lute players are even rarer than female singers. Traditionally, the moon lute has male gender associations, and this has ensured that bands are a male domain. In the past, the moon lute was known as the instrument "held by noblemen" (*quan tu cam*), and it is still commonly thought of as a "male" instrument. As one musician once commented, the moon lute is not considered suitable for women because it is not "soft" (*em diu*) and its shape is not "feminine" (*nu tinh*), unlike instruments frequently played by women, such as the pear-shaped lute (*ty ba*) and the sixteen-stringed zither (*dan tranh*).

The membership of bands is often quite fluid. Although certain groups of musicians regularly perform together, the band for any particular ritual may have different members depending on the occasion, the availability of the musicians, and the preferences of the medium. Usually the medium holding the *len dong* invites the band members to perform, and well-liked musicians are in high demand. Some bands are connected to a specific temple as "resident bands" (*cung van truong*).[2] These bands perform for most *len dong* held at the temple and tend to have a more fixed membership than bands formed for a specific ritual occasion. When holding a ritual at a temple with a resident band, mediums do not have the same freedom to choose musicians, but occasionally they invite an additional performer to join the resident band.

The core instruments of *chau van* bands in northern Vietnam are the two-stringed moon lute (*dan nguyet*) and a set of percussion (*bo nhac cu go*). The Vietnamese moon lute, which is related to the Chinese *yueqin,* has a long neck with between eight and eleven—most commonly ten—high frets. The frets are positioned to produce an anhemitonic pentatonic scale (Nguyen Thuyet Phong 1986). Other pitches can be obtained by pressing the strings more deeply against the high frets. The two strings of the moon lute—the small string (*day tieu*) and the big string (*day dai*)—used to be made of silk but are now nylon. For most songs the two strings are tuned to the interval of a fourth (*day lech*) or a fifth (*day bang*); on very rare occasions the interval is a minor seventh (*day to lan*) or an octave (*day song thanh*). The basic set of percussion used for *chau van* consists of the bamboo clappers (*phach*), a small two-headed barrel drum (*trong*), and a small cymbal (*canh*). All of these instruments are placed on the floor and are struck with three wooden beaters (*dui*). Two beaters are held in one hand—one used to strike the small cymbal and the other the clappers—and the third beater is held in the other hand to strike the clappers and drum. To this basic set of percussion a knobless small gong (*thanh la*) and the "wooden fish" slit drum (*mo*) are often added. For some melodies the gong is laid flat on the face of the drum; for others it is handheld. The large double-headed barrel drum found in some temples may also be played during rituals.

Three main rhythms are played on these percussion instruments: the one-beat (*nhip mot*), two-beat (*nhip doi*), and three-beat (*nhip ba*) rhythms. Each of these rhythms consists of a basic pattern:

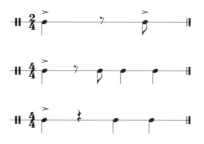

Figure 3.1. The one-beat, two-beat, and three-beat rhythms

Although complex rhythms are added in performance, the basic rhythmic pattern is sounded on the small cymbal or, in the case of the one-beat rhythm, on the clappers, cymbal, or small gong. A few songs do not use the three basic rhythmic patterns. The various types of "Bi" melody, for instance, do not have a regular pulse; they are in "free rhythm" (*nhip tu do*). Some other melodies follow a regular beat but do not utilize a recurring rhythmic framework like the one-, two-, and three-beat rhythms. These include "Thinh Bong," "Trong Chien," and "Sai," which all have their own rhythms, *nhip thinh bong, nhip trong chien,* and *nhip sai,* respectively.

The minimum number of musicians necessary to form a band is two: a moon-lute player and a percussionist, one or both of whom also sings. This core band may be augmented to form a larger band of four or five musicians, especially when mediums can afford more than two musicians. Additional instruments frequently included in larger bands are the sixteen-string zither (*dan tranh*), the two-string fiddle (*dan nhi*), and various bamboo flutes, including the *sao* and *tieu.*

Three Musicians: Pham Van Ty, Dang Cong Hung, and Le Ba Cao

Shortly after arriving in Hanoi in the summer of 1996, I went to some record shops to see if I could find any *chau van* recordings. One of the first places I tried was a strip of shops selling CDs and tapes on the busy Hang Bai street in the center of Hanoi. The music blasting out of the speakers, which pointed out of the shop fronts into the busy throng of passing motorbikes and bicycles, was Vietnamese popular song, and I doubted they had what I was looking for. In one of the shops, I asked an assistant if they had any "traditional music" and was directed to an area that had various recordings, mostly of the theater music genres *cheo* and *cai luong.* To my surprise, among

Figure 3.2. Members of the *chau van* band at the Mulberry Temple in 1997. From left to right: Pham Quang Dat (percussion including a drum, bamboo clappers, a small cymbal, and a small knobless gong); Pham Van Ty (moon lute); Trong Kha (sixteen-string zither); Truong Manh Linh (voice)

these recordings was a set of four *chau van* tapes. On the cover of each tape there was a picture of Pham Van Ty—referred to as "artist Van Ty"—holding a moon lute and dressed in a tunic and stiff turban-shaped hat traditionally worn by Confucian literati. On listening to the tapes, I found Ty's strong, distinctive voice immediately appealing, and I asked some musician friends in Hanoi whether it was possible to meet him in person. After some negotiation by phone, I found myself sitting in Ty's home in the old quarter of Hanoi. My Vietnamese was not very fluent at our first meeting, but I managed to communicate my interest in studying music and asked him whether he had time to teach me. On first meeting Ty seemed a little reserved, but he was tolerant of my language inadequacies and agreed to meet me again. Over the next year, from 1996 to 1997, I met with Ty many times at his home for music lessons and accompanied him when he performed at rituals in Hanoi and in the countryside. On subsequent trips to Vietnam in 1998 and 2004–5, he also accompanied me on trips to Phu Giay close to his home province of Nam Dinh. Over the years, my friendship with Ty has grown and developed beyond a formal teacher–student relationship.

Since the 1980s, Ty has been the main moon-lute player and singer in the resident band at the famous Mulberry Temple (Den Dau) on Hang Quat street in the old quarter of Hanoi. Presided over by a powerful male medium, the temple is extremely opulent and popular. For about five months of the year during auspicious periods, one or two *len dong* are hosted at the temple every day. The Mulberry Temple band is one of the most respected in Hanoi. The two oldest members of the band, Pham Quang Dat and Trong Kha, are skilled at Sino-Vietnamese ritual invocations and prayers, as well as having an authoritative knowledge of the *chau van* melodies and song texts, and have passed on their expertise to younger members of the band.

Ty was born in 1956 in a village near the city of Nam Dinh about one hundred kilometers south of Hanoi. He moved to the capital in 1973, when he became a student at the Hanoi Music Conservatoire. Ty was not born into a musical family, but his father was interested in the arts and encouraged his interest in music. From an early age Ty learned the moon lute and picked up songs from local musicians. In 1971, at the age of fifteen, he joined the Nam Dinh Folk Song and Dance Troupe, where he developed a close friendship with Nguyen The Tuyen, the moon-lute player who devised the first revolutionary *chau van* suites. It was during his time with the troupe that he developed a strong interest in *chau van* under the guidance of Tuyen. As Ty once commented, he became "infatuated" or "obsessed" (*me*) with the moon lute and "had a heart" (*co tam*) for mediumship music. After two years in the Nam Dinh troupe, he entered the Department of Traditional Instruments at the Hanoi Music Conservatoire, where he studied the moon lute for nine years with the neotraditional composer and instrumentalist Xuan Khai. He received a high school diploma after four years and an undergraduate degree after five more years. Alongside his formal study of neotraditional music with Xuan Khai, he continued his own study and research of *chau van* and other genres, such as *hat xam*. After graduating from the Hanoi Music Conservatoire, he did some teaching at the Department of Traditional Instruments before joining the Folk Culture Institute, where he is still employed as a researcher. At the institute he completed a master's degree on *chau van* and was one of the main contributors to the groundbreaking publications on mediumship coordinated by the institute (Ngo Duc Thinh 1992; Pham Van Ty 1992; Vu Ngoc Khanh and Pham Van Ty 1990).

As one of the most accomplished musicians of his generation, Ty has often performed widely in Asia, Europe, and America. In April 1998, I invited him to perform in the UK on the Asian Music Circuit tour. His contribution to Vietnamese culture was officially acknowledged in 2001 when he was awarded the prestigious title of "Artist of Merit" (Nghe Si Uu Tu) by the Ministry of Culture.[4] Throughout his life, Ty has taken advantage of the opportunities provided by government institutions while at the same time being committed to "traditional" performance practices. Over the years he has acquired an authoritative knowledge of *chau van* and other music connected to spirit worship, such as the invocation of prayers, known as *doc canh*. Following the tradition of spirit priests, he has also taught himself how to read and write Sino-Vietnamese characters.

The other musician with whom I had regular one-to-one music lessons was Dang Cong Hung. Born in 1955 in Hai Hung province southwest of Hanoi, Hung is a contemporary of Ty, and from 1971 to 1975 he also studied with Xuan Khai at the Hanoi Music Conservatoire. Since 1977 he has been an instrumentalist at the Vietnam Cheo Theater (Nha Hat Cheo Viet Nam), based in Hanoi. Hung was introduced to mediumship by his father, who was a *chau van* and *cheo* musician. In the mid-1970s Hung went with his father to *len dong*, but he was reluctant to enter the world of mediumship because he knew many musicians who had been arrested for their ritual activities. According to Hung, his father did not teach him *chau van* to a "professional level" (*muc do nghe nghiep*). It was not until the mid-1980s, when antisuperstition was less vigorously enforced, that he committed himself more fully to learning the genre. Encouraged by another instrumentalist at the Vietnam Cheo Theater, he started to play the moon lute for a spirit priest, called Chen. By accompanying Chen, Hung gradually picked up the songs and became an accomplished singer. Since then, he has regularly performed *chau van* at different temples when invited to do so by mediums; he is not a member of a resident temple band.

Hung is an extremely versatile multi-instrumentalist and singer. Not only a performer of *chau van* and *cheo*, he also plays the *dan day*, the three-stringed lute used in performances of the northern chamber music genre *ca tru*. He has performed widely within Vietnam and toured internationally with the Vietnam Cheo Theater, and with a troupe formed by the Vietnamese choreographer Ea Sola in the 1990s.

Hung lives in a modest house in the Mai Dich area on the outskirts of Hanoi with his wife, who is also a *cheo* musician, and daughter. Mai Dich is home to several large theaters, and a large community of actors and musicians live in the Soviet-style cement housing blocks that dominate the area. Every week for several months I went to his house for lessons. Hung is an excellent teacher, as he has a gift for communicating complex musical concepts in a clear and simple way and he has reflected deeply on his own process of music learning. I had difficulties learning to sing *chau van* mainly because the vocal melody of each verse of a song changes when a different song text is used. However, as we shall see in Chapter 5, Hung had his own imaginative ideas about how to overcome this problem based on understanding the underlying melodic identity of songs.

Le Ba Cao follows in a line of five generations of spirit priests. Now in his seventies, he acquired the specialist expertise of spirit priests from his father in the 1940s. As a spirit priest, Cao is not only a *chau van* performer, he is also skilled at writing spirit petitions in Sino-Vietnamese characters, reading horoscopes (*tu vi*), and reciting prayers to the spirits (*doc canh*). After I was introduced to Cao in November 1996 by another Hanoi-based musician, I often went to visit him at his home in a village not far from the town of Thuong Tin in Ha Tay province, about an hour's motorbike ride to the west of Hanoi. A father of nine children, Cao lives in a spacious house fronted by a large courtyard. Some members of his large extended family live in adjacent buildings, and my visits were invariably punctuated by the coming and going of relatives and friends. On several occasions mediums also came to ask him to perform at their *len dong*, to consult him about their ritual practices, and to get horoscope readings. Cao is a great talker and entertainer and always

Figure 3.3. Dang Cong Hung teaching me at his Hanoi home in 1998

Figure 3.4. Le Ba Cao playing the moon lute at a *len dong* in 1998

seemed to be in a buoyant mood. Sitting on a mat on the floor in his guest room, we chatted for hours about the Four Palace Religion and *chau van* and the changes he had seen during his life. He would often sing extracts of songs to illustrate his points and encourage me to accompany him on the moon lute. He was also fond of reciting old Sino-Vietnamese poetry, now rarely used as song texts, and pointing out the artistry and profound sentiments of the poems. Cao has strong opinions about the *chau van* repertoire, and he did not accept some of the recent innovations and changes to it.

As a young man, Cao performed *chau van* with his father and other spirit priests. He stopped playing at rituals toward the end of 1952 when the local authorities clamped down on the practices of mediums and spirit priests. During the 1950s and 1960s he did a number of jobs, including bookkeeping for a local company and working in the agricultural collectives. He did not start playing again until 1971, and even then it was possible to perform only secretly in remote rural areas. After a gap of nearly twenty years, Cao recalled in one of our conversations how he practiced with another older musician so they could help each other remember all the song texts they used to sing in the 1940s. Since the late 1980s, Cao has resumed his position as the local spirit priest and regularly officiates at numerous ceremonies. He is much respected by the younger generation of musicians for his deep knowledge of all aspects of mediumship. Although one of Cao's sons, who lives on the outskirts of Hanoi, is a *chau van* musician, he has not been trained in the wide range of practices required of a spirit priest: Cao will likely be the last in his family's line of spirit priests.

I met numerous musicians during my research, all of whom shaped my understanding of mediumship music in different ways. But as I spent a great deal of time with Ty, Hung, and Cao, they were formative influences. As a hereditary spirit priest, Cao is a representative of the prerevolutionary tradition and is seen as an important link to the past by younger musicians who treat him as their "master" (*thay*). Hung is one of a growing number of professional musicians who learned *chau van* in the reform era, although in Hung's case, hereditary connections also predisposed him to the genre. Like Hung, Ty is a formally trained musician who has applied his musical knowledge and skills across genres. He has mastered a wide range of ritual practices, and his research into mediumship has also given him a somewhat unique position as a cultural authority, as a "folklore expert."

Despite Hung, Ty, and Cao's different backgrounds, they all share a deep respect for sacred practices and the responsiveness of spirits. Ritual musicians, like mediums, must have a "true heart" (*thuc tam*) for the spirits. Two female *chau van* musicians, who were farmers before becoming the band at one of the temples in Phu Giay, made this point forcefully when they said the "spirits had entered their hearts" and taught them to sing and play. Few musicians I met attributed their knowledge so directly to the spirits, but all wished to serve them in song.

The Chau Van Repertoire and Hat Tho

Chau van is predominantly a vocal genre. Except for two instrumental pieces, "Luu Thuy" and "Trong Chien," the repertoire consists of a large corpus of over forty strophic songs. For *chau van,* as is the case in most genres of Vietnamese music, the vocal melody is at the heart of performance practice. The purpose of the instrumental accompaniment during verses is to support and complement the voice. Short instrumental phrases "link" successive vocal phrases within each verse.[5] Longer instrumental sections, known as *luu khong* (lit. "flowing without [words]"), are interspersed between each sung verse. Each song has its own characteristic *luu khong* and "linking phrases," but the length of these sections is not fixed, and there is considerable variation in their realization.

The two terms for mediumship music—*chau van* (lit. "serving literature") and *hat van* (lit. "singing literature)—emphasize the importance of sung text. To be a *chau van* singer it is necessary to memorize a large body of "literature that serves [the spirits]" (*van chau*). This "literature" consists of poems dedicated to the spirits. Musicians are skilled at setting poems to songs and adapting the contour of the vocal melody to suit the song text. For most songs, any poem in a particular poetic form may be used as a song text, so numerous poems dedicated to different spirits in the pantheon may be inserted into the same song. *Chau van* poems use conventional forms of Vietnamese poetry: most use the *luc bat* ("six, eight") form, and a smaller number use the *song that luc bat* ("two sevens, six, eight"), *song that* ("two sevens"), and *bon chu* ("four syllables") forms. The names of these poetic forms refer to the number of syllables in each line of text, and each has its own speech-tone and rhyming scheme (see Nguyen Xuan Kinh 1992).

Recent work by Vietnamese scholars provides lists, descriptions, and transcriptions of *chau van* songs, but there are considerable differences in the number and names of songs included in the repertoire (see Ngo Duc Thinh 1992; Bui Dinh Thao and Nguyen Quang Hai 1996; Thanh Ha 1996). Like the pantheon of spirits of the Four Palace Religion, the repertoire of *chau van* songs is continually changing. Songs fall into disuse, melodies are adapted from other genres, innovations are made to songs, and occasionally, entirely new songs are composed. Classification of the repertoire is further hampered by regional differences, by the lack of standard nomenclature for songs, and by the fact that musicians have differing opinions about which songs constitute the repertoire. *Chau van* is a living folk tradition, which has not been centrally systematized. Table 3.1 lists the main songs of the repertoire. The list draws on over thirty *len dong* I attended in Hanoi and in provinces in northern Vietnam. Table 3.1 therefore provides an overview of the core songs discussed in this book; it is not intended to be a comprehensive list of all the melodies that might be considered to be part of the *chau van* repertoire in different regions. Four melody "groups" (*nhom*)—"Doc," "Con," "Xa," and "Phu"—are listed separately in the left-hand column of the table. Some recent additions to the repertoire, which are discussed in Chapter 5, are not included because they have yet to be widely adopted by bands.

The body of poems dedicated to the spirits, like the song repertoire itself, is not fixed and has evolved over a considerable length of time. Maurice Durand's book on mediumship includes a reproduction of twenty-four poems written in Sino-Vietnamese characters (*chu nom*) and a transcription of the poems in romanized Vietnamese script (*quoc ngu*) (Durand 1959:221–327).

Table 3.1. The *chau van* repertoire

Four groups of melodies	Other melodies
"Doc"	"Thinh Bong"
"Doc (Song That Luc Bat)"	"Luu Thuy"
	"Nhip Mot"/"Bo Bo"
"Con Giay Lech"	"Nhip Mot Chuoc Ruou"
"Con Xuan"	"Bi"/"Bi Tho"
"Con Luyen"	"Bi Tho Cheo Do"
"Con Luyen Tam Tang"	"Bi Tho Chuoc Ruou"
"Con Oan"	"Sai"
"Con Hue"	"Kieu Duong"
	"Ham"
"Xa Thuong"	"Van"
"Xa Quang"/"Xa Bac"	"Ho Hue"
"Xa Giay Lech"	"Ho (Nhip Mot)"
"Xa Mua Moi"	"Don"
["Xa Vao Lang"]	"Cheo Do"
["Xa Giay To Lan"]	"Trong Chien"
["Xa Ke Noi"]	"Ban Chim Thuoc"
["Xa Tay Nguyen"]	"Cac Ban Tien"
	"Suoi Oi"
"Phu Noi"	"Ly Tam That"
"Phu Binh"	["Muou (Nhip Ba)"]
"Phu Chuoc Ruou"	["Dua Thu"]
"Phu Van Dan (Nam Than)"	["Thien Thai"]
["Phu Van Dan (Nu Than)"]	
["Phu Chenh"]	
["Phu Dau"]	
["Phu Ha"]	
["Phu Giay Lech"]	
["Phu Bac Phan"]	
["Phu Ty Ba"]	

Table key: The melodies rarely heard during *len dong* are placed in square brackets. Common alternative names for songs are divided by a diagonal slash. Optional extended names for songs are placed in brackets. These extended names describe a defining characteristic of the song: *song that luc bat* refers to a poetic meter; *nhip mot* and *nhip ba* refer to the one-beat and three-beat rhythms, respectively; *nam than* (lit. "male spirit") and *nu than* (lit. "female spirit") differentiate between the two versions of "Phu Van Dan," which are performed for male and female spirits.

In the reform era, Vietnamese folklorists have also compiled numerous *van chau* (Ngo Duc Thinh 1992:147–252; Ngo Duc Thinh 1996b; Bui Dinh Thao and Nguyen Quang Hai 1996:70–142). Most of these published poems are anonymous and have been transcribed from oral sources. Only a few, which were written in living memory, are accredited to specific individuals (e.g., see Ngo Duc Thinh 1996b). The versions of *chau van* poems published in French and Vietnamese sources are quite long, typically between forty and one hundred lines. Most of the poems consist of pairs of lines in the *luc bat* form, which are usually semantically complete in themselves. Poems do not have an overarching, progressive narrative, so short, semantically independent sections can, within certain limits, be freely arranged in performance.

Songscapes are intimately connected to possession, but sequences of *chau van* songs are sometimes performed before *len dong* in order to prepare for the incarnation of spirits or on separate occasions when offerings are made to the spirits. Such performances are known as *hat tho,* or "worship singing" (Thanh Ha 1996:11; Ngo Duc Thinh 1992:47). At most *len dong,* the band sing *hat tho* while the final preparations are being made. As soon as the medium sits in front of the altar and places the red scarf over her head to signal the imminent incarnation of the first spirit, the band starts to perform the spirit's songs. In contemporary practice it is not common for *hat tho* sessions to be arranged the day before a *len dong;* older musicians said this was more common in the past.

Hat tho sessions, which are organized independently of *len dong,* are held in temples on important days of the ritual calendar, such as the "death anniversaries" (*ngay gio*) of spirits, on the first and the fifteenth of the lunar month, and at the beginning and end of the year or summer. They are either devoted to the entire pantheon or one or more spirits who are the focus of worship at a particular temple. As a form of devotional singing, the audience for *hat tho* is divine rather than human. For followers of the Four Palace Religion, *hat tho* sessions are a time for worship and making offerings.

Musicians proficient at *hat tho* are highly regarded for their specialist knowledge of songs and texts. The poems sung during *hat tho* are quite distinct from those used during *len dong.* They include long texts that pay homage to the mother spirits and Van Cong Dong, a poem dedicated to the whole pantheon (see Ngo Duc Thinh 1996b:5–76). There are numerous *hat tho* song arrangements, and the length of performances can vary from about twenty minutes to over an hour. An example of a song sequence commonly used for the poem dedicated to the Third Mother Spirit, Van Mau Thoai, is as follows: (1) "Bi," (2) "Muou," (3) "Thong," (4) "Phu Binh," (5) "Phu Chenh," (6) "Phu Dau," (7) "Phu Noi," (8) "Dua Thu," (9) "Van," (10) "Doc," (11) "Con Giay Lech," (12) "Ham," (13) "Don." Many of the songs in this sequence are also performed during *len dong,* but some songs, like "Muou" and "Thong," are unique to *hat tho,* and others are rarely performed for spirit possession (e.g., "Phu Chenh," "Phu Dau," and "Dua Thu").

Songscapes for Four Spirits at Two Rituals

The "Ritual Songscapes" menu of the DVD features video extracts of incarnations of four spirits at two *len dong*, labeled as Ritual 1 and 2. The four spirits—the Third Mandarin (Quan De Tam), the Second Lady (Chau De Nhi), the Tenth Prince (Ong Hoang Muoi), and the Third Princess (Co Bo)—have been selected because their songscapes encompass the maximum possible diversity. Each of these spirits belongs to a different rank and, because the ritual actions and songscapes within each rank of spirits bear similarities, they provide a good insight into the songscapes of rituals as a whole.[6] For each of the four spirits, the different songscapes performed at each ritual are outlined in tables. The video extracts are arranged in a table format to facilitate nonlinear comparison of the two rituals and to make it clear where they are situated within the overall progression of the possession. Because the arrangement of the poems is inherently flexible, there are differences in the song texts used for each spirit at each ritual. The translations of the song texts, which appear after each video extract, enable the different texts sung for the four spirits to be compared. For additional information about the table layout and directions about how to access the video extracts in the tables, see "DVD Contents."

Ritual 1 was held on the eighteenth day of the third lunar month (April 24, 1997) by Nguyen Thi Lai at the Mulberry Temple in the center of Hanoi (see Figure 3.5). The third lunar month is one of the most popular periods for *len dong* because many of the "death anniversaries" of female spirits occur in this month. At the Mulberry Temple, rituals are held continuously throughout the third lunar month. The date of Lai's *len dong* was arranged to fit in with the busy schedule at the temple and to avoid her menstrual cycle. The actual date of the ritual did not coincide with a particular spirit's death anniversary. The music was performed by the resident temple band: Pham Van Ty (moon lute and voice), Pham Quang Dat (percussion and voice), Trong Kha (voice, sixteen-string zither, moon lute, and two-stringed fiddle), and Doan Nhung (bamboo flute). At some points, Trong Kha played the moon lute in order to give Ty a break, and Ty then played the percussion formerly played by Pham Quang Dat. One other musician also performed at Lai's ritual: Truong Manh Linh (voice and percussion). Linh usually performs at another temple in Hanoi and is not a member of the resident band; Lai asked him to sing on this occasion because she is fond of his voice.

Ritual 2 was held by Nguyen Thi Hang on the fourth day of the sixth lunar month (July 8, 1997) at An Tho temple on Yen Phu street in Hanoi. Hang's

Figure 3.5. The Mulberry Temple (Den Dau) in 2005

ritual was held in the sixth lunar month to mark the "the feast of the mandarins of the three palaces" (*tiec quan tam phu*). The climax of the "feast" is on the twenty-fourth day of the sixth lunar month. The band at Hang's *len dong* was made up of Dang Cong Hung (moon lute and voice), Cao Mon (voice and percussion), Le Tu Cuong (bamboo flutes and voice), Tran Chung Sinh (sixteen-string zither), and Nguyen Ngoc Thu (large drum).

The two rituals featured on the DVD were held by wealthy Hanoi-based mediums. One of the main reasons why I have chosen these two rituals for comparison is because I had the opportunity to discuss the songs performed in detail with my music teachers Pham Van Ty and Dang Cong Hung, and other band members, particularly Cao Mon and Le Tu Cuong. The opulence of these *len dong* contrasts with those held by poorer mediums, especially in rural areas. A third ritual from a rural area might have been included for comparison, but the fundamental features of all the rituals I attended were the same, and the addition of another would unduly lengthen the discussion. Taking each spirit in turn, the following commentary describes the performative interaction that occurs and points out the main differences and similarities between the songscapes of Rituals 1 and 2.

Commentary on the DVD Video Extracts

THE THIRD MANDARIN (VIDEO EXTRACTS 1–12)

The songs performed during Ritual 1 and 2 for the incarnations of the Third Mandarin are the same until the mediums dance with swords. From then on they are substantially different. For both rituals, the bands "invite" the Third Mandarin with the "Thinh Bong" melody. Also, they both perform "Doc" while the mediums are being dressed, "Luu Thuy" when the mediums are presenting incense to the altar, and "Sai" for the action of "waving incense." For all of these actions there is a corresponding melody. The first difference in the songscapes of the two rituals occurs when the mediums dance with swords: the Ritual 1 band plays "Luu Thuy," whereas the Ritual 2 band plays "Trong Chien." The Ritual 2 band was able to play the loud percussion of rhythms of "Trong Chien," meaning "War Drums," because the ensemble includes a large temple drum.

Up until the sword dance, both bands change melodies according to the ritual action. Once the mediums sit down after dancing, the songs are not linked to specific actions in the same way and there is greater flexibility for the bands to choose which songs to perform. Most of the "Phu" melodies, and "Kieu Duong" and "Don," may be performed for mandarins once the dancing finishes. The Ritual 1 band chooses to perform "Phu Van Dan," "Phu Noi," and "Don" while Lai distributes gifts. The moon-lute player/singer Pham Van Ty initiates the change from "Phu Van Dan" to "Phu Noi," and this song change is not made in response to Lai's movements (Video Extract 10). The transition from "Phu Noi" to "Don" (Video Extract 11) is initiated by Ty when he becomes aware that the spirit is about to leave Lai's body. "Don," which means "fast," has a faster tempo than "Phu Noi" and increases the excitement at the close of the possession. The band can tell the spirit is about to "return" because one of Lai's assistants picks up the red scarf. When this scarf is thrown over Lai's head (Video Extract 12), the spirit leaves her body and the musicians sing the phrase *xe gia hoi cung,* "the spirit's carriage returns to the palace." This phrase is sung at the close of every possession to mark the spirit's return to the celestial "palaces" in the other world.

In addition to "Phu Van Dan," "Phu Noi," and "Don," the Ritual 2 band also performs "Kieu Duong" and "Cao Mon's Melody," which was recently devised by the singer/percussionist in the band, Cao Mon. "Cao Mon's Melody" is included in the songscape because of a request made by Hang, to make the "singing more happy" (*hat vui len*). Hang told this to one of her assistants, who passed the message on to the band. In Video Extract 2, this assistant turns to the band and calls out "*thay do,*" meaning "change," and the band immediately obliges by changing from "Phu Van Dan" to "Cao Mon's Melody." The latter song has a fast tempo and is "happier" than "Phu Van Dan." Hang shows her appreciation for the new song by striking a cushion with her hand and giving the band money. Throughout the period when she is sitting and interacting with other ritual participants, the band intersperse "Cao Mon's Melody" between renditions of the more conventional songs "Phu Van Dan," "Phu Noi," "Don," and "Kieu Duong," to ensure the musical momentum and interest are maintained.

THE SECOND LADY (VIDEO EXTRACTS 13–17)

The songs performed for the Second Lady are the same for both Ritual 1 and 2, so video extracts from just one of the rituals, Ritual 1, are included on the DVD. With the exception of "Thinh Bong," which is used for all spirits at the onset of possession, all the melodies performed for the Second Lady belong to the "Xa" group. For both Ritual 1 and 2, the following "Xa" melodies are performed at different stages of possession: "Xa Thuong" when the mediums are being dressed; "Xa Mua Moi" to accompany the lit-rope dances; and "Xa Giay Lech" when the mediums sit down to distribute gifts.

THE TENTH PRINCE (VIDEO EXTRACTS 18–25)

The songscapes of Ritual 1 and 2 start with the same four melodies, "Thinh Bong," "Doc," "Luu Thuy," and "Sai." As for the Third Mandarin, these songs are performed for specific ritual actions: the onset of possession, dressing in the spirits clothes, presenting incense to the altar, and waving incense respectively. After this, Lai and Hang carry out different movements. Lai imitates writing a poem with a stick of incense and then dances with a fan, whereas Hang dances with bell sticks. For bell-stick dances, "Luu Thuy" is usually performed. Thinking that Lai will also perform this dance after the ritual action of waving incense, the Ritual 1 band begins to play "Luu Thuy." But once they see Lai "writing a poem"—with a stick of incense as the "quill" and an outstretched fan as the "manuscript"—the band switches to a song appropriate for this action (Video Extract 18). The band "recites" the poem being written by the Tenth Prince by singing "Bi Tho" (Reciting a Poem) as a prelude to "Nhip Mot." After "writing a poem," Lai puts down the stick of incense and briefly dances with a fan, and the band begins to play "Luu Thuy." However, the dance is short-lived, and Lai summons "Luu Thuy" to a close by raising her arms. She then sits down to drink rice wine and the band plays a special "Phu" melody, "Phu Chuoc Ruou" (lit. "Wine-Pouring

Phu"). Each of the three verses of "Phu Chuoc Ruou" invites Lai to drink one cup of rice wine, and Lai waits for each verse before drinking each cup (Video Extracts 19 and 20). In this instance, it is Lai who follows the band rather than the reverse.

In contrast to Lai, Hang does not write a poem. Following the bell-stick dance, she sits to drink rice wine and the band sings "Bi Tho Chuoc Ruou" (Reciting a Poem for Pouring Rice Wine), followed by "Nhip Mot Chuoc Ruou" (Wine-Pouring One-Beat Rhythm Melody). Cao Mon sings these melodies, and he has chosen to sing them because he thinks they are "lighter" and more suitable for the "romantic" character of the Tenth Prince than "Phu Chuoc Ruou," which is associated with serious mandarins.

Having drunk three glasses of rice wine, both Lai and Hang remain seated, smoke cigarettes given to them by their assistants, and distribute gifts to their disciples. At this stage, the songs performed do not correspond to specific ritual actions, and the bands have more flexibility in choosing melodies. The Ritual 1 band performs the following sequence of melodies: "Bi Tho," "Con Hue," "Ho Hue," and "Nhip Mot." The Ritual 2 band also performs this sequence of songs but is prompted by Hang to include two further songs, "Ly Qua Cau" and "Ly My Hung," before "Nhip Mot." Shortly before the possession draws to a close, Hang again calls over to the band, who at that point are performing "Ho Hue," to change to a "happier" melody. Cao Mon immediately responds by performing the two "Ly" folk songs. Both of these songs are not usually included as part of the *chau van* repertoire, but Cao Mon has written new words for them and incorporated them into *len dong*. Hang shows her appreciation for "Ly Qua Cau" and "Ly My Hung" by letting out a cry and giving the musicians money at the end of each song.

THE THIRD PRINCESS (VIDEO EXTRACTS 26–30)

Like the songscapes for the Third Mandarin and Tenth Prince, the songs for the Third Princess correspond to specific ritual actions until the dancing finishes. The first three melodies of the songscapes for the Third Princess— "Thinh Bong," "Doc," and "Sai"—are also performed, although with different words, for the Third Mandarin and Tenth Prince. The Third Princess is famous for the Boat Rowing Dance, "Mua Cheo Do," in which mediums dance with a pair of oars. This dance is associated with a special melody, "Cheo Do" (Boat Rowing). The prelude to the "boat rowing" melody, "Bi: Tho Cheo Do"), is performed as the medium is given the oars by her assistants. This gives the medium enough time to bless the oars with incense and position herself for the rowing dance.

Following her performance of the Boat Rowing Dance, Hang puts down the oars and dances with empty hands, and the band changes from singing "Cheo Do" to "Nhip Mot." Once she finishes dancing, Hang sits to drink water and distribute gifts to her disciples, while the band sings the "lyrical" "Con" melody, "Con Giay Lech," appropriate for the graceful Third Princess (Video Extract 29). Unlike Hang, Lai does not dance without oars: she sits down immediately after the Boat Rowing Dance. While Lai is sitting in front of the altar, the band performs four melodies—"Bi Tho," "Van," "Con Oan," and "Nhip Mot"—rather than "Con Giay Lech." "Van" and "Con Oan" are known as sad melodies and are avoided by the Ritual 2 band because they know Hang prefers lively, happy songs. "Nhip Mot," which is also used for some dances and has a faster tempo than "Van" and "Con Oan," is performed by the Ritual 1 band shortly before the spirit leaves Lai's body to make the conclusion of the spirit possession more animated (Video Extract 28). The Ritual 2 band creates the same effect by increasing the tempo of "Con Giay Lech"; the spirit's imminent departure is signaled when Hang picks up a fan (Video Extract 30).

Musical Interaction

Now that the songscapes for four spirits featured on the DVD have been described, it is possible to draw some conclusions regarding the processes of musical interaction involved in the creation of songscapes. To this end, I employ four of Benjamin Brinner's analytical concepts—interactive network, interactive system, interactive sound structure, and interactive motivation—to frame the discussion of the performative interactions during *len dong.* These four concepts are defined by Brinner as follows: "*Interactive network* comprises the roles assumed by performers and the relationships or links between them, *interactive system* refers to the means and meanings of communication and co-ordination, and *interactive sound structure* is a constellation of concepts associated with the constraints and possibilities inherent in the ways sounds are put together . . . the 'why' of interaction, the goals, rewards, pitfalls, and sanctions . . . may be subsumed under the rubric *interactive motivation*" (Brinner 1995:169, emphases in original).

INTERACTIVE NETWORK

A good relationship between the medium and the band is extremely important to ensure a successful ritual. Throughout possession, mediums show their "appreciation" (*thuong thuc*) for the music by giving the band money and gifts.

The giving of money is often accompanied by ebullient cries and vigorous hand slaps on a big floor cushion, which is usually placed next to the medium when she is sitting in front of the altar. Over the course of rituals, which usually last several hours, the medium and band feed off each other's energy. As Nguyen Thi Hien has commented, the interaction between the medium and the band "creates mutual strength for performance" (2002:156).

The assertion of musical preferences by the possessee is not a standard feature of ritual practice. Lai arranged for one of her favorite singers, Linh, to perform with the resident band but did not express her musical preferences during the ritual itself. Lai did not have a close relationship with the resident band, and the band members were not influenced by Lai in their choice of melodies. Lai's control of the band was limited to dictating the approximate timing of song changes at some stages during possession when the band followed her movements. Hang exerted more influence over the musical decisions made by the band than Lai. However, even when the medium expresses music preferences, as was the case during Hang's ritual, this is done in general terms: a change in song, rather than a specific song, is requested.

When I met Hang in December 2004, I asked her about the musical requests she made while possessed. She said that "if the spirits want to hear any song they say so," and she thought musicians should follow the "ideas" of the spirits. She also made her own musical tastes clear: "There are some old and young people who serve [the spirits] who like the old texts (van co), but me and my friends like happy texts . . . some chau van is slow (cham cham), leisurely (tu tu), it drawls (am i) and groans (ren ri) . . . I like happy music and song (ca nhac vui), pop and rock music (nhac pop, nhac roc)." On hearing these comments, I asked Hang whether pop and rock music could be used during len dong, to which she said, "No! The spirits wouldn't like it. They would laugh! Should the spirits dance in a European style (nhay dam)? No, that's not allowed."

Hang's reference to nhay dam, or European dancing, is interesting in the context of the history of comment on mediums' behavior. Female mediums' exuberant dances have been ridiculed by critics since the early twentieth century. The modernist critic Phan Ke Binh, for instance, refers in derisory terms to mediums' dances as an imitation of nhay dam motivated by vanity: "People say mediums dance in an affected, finicky way like the nhay dam of women in Europe. This European dancing is an opportunity for women to show off their graceful figure and affected manner. We do not have the custom of dancing like that, so it was adopted into the dances of mediums; that's the particular character of women, they want to flaunt their beauty for the whole world to see" (1987 [1913/1914]:300). Such comments about mediums' dancing are still aired by people critical of *len dong* in contemporary Vietnam, and by asserting that *len dong* does not imitate European music and dance styles, Hang both points out the limits of change that are acceptable within the tradition and implicitly defends mediums' practices against mocking criticisms.

Although Hang stopped short of requesting pop and rock music to be performed during *len dong*, Cao Mon and Hung were aware of Hang's preference for "happy music and song," as they had performed at her rituals on numerous occasions, and this informed their musical decisions. At points when they could choose between songs, they opted for "faster," "happier" ones. These songs are less "drawling" because the song texts are sung at a high rate of delivery, without extended melisma between each word.

Within the band itself, the two core members—the moon-lute player/singer and main percussionist/singer—perform the most crucial roles. Non-core members of bands, who play other instruments, such as bamboo flutes and the sixteen-string zither, tend to follow the lead of the core members and are not usually responsible for musical decisions made in the course of performance. The core band members usually sit in front of the rest of the band, so they have a clear view of the medium. This spatial arrangement aids the coordination of musical changes made in response to the medium's movements.

The leadership role in a band is usually assumed by the moon-lute player/singer (as in Ritual 1) but is sometimes shared between the two core members (as in Ritual 2). The band leader at any point during a ritual is responsible for leading song, tempo, and dynamic changes, which may or may not be prompted by the medium's movements, and for making decisions about which song to perform. The band leader does not exercise influence over other aspects of performance, such as the musical texture. Non-core band members, for example, make their own decisions, within limits established by performance conventions, about whether or not to play or sing at any particular point.

From a practical point of view, it makes sense for the moon-lute player to be the "leader," because the moon lute is the main melodic instrument. As most song changes are carried out during instrumental sections, the moon-lute player is able to indicate a song change by playing the instrumental phrase of the new song. The band member who leads song transitions also usually sings the first verse of the new song. For most of Lai's ritual, Pham Van Ty played the moon lute and initiated most of the song changes (e.g.,

Video Extracts 19, 20, 21, 22). However, at some points Trong Kha played the moon lute instead of Ty (Video Extract 26) and therefore took over the leadership role. Owing to the importance of the moon lute within bands, competence at playing the moon lute, rather than status, is the most important factor in determining the band leader. In the Mulberry Temple band, for instance, Trong Kha and Pham Quang Dat are respected because of their seniority and extensive knowledge of *chau van*. Yet Ty usually performs the leadership role because he is the main moon-lute player.

Although the moon-lute player tends to assume the leadership role, it would be misleading to give the impression that bands conform to a rigid hierarchy or that band members have fixed, narrowly defined roles. Musical decisions are frequently negotiated in the course of performance, and the roles assumed by band members may shift from one moment to the next. During Ritual 1, for instance, Pham Van Ty was responsible most song changes, but some were led by the percussionist/singer Pham Quang Dat. One example of this can be seen in Video Extract 23, when Dat signals the change in melody from "Ho Hue" to "Nhip Mot" by increasing the tempo. The more or less equal sharing of the leadership role between Cao Mon and Dang Cong Hung during Ritual 2 is indicative of the even greater flexibility in role taking that can occur between core band members. Cao Mon, for instance, led the changes between melodies and made the decision to introduce his own innovations, such as the "Cao Mon's Melody" (e.g., Video Extracts 2, 3, 6, and 7), "Ly Qua Cau," and "Ly My Hung" (Video Extract 25). At other times Dang Cong Hung led song transitions (e.g., Video Extracts 4 and 5).

It should also be noted that the core band and other band members do not just have a "leader–follower" relationship. The primary purpose of the instrumental parts is to support the voice, and non-core instrumentalists often anticipate the vocal line as well as following, imitating, and embellishing it. They therefore do not just "follow" the vocal part. For example, the flute players sometimes introduce the vocal melody before the voice enters (see the performances of the "Bi" melodies in Video Extracts 24 and 26). Non-core band members also take a prominent role when they sing verses of songs.

INTERACTIVE SYSTEM

To coordinate ritual music performances, mediums and musicians communicate through the use of a range of cues. Brinner defines a *cue* as "a musical, verbal, visual, or kinetic act specifically produced for the purpose of initiating an interaction—that is, bringing about a change in the performance of others in the ensemble—that would not occur otherwise" (1995:183, emphases omitted). During *len dong,* bands respond to some of the medium's actions as if they are kinetic–visual cues. At some points, musicians respond to ritualizing by changing to a different song or altering other aspects of their performance, such as the tempo and dynamics. The precise timing of the musical response to the kinetic-visual cues is quite flexible. For instance, the band may change to the "Sai" melody when the lit incense is being prepared by the assistants or, as is the case in Video Extract 1, at the moment the medium starts waving the incense. The translation of the medium's visual cue into an aural response is carried out by the person leading the band and is reinforced by the other musicians.

The hand signals mediums make at the onset of possession are an interesting example of communication between the medium and musicians. If the medium raises her right hand when being possessed by a spirit, the spirit is male, if she raises her left hand the spirit is female. The fingers (and thumb) indicate the number of the spirit. For instance, when the medium raises her right hand with one finger outstretched, the musicians know that a "first male spirit" is being incarnated. This could be the First Mandarin, First Prince, or First Young Prince, but because the spirits are usually incarnated in sequence following the hierarchy of the pantheon (i.e., the mothers, mandarins, ladies, princes, ladies, and young princes), musicians know which male spirit is being incarnated. For spirits numbered above five, both hands must be raised. For example, for possessions by the Tenth Prince, the medium raises both hands with all fingers and thumbs outstretched, and because the sequence of possessions is established by convention, musicians know that the spirit is male. Ambiguities do, however, arise when mediums are possessed by regional spirits. For example, musicians are not able to tell from the hand signal whether a medium is being possessed by the Second Princess of the Mountains and Forests or the regional spirit the Second Princess Cam Duong. If musicians are unsure of the deity being incarnated, they sometimes sing a general invitation that can be used for the particular spirit rank.

In both the video clips of the onset of possession included on the DVD (Video Extracts 1 and 13), the musicians are able to predict which spirit is emerging because the incarnations follow the conventional sequence, so the singers call out the spirit's name before the hand signal is made. In these cases the signal merely confirms the assumption made by the musicians. However, the spirit to be incarnated is not always fully determined by the conventional sequence, and in these ambiguous cases the medium's hand signal is an important visual-kinetic cue that the musicians observe before calling the spirit.

For the most part, the band must respond to the medium's movements. But the timing of ritual action is sometimes dictated by the music. In Video Extract 25, for example, Lai takes the oars in preparation for the rowing dance while the musicians perform the "Bi Tho Cheo Do" melody, and Lai waits until the band switches to "Cheo Do" before beginning the rowing dance. While dancing, Lai also speeds up her rowing movements in time with the gradual accelerando that occurs throughout "Cheo Do." At another ritual I attended, the medium began the rowing dance of the Third Lady before the band had finished "Bi Tho Cheo Do." The musician who was singing was clearly irritated and shouted out to the medium to listen to the music. This incident illustrates that it is not just mediums who dictate proceedings: bands also affect ritual action.

Within the band there are no preparatory cues made by the musician leading the song change: the other members of the band usually follow the musical cue of the leader as soon as they hear the song change being made. Bands rarely make use of verbal cues, although in Video Extract 5, Hung tells Cao Mon to make the song change from "Don" to the "Cao Mons Melody" before it takes place, instead of relying on a musical cue.[7]

When song changes are made in response to the medium's movements, there is little or no song choice, so band members usually know which song will be performed. However, there is a greater degree of choice when song changes are not made in response to the medium's actions.

Several factors help ensure smooth transitions between songs when there are several song options. First, band members are usually aware of the likely timing of song changes and favored song sequences because of their previous experience of playing together. Second, non-core band members are not always playing during song transitions, so only the core band need carry out the song change. Third, as most songs employ the one-, two-, or three-beat rhythm, some song changes do not require a change in the basic rhythm or tempo. In such cases, the moon-lute player is free to make a song change without necessarily coordinating the change with the percussionist. An example of this occurs during Video Extract 10 when Pham Van Ty makes the transition between "Phu Van Dan" and "Phu Noi," which both use the three-beat rhythm. While these factors apply to many song transitions, there may still be occasions when a song change is not made at precisely the same moment by all the members of a band. However, even on such occasions musicians are quick to respond, and slight differences in synchronization are tolerated because they do not seriously affect the realization of songscapes or the progress of the ritual.

INTERACTIVE SOUND STRUCTURE

Songscapes are constructed within the interactive sound structure of the *chau van* musical system. At the level of the progression of song sequences, this structure consists of associations between songs and spirits, and between songs and ritual action. For each spirit, certain songs can be performed, although many songs are shared between more than one spirit or group of spirits. In addition to the constraints on the use of songs according to the spirit incarnated, some songs are only performed for specific ritual actions.

The links between songs, spirits, and ritual action affect the degree of song choice available for musicians for each spirit possession and at each stage of possession. At one extreme, only one song may be performed, while at the other, musicians may perform one of several songs.

In general, the song choice for female mountain spirits is more restricted than for other spirits, as the identical songscapes of Rituals 1 and 2 for the Second Lady indicate. With the exception of "Thinh Bong," only "Xa" melodies are performed for female mountain spirits. At some rituals, I heard "Xa Quang" performed instead of "Xa Giay Lech" for the Second Lady, but the sequence of songs for female mountain spirits like the Second Lady is largely predetermined.

For spirits other than female mountain spirits, the spectrum of song choice is much broader. Musicians have the least choice when song changes are made as a consequence of the medium's movements and the greatest when songs do not correspond to particular ritual action. Three examples that give an impression of the range of song choice are (1) the compulsory performance of the "Sai" melody for the action of waving incense; (2) the performance of either the "Luu Thuy" or "Trong Chien" melodies for the Third Mandarin's sword dance; and (3) the choice of at least five different songs when the Third Princess is drinking and distributing gifts. Up until the time when the medium sits down after dancing, the songs are linked to the medium's movements: it is only after the medium finishes dancing that musicians may change melodies of their own accord.[8] Therefore, songscapes are the most diverse after the medium stops dancing.

INTERACTIVE MOTIVATION

The aim of the interaction between the medium and the band is to ensure the spirits are served well. Coordination between the band and the possessee is necessary for correct ritual practice, yet there is some flexibility in the timing of song changes. Close coordination between the members of the core band is the ideal, but a certain degree of looseness is accepted during song transitions as long as the ritual momentum is maintained. The parts of non-core band members are less essential than those of the core band and are generally less tightly synchronized.

As the progression of acts is quite fixed, spontaneity is not a crucial part of ritual practice. Mediums rarely deviate from the conventional sequence, but bands adjust when unusual actions do occur. This was the case during Ritual 1 when Lai, while possessed by the Tenth Prince, wrote a poem with an incense stick instead of dancing with bell sticks, and the musicians had to quickly change to a different melody to suit Lai's actions (Video Extract 18). However, songscapes are constructed with the ideals of diversity and musical interest in mind rather than spontaneity. Band members strive to perform songscapes with an "abundance" of songs to make them "interesting," "lively," and "enjoyable."

The performance aesthetics of *chau van* rely on a combination of "sweet playing and interesting singing" (*dan ngot hat hay*). The main purpose of "interesting singing" is to flatter the spirits and the instrumental parts provide support for voice.

* * *

Chau van is an elaborate musical system based on interrelationships between songs, spirits, and ritual action. Through comparison of the songs performed for four spirits at two different rituals on the DVD, a picture emerges of how songscapes are created. Songscapes are flexible entities. They are often realized differently for each ritual, although the degree of difference varies depending on the spirit and the stage of possession. The creation of diverse songscapes depends on numerous types of musical interaction both between the medium and the band and among band members.

The discussion of songscapes and musical interaction in this chapter paves the way for the examination of the significance of music and spirit possession in the next. The term songscape encourages the music performed for each spirit incarnation to be viewed as a coherent "whole" with many parts, rather than as a series of discrete, unrelated songs. This view is useful because, although the relationship between musical performance and other ritual elements varies at different stages of possession, the individual songs that constitute a songscape have a unity, as they are linked to the identity of the incarnated spirit.

Judith Vander has used the term songprint to refer to the song repertoires of five Shoshone women (1996 [1988]). She describes the songprint of each

Shoshone woman as being "distinctive to her culture, age, and personality, as unique in its configuration as a fingerprint or footprint" (1996 [1988]:xi). Songprints endeavor to map the musical knowledge of particular singers for the purposes of drawing "historic conclusions about song genres and the participation and role of Shoshone women in music" (1996 [1988]:287). The comparison of songscapes in this chapter has focused on the processes of musical interaction and the construction of songscapes. The notions of songprint and songscape are therefore quite different. However, they might usefully be compared, in that both are concerned with identity, albeit in different ways: a songprint reflects the particular personality, culture, and life experiences of a singer; a songscape evokes the presence of the divine and expresses aspects of a spirit's character and identity. How the identities of spirits are musically constructed is a theme that is taken up in the next chapter.

4

The Musical Construction
of the Spirits

This chapter examines the role of music during *len dong*. It begins with a consideration of rituals conducted without a *chau van* band. This is followed by a more detailed investigation into how the aural invocation of the spirits relates to possession experiences and emotional arousal, and how music and sung text structure ritual time and entrain bodily movement. I go on to argue that music is constitutive of spiritual presence through various imaginings that relate to place, gender, and ethnicity, and I discuss how these imaginings relate to nationalist discourse. Finally, I illustrate the ways in which song texts describe the place and gender of spirits and recall the past.

Rituals without Bands?

When I spoke with mediums about the role of music during *len dong*, they emphasized the importance of *chau van*. Yet some claimed they could hold rituals without a band being present. The possibility of possession occurring without music is a useful point of entry for discussing *chau van*, because it raises a fundamental question: If it is possible for possession to occur without music, is music an epiphenomenon in possession practice? In other words, is *chau van* an optional accompaniment to other, more important ritual practices?

The practice of conducting rituals without a band arose when the Vietnamese Communist Party vigorously condemned and prohibited *len dong* from the 1950s to the late 1980s. Although people who were caught participating in mediumship were often subjected to some form of punishment, including imprisonment, mediums continued to secretly worship the spirits. Mediums who held "secret rituals" (*hau vung*) said they did not always ask a band to perform, for fear the sound would alert the authorities. *Len dong* conducted without bands were known as *hau vo* (lit. "serving [the spirits] without [a band]"). By definition, *hau vo* do not include a band, but mediums' descriptions of them indicate that sound was not entirely absent. It was still necessary for the assistants to "call out" (*keu*) by clapping and singing phrases of songs, especially when inviting the spirits. The medium's assistants had to call out to "satisfy" (*thoa*) the spirits and to ask their permission for worship.

Hau vo have not been held since the Party's restrictions were relaxed in the late 1980s, because no medium would conduct a ritual without a band out of choice. At best, *hau vo* were described as dull and miserable, and they were much shorter than conventional *len dong*. Some mediums even said *hau vo* were "worthless" (*ra gi*) and that, in fact, rituals could not be carried out without a band. Although *hau vo* were no longer occurring by the time of my fieldwork in Vietnam, I was intrigued by their existence in the past because they seemed to raise important issues about the role of mediumship music. In May 1998, Doan, whom we have already come across in previous chapters, suggested she hold a *hau vo* on condition that I "sponsor" it. This suggestion was an attempt to persuade me to financially support a ritual, but Doan had always maintained that she could hold *len dong* without a *chau van* band. For my part, I was keen to see what a *hau vo* would be like, and I also wanted to show my appreciation for Doan's help and kindness. So, despite my reservations that financial involvement would be disruptive, I decided to contribute 20 U.S. dollars to help cover the expenses of holding a ritual. An auspicious date was then chosen, close to the festival day of the Third Lady, and preparations for the *hau vo* were made.

Doan invited a small group of her friends and disciples to participate in the *hau vo*. Though she did not invite a band, she in fact asked an apprentice female musician to sing and play some percussion. Contrary to her previous claims, Doan requested music for the ritual. Just as in the past *hau vo* were not silent, neither was Doan's ritual.

While Doan was possessed by General Tran Hung Dao, who is also known as Tran Trieu, the spirit spoke of the contradiction of holding a *hau vo* with music:

> Today the wishes in the hearts of the mortals are that . . . they "address me with their mouths" and bow their heads in worship, so why is there still the sound of the drum and singing? How can this be a *hau vo?* . . . But I forgive

the mortals whose words "cross over" to the spirits and the four palaces. I, Tran Trieu, do not need singing or musical instruments. . . . The spirits of the four palaces have a childlike deception, because they must be presented with words, playing, and song, but remember the spirits of the four palaces are different from Tran Trieu.

According to these remarks, song is necessary for other spirits, but the general—who does not belong to any of the four palaces—needs only to be addressed with the spoken word. These comments highlight a tension: theoretically *hau vo* should be without music, yet at the same time, it is vital to "present" music to the spirits of the four palaces.

The importance of sound during rituals—whether or not it is played by a band or, indeed, whether it is strictly considered to be "music"—has been highlighted by Yung in his discussion of Chinese ritual sound: "The study of ritual music must include all ritual sound. Whether the sonic event is closer to noise, to speech or to music is of less significance than the particular role it plays in the context of ritual" (1996:17). In the case of *len dong,* there is a similar emphasis on sound and its ritual role. In order for aware possession to take place—even during *hau vo*—it is crucial that the spirits be aurally invited, either with speech or song. Following the onset of possession, rhythm and song are necessary for ritual actions to be carried out, as demonstrated by Doan's *hau vo. Chau van* songs are therefore necessary for the maintenance of possession, even if, in exceptional circumstances, they are not performed by a specialist band.

Inviting the Spirits: Music and Emotion

> Music makes translucent the boundary between human and spirit.
> —Friedson 1996:100

Even for *hau vo,* the aural invocation of the spirits is necessary to establish contact between the human and spirit worlds. When a band is present at rituals, the spirits are invoked with "Thinh Bong" (Inviting the Spirits), which is characterized by short vocal phrases sung in a high register over rapid drumming and a flurry of vigorous instrumental phrases. The rhythms and melody of "Thinh Bong" are essentially the same for each incarnation, but the song text is particular to each spirit. When the Second Lady possessed Lai during Ritual 1 (Video Extract 13), for instance, the text for "Thinh Bong" names and evokes the spirit's presence in the human world by referring to the famous temples, which are devoted to her, in Lang Son province in northeast

Vietnam: "Offer poems to the Second Lady of the Forest, The spirit descends to the temples in Dong Cuong and Tuan Quan."

The frequent association of loud, fast drumming with the onset of possession in many different rituals around the world has led to the common assumption that there is a causal connection between drumming and trance. The idea that drumming physiologically "triggers" trance, advanced by Neher (1962) and others, has been emphatically refuted by Gilbert Rouget in his exhaustive survey of spirit possession rituals (1985 [1980]:172–76). Drumming undoubtedly has physical effects on the body and brain (Erlmann 1982), but the fact that different people do not automatically go into trance when listening to the same rhythmic stimulus clearly indicates that drumming alone cannot trigger trance. In place of causal theories of the interrelationship between music and trance, Rouget maintains that the function of music in any particular ritual is culturally defined. He argues that music's primary role of music is to socialize trance (Rouget 1985 [1980]:323, 326). This socialization, Rouget maintains, is achieved through music's identificatory role. In other words, music exteriorizes possession by signaling the new identity of the possessee so that it is "recognized by everyone" (Rouget 1985 [1980]:324). By naming the spirit at the onset of possession—both in the aural invocations during *hau vo* and performances of "Thinh Bong"—and by singing about the spirit throughout the possession, the spirit incarnated is identified for ritual participants. As the musician Le Ba Cao said: "The members of *chau van* bands are musicians, but at the same time they are directors: they tell of the virtues of the spirits and sing for everybody to know which spirit is present" (pers. comm., January 1997). However, music during *len dong*, and in other rituals in different parts of the world, is not merely an "instrument of communication"; it also has other effects.

In *Deep Listeners,* Judith Becker attempts to move beyond the "long-standing argument between trance as basically physiological or as culturally constructed" and thereby overcome the rigid opposition between physiological and culturally defined effects of music (2004:37). By bringing together scientific theories of emotion and consciousness with cultural, humanistic perspectives on spirit possession, she aims to demonstrate that "sound properties of music accompanying trancing can be both biological and cultural" (2004:38). One of the central questions Becker poses is, "How are the outward characteristics of religious trance (dance, prophecy, speaking in tongues, speaking in voices of spiritual beings) correlated with inner physiology and what is the role of music in facilitating these events?" (2004:4). In answering this question, Becker covers a great deal of ground, juxtaposing theories of trancing, the self and embodiment, and phenomenological, biological, cognitive, and neurophysiological approaches to consciousness. She argues that high emotional arousal is central to trance consciousness and that the power of music to stimulate emotions is key to understanding its role in possession experiences. Rouget also emphasized how music in ceremonies "creates a certain emotional climate for the adepts" (1985 [1980]:325), but Becker goes further than Rouget by linking music-induced emotional arousal to theories of emotion and consciousness developed by neuroscientists.

In Chapter 2, Becker's hypotheses regarding the neurophysiology of trance consciousness based on Antonio Damasio's distinction between core consciousness and extended consciousness were discussed. Emotions are integral to the Damasio's theories on consciousness, and Becker suggests trancers learn to voluntarily control their emotional responses and therefore learn to change their extended consciousness at will. The effects music has on core and extended consciousness are speculative in Becker's account. But trancers' moment-to-moment sensitivity to, and coordination with, ritual music is thought of as a kind of "'musicked' core consciousness," and Becker hypothesizes that the power of music to stimulate emotion is one of the main factors that "helps propel the trancers into an alternate extended consciousness" (2004:147).

According to mediums' verbal reports, *chau van* stimulates the emotional arousal of aware possession. If Becker's hypotheses about the importance of emotional arousal for states of trancing are correct, then it is possible that *chau van* induces aware possession in part through music's power to arouse emotions. When listening to music during *len dong*, mediums said they were "profoundly moved" (*xuc dong*). They spoke of how music facilitated their euphoric emotions of "happiness" (*vui*), "joy" (*sung suong*), "elation" (*sang khoai* or *phan khoi*), and "intoxicating passion" (*say*). The experience of aware possession, in which the heart and heart-soul feel buoyant and light, were linked to musical experiences. The following comments by mediums were typical: "When I hear the invitation to the spirits before the spirit enters, my heart-soul flies, I feel elated"; "When I listen to *chau van* I find that I am charmed, my heart-soul is charmed, then the spirits enter me"; "Listening to *chau van* is profoundly moving, it makes me joyous." The interaction between music, the heart-soul, and the spirits is also alluded to by Vietnamese scholars of *chau van*: "there are people who think that *chau van* . . . leads the heart-soul into the supernatural world" (Bui Dinh Thao and Nguyen Quang Hai 1996: 68); "[*Chau van*] affects the heart-soul of the person serving the spirits and the people participating [in rituals], to create an atmosphere for possession" (Ngo Duc Thinh 1992:82). Music, then, moves the heart-soul so that bodily possession of the spirits is possible. The aural invocations of the spirits bring forth the spirits into the human world by evoking euphoric emotions.

Ritual Time and Musical Entrainment: "Animating" Possession and "Inciting" Dance

> "If there is no music, you cannot do the work of the spirits"
> —Pers. comm., medium Lai, May 1998

John Blacking noted the capacity of music to frame experiential time when he commented that "ordinary daily experience takes place in a world of actual time. The essential quality of music is its power to create another world of virtual time" (1973:27). Following Schutz's reflections on how music involves a "mutual tuning-in process," a sharing of "inner time," between performer and listener (Schutz 1977), phenomenologically oriented accounts of musical performance have expanded upon the ways music shapes shared experiences. Christopher Waterman discusses how in jùjú performance, Yoruba musicians "established a special flow of lived time" through which social organization and interaction are ordered (1990:215). In the context of Tumbuka healing and spirit possession in northern Malawi, Steven Friedson asserts that music has a "powerful effect on the processual nature of lived experience" and draws on Heidegger's theories of being-in-the-world to suggest that "music making projects a clearing, a place in which people can encounter the world and each other in all their reflexive immediacy" (1996:126). From a phenomenological standpoint, musical experience involves the collapsing or blurring of temporal boundaries. Bruce Kapferer makes this point when he states that "*music demands the living of the reality it creates.* Engaged in music, a listening subject is opened up to the experiential possibility internal to its structure, its duration, change and movement through successive and repeated nows, and to a sonorous past continuous with the present and moving to its future" (1991 [1983]:258, emphases in original). In his discussion of Malagasy *tromba* ceremonies, Ron Emoff also emphasizes how "musical performance facilitates the actual evanescence of temporal delimitations between past, present, and future . . . as it reorders the feel of the passing of present time in bringing up past times and events" (2002:8).

The intimate relations between songscapes and ritual action suggest that the potential of music to affect lived experience and experiential time is nothing new to participants of *len dong*. *Chau van* performance has effects on mediums' possession experiences, and their assistants and disciples engage or "tune in" with the progression of ritual time through listening to songscapes.

Following the onset of possession, the ritual time of *len dong* unfolds musically. As discussed in the previous chapter, some songs are strongly linked to particular ritual actions. This is the case for some dances (Video Extracts 16, 26, and 29) and for actions such as waving incense (Video Extracts 1, 18, and 24), drinking rice wine (Video Extracts 19, 20, and 24), and writing poems on a fan (Video Extracts 18 and 19). Such coordination between ritual progression and the musical flow of songscapes enables mediums to carry out their ritual practices. Songs embody ritual action. As Lai succinctly observed, without music it is not possible to maintain possession and carry out ritual acts. Even those mediums with a particularly "high aptitude and a heavy fate," who maintained they could hold *hau vo*, admitted that possession without a full band was short-lived.

Ritual acts are narrated in sung text. For instance, when the Tenth Prince imitates writing a poem on a fan with a stick of incense and when the spirit drinks rice wine, the medium must time her movements to coincide with the sung verses. In Ritual 1 (Video Extracts 18 and 19), as Lai "writes," the band members sing the poem inscribed on the fan by the Tenth Prince; when she is offered wine by her assistants, the song invites the Tenth Prince to drink:

> The bunch of incense is a powerful pen.
> It makes the army generals return to protect;
> It orders the ministries of war.

> The sacred pen performs miracles.
> The flowers open for a thousand springs.
> The Tenth Prince's pen brings peace to the world.
> Everybody sings the ancient song of peace.

> A fan inscribed with a poem,
> The Tenth Prince walks in a ceremonial style.
> He is a hero of the past and present.
> Recite poetry of the past masters.

> The Tenth Prince returns and the pen from the heavens brings peace
> to everyone.

> The maidens pour the first glass of delicious peach wine.
> The maidens offer rice wine and invite the Tenth Prince to drink.

As well as narrating actions, music affects mediums' experience of time through making possession "animated" (*boc*) and "impulsive" (*boc dong*). One elderly medium, who was ninety-two when I met her, became remarkably energetic and agile when possessed, even though in everyday life she was frail and weak. She said she felt extremely strong when possessed and attributed her vigorous behavior and strength to the music, which made her animated. The term *boc* literally means "rise up"/"emanate" (e.g., smoke, vapor), but it is also used metaphorically to express "excess," "heat," or "animation" regarding a person's behaviour or character. *Boc* may be used to describe a person's "fiery" or "tumultuous" character (*tinh hay boc*) or the "rising up" (*boc len*) of emotion. The compound word *boc dong*—rendered as "impulsive"—is commonly used to refer to the impetuous character of mediums and their behavior when possessed. Music, then, heightens the rising up of energy when mediums are performing rituals and brings out their impulsive character, which is necessary to carry out the work of the spirits.

The experience of musical and ritual time involves a synchrony between gesture and rhythm. The coordination of bodily and musical rhythms during *len dong* is a case of rhythmic entrainment. The idea of entrainment broadly refers to "the alignment or integration of bodily features with some recurrent features in the environment" (DeNora 2000:77–78). Studies have explored the diverse ways in which sound entrains. For example, research has examined how the sonic environment influences the physiological states of neonatal infants, and microbehavioral analyses of teachers and students in the classroom have shown that successful teaching relies on mutual synchronization of body and speech rhythms (DeNora 2000; Becker 2004). In the case of ritual trancing, Judith Becker suggests that "musical rhythmic entrainment can be seen as structural coupling, of a changed interior, personal consciousness in a musical domain of coordination" (2004:127). Musical entrainment is an important factor in ritual experiences, she argues, because it brings about changes in individual being and consciousness, while at the same time interconnecting ritual participants through "structural coupling," a biological notion that refers to how organisms become linked through repeated interaction.

Rhythmic entrainment during *len dong* occurs most directly when mediums dance and perform actions such as "presenting incense," which involves processing and kneeling in front of the altar in time with *chau van* rhythms. The power of music to animate possession applies to all ritual acts, but religious devotees used a specific term for the effect of music on "dance" (*mua*): they said that the rhythm "incites" (*kich dong*) dance. To illustrate how rhythmic entrainment incites mediums to dance, it is necessary to briefly examine the relationship between musical rhythms and dance movements.

The dance performed by mediums depends on the spirit incarnated. Most dances are shared between a group of spirits; only a few are reserved for individual spirits. In terms of Rouget's classification, *len dong* dances are figurative dances "whose function is to manifest the possession state," rather than abstract dances "whose function is to trigger trance" (1985 [1980]:114). Three different rhythms are used for these figurative dances: the one-beat and three-beat rhythms, and *nhip trong chien,* which is used for the "Trong Chien" or "War Drums" melody. The one- and two-beat rhythms adhere to a basic rhythmic framework (see Chapter 3), but *nhip trong chien* does not follow a standard recurring pattern. As the name "War Drums" suggests, the driving rhythms of "Trong Chien"—which usually features loud, tremolo-like rolls on a large drum and handheld gong—evoke the atmosphere of war.

Dances are named according to the different objects used for dance. Table 4.1 lists the most common dances, the song(s) used for each dance, and the rhythm of each song(s). The numbers of the video extracts on the DVD that include examples of the dances are also provided.

Table 4.1. Spirit dances and percussion rhythms

Dance	Spirit(s)	Song(s)	Rhythm(s)	DVD Video ext.
Lit-rope (*mua moi*)	Female spirits belonging to the Mountains and Forests Palace	"Xa Mua Moi"	One-beat	15
Bell-sticks (*mua heo*)	Prince spirits and the young prince spirits	"Luu Thuy"	Three-beat	24
Sword (*mua kiem*)	Second and Third Mandarin	"Luu Thuy" / "Trong Chien"	Three-beat / *nhip trong chien*	1, 9
Sabre (*mua dao*)	Fifth Mandarin Trong Chien	"Luu Thuy" / "Trong Chien"	Three-beat / *nhip trong chien*	
Fan (*mua quat*)	Ninth Princess (also some other princess and lady spirits)	"Nhip Mot"	One-beat	15
Rowing (*mua cheo do*)	Third Princess	"Cheo Do"	One-beat	26, 29

Female spirits dance to the one-beat rhythm, whereas male spirits dance to the three-beat rhythm. Both of these rhythms are used for songs that do not accompany dance, so they are not unique dance rhythms. However, both the one-beat and three-beat rhythms incite dance when played at the appropriate point in the ritual. Musicians and mediums consider the one-beat rhythm to be the most "lively" (linh hoat/soi noi) rhythm for dance and the three-beat rhythm to be "stately" or "majestic" (oai nghiem). This is in accordance with the character of the dances for male and female spirits: the dances of female spirits are more "fun" than the dances of male spirits. This is especially the case when comparing the dances of female mountain spirits with the "serious" (nghiem tuc) martial dances of mandarin spirits. When dancing, mediums do not follow a standard sequence of movements, but some characteristic movements can be identified.

The basic movements of the female-spirit dances and the bell-sticks dances of the prince and young-prince spirits follow the percussion rhythm. A core movement of most of the female-spirit dances (except the rowing dance) is a "jogging step" consisting of bouncing from one foot to the other in time with the pulse of the one-beat rhythm. Arm movements are also usually linked to the pulse of the one-beat rhythm and the jogging step. Similarly, the imitation of boat rowing, which forms the basis of the rowing dance, follows the pulse of the "Cheo Do" song. Mediums follow the accelerando of "Cheo Do" by increasing the speed of their rowing. The bell-sticks dances of the prince and young prince spirits are linked to the rhythm of the music to the extent that mediums usually beat the two bell-sticks together in time with the beat of the drum.

The mandarin dances do not usually follow the pulse of the music as closely as those for female and prince spirits. During these dances, mediums usually "bob up and down" in the vertical plane by bending their knees, without lifting their feet completely from the ground. This movement is not always strictly linked to the pulse of the music: it usually slips in and out of phase with the percussion rhythms. When Lai dances with swords (Video Extract 9), she begins with a variation of the jogging step, which follows the three-beat rhythm of "Luu Thuy." But when she starts to "bob up and down," with one hand placed on her hip and the other wielding the sword in a circular motion, her movements are not directly coordinated with the pulse. Similarly, in Ritual 2, Hang's sword dance to "Trong Chien" (Video Extract 1) is not always in sync with the percussion. "Trong Chien" incites dance by creating a percussive, warlike atmosphere appropriate for showing military strength, and precise synchronization of bodily movement and rhythm is not required.

Movement is coordinated with the rhythms of music during dances, but even when mediums are seated, their bodily movements are musically regulated. They swing their arms, sway their torsos, drink, smoke, make vocal noises, utter words, distribute gifts, and interact with the band and disciples in ways that are musically enveloped and coordinated. Video Extract 21, which shows Lai smoking and distributing gifts while listening to the "Bi Tho" melody, provides a good example. Lai becomes more contemplative as she listens to the soaring, unmetered vocal of "Bi Tho" sung by Pham Van Ty. She becomes calmer and her movements more deliberate in response to the sung poem and the flute part that weaves around the vocal melody. At the end of Pham Van Ty's verse, Truong Manh Linh sings: "The beauty of the world is far away, / Dreaming for a thousand years in the light of the moon." For this verse, Lai stops smoking, and disciples offer gifts for her to bless. Although she is busy interacting with the disciples, she shows how attentive she is to the music and the poetic imagery by letting out a cry of appreciation and giving the musicians "reward money" at the end of Linh's verse, just before the band changes to a new song, "Con Hue." The musical entrainment evident during the performance of "Bi Tho" relies on a deep appreciation of the whole auditory experience and is not driven just by the rhythm of the music.

The phenomenon of musical entrainment during *len dong* pertains primarily to the bodily rhythms of mediums. At some rituals I have seen disciples clap along with the one-beat rhythm, but *len dong* does not usually involve participatory music making by all those present. However, the modes of interaction between mediums, assistants, and disciples are numerous, and the shared listening experience influences these interactional modes. The assistants who attend to the possessee must "tune in" to songscapes to ensure that ritual action is musically coordinated. As assistants are usually also mediums, they have already learned to respond in particular ways to *chau van* while possessed. This embodied knowledge of musical and ritual practices makes assistants ideally suited to ensure that the possession progresses smoothly. Assistants are expected to give their full attention to the unfolding ritual event and to facilitate the interactions between the possessee and other participants. Disciples interact with mediums more intermittently than assistants, but they, too, must time their physical and verbal interactions with the possessee appropriately, as they are permitted to approach the medium only at certain points in the ritual. The sonic environment of possession, while it only rarely entrains the overt physical movements of disciples, encourages religious devotion. The styles of listening among disciples of course varies depending on personal biographies and other factors, but disciples often expressed to me how much they enjoyed *chau van* because it created a "spiritual atmosphere" (*khong khi tam linh*).

The Musical Construction of Place, Gender, and Ethnicity

Martin Stokes has suggested that "music is socially meaningful not entirely but largely because it provides a means by which people recognise identities and places, and the boundaries which separate them" (1994:5). With roots in Barth's analysis of ethnicity, Stokes explores how music both marks out and "preforms" boundaries—not only geographical boundaries, but also the boundaries that define and maintain ethnicity, national identity, and class and gender differences. The idea of boundaries is useful because it denies essences and provides scope for analyzing how different social categories overlap. This is particularly important in regard to the *chau van* musical system and the spirit pantheon of the Four Palace Religion, because they involve complex entanglements of place, gender, and ethnicity.

In Vietnamese speech, there are two opposing expressions of orientation: *mien xuoi,* meaning "the lowlands" or "downstream," and *mien nui,* meaning "the mountainous regions." The same polarity is also present in one of the terms for nation, *nui song* (lit. "mountains and rivers"). This has obvious similarities with the opposition of the Mountains and Forests Palace and the Water Palace in the Four Palace Religion.

The prosperous "downstream" is the heartland of the Viet majority, the Kinh, and the mountains have, at least in the past, been predominantly the domain of so-called ethnic minorities. Official classifications denominate fifty-four ethnic minority groups in Vietnam. Having set up ethnic diversity, nationalist discourse combines this diversity again into a "cultural unity" with a "unified core" (Dang Nghiem Van et al. 1984:13). Ethnic minorities in Vietnam, according to the nationalist project, are incorporated for the good of creating a unified state, a "higher community," a "community of the Vietnamese nation" with the Viet majority, the Kinh, at the "center" (Dang Nghiem Van et al. 1984:13).

Place and ethnicity are therefore explicitly linked through the opposed double pairings of the mountains/ethnic minorities on the one hand, and the lowlands/Kinh on the other. This pairing has a parallel in the *chau van* repertoire through the use of a particular group of melodies, the "Xa" melodies, for certain spirits connected to the mountains. Spirits are linked to the mountains through belonging to the Mountains and Forests Palace and/or through being associated with mountainous regions in Vietnam, and some mountain spirits are "ethnic minority" spirits. For followers of the Four Palace Religion, the "Xa" melodies evoke the mountains and the sound of the ethnic minorities who live in the mountainous regions.

However, the "Xa" melodies are not performed for all mountain spirits: the issue is also complicated by gender. The only male mountain spirits who are incarnated regularly are the Seventh Prince and the Second Mandarin. "Xa" melodies are not usually performed for these two spirits, so only female spirits are musically constructed as mountain spirits.[1]

So why are female mountain spirits, and not male mountain spirits, linked to the mountains through song? In general, female spirits are more explicitly linked to the environment than male spirits. For example, the Third Lady of the Water Palace is connected to the water, through ritual actions such as rowing down a river, whereas the actions of the Third Mandarin of the Water Palace do not make explicit references to the environment. It would therefore seem that the classic male/female, culture/nature dichotomies (Ortner 1996) are, to a certain extent, embedded in the *chau van* musical system and the behavior of spirits. Certainly, this view is supported by the folklore scholar Ngo Duc Thinh when he claims that "many cosmic and natural phenomena are connected with the female character" (1996a:12).

The connections among place, gender, and ethnicity outlined so far may be summarized as follows:

Male spirits, female lowland/Kinh spirits = non-"Xa" melodies
Female mountain/ethnic minority spirits = "Xa" melodies

In addition to the musical construction of female mountain spirits through the use of the "Xa" melodies, the gender boundary between male spirits and lowland female spirits is musically denoted. Although the songscapes of female lowland spirits have some melodies (e.g., "Doc," "Sai," and "Luu Thuy") in common with male spirits, certain groups of songs and individual songs are linked to the gender of spirits. In the broadest terms, female lowland spirits are musically differentiated from male spirits by the use of the "Con" and "Phu" melodies, respectively.[2] Each "Con" and "Phu" melody has its own distinctive aesthetic, but generalizing at the level of the group, the "Phu" melodies imbue "masculinity" (*nam tinh*), "authority" (*uy nghi*), and "seriousness" (*nghiem tuc*), and the "Con" melodies imbue "femininity" (*nu tinh*), "smoothness" (*muot ma*), and "lyricism" (*tru tinh*). Other melodies that are divided according to the gender of spirits include "Van" and "Ham," which are performed for lowland female spirits, and "Kieu Duong," which is performed for male spirits.

Status and age also have a bearing on the division of melodies on gender lines. The "Phu" melodies and "Kieu Duong" are particularly appropriate for the mandarin spirits, who are the highest-ranking male deities. The song-scapes of prince spirits sometimes include "Phu" melodies, but many bands favor alternative melodies, such as "Nhip Mot," which are less serious than the "Phu" melodies and therefore more in keeping with the lower status of the princes compared to mandarins. "Phu" melodies are never played for the young princes, because they are children and therefore cannot assume the same gender position as adult male spirits.

The musical construction of mountain spirits—in contrast to that of lowland spirits—has already been noted. Apart from this broad division, in some instances the places of lowland spirits are more specifically delineated in song. Two examples are the musical construction of the Water Palace of the Third Lady and the Tenth Prince's home province in the human world, the central Vietnamese province of Nghe An. When the Third Lady dances with oars, the musicians sing the "Cheo Do" melody to musically evoke the Water Palace to which the Third Lady belongs; "Cheo Do" directly references rowing by including a "rowing call" refrain, *khoan khoan ho khoan*. The Tenth Prince's native province is musically constructed through the use of "Ho Hue" and "Con Hue." These melodies are recognized by ritual participants as being influenced by the musical style of the city of Hue and, more generally, that of central Vietnam as a whole. They therefore musically evoke the Tenth Prince's native province in central Vietnam, Nghe An.

Ho is a generic term for a large body of folk songs found throughout Vietnam. They are associated with acts of labor, especially rowing, but some "Ho" songs are also love songs, and others are performed at festivals (Pham Duy 1975:27–47). "Ho Hue," which is performed for the Tenth Prince, is thought to have been devised in the 1980s by the musician Doan Duc Dan (pers. comm., Dang Cong Hung, May 1998). "Con Hue" is related to a type of "Con" melody performed by *chau van* musicians in central Vietnam. The central Vietnamese musical characteristics that musicians pointed out as being evident in "Ho Hue" and "Con Hue" were the frequent use of a wide vibrato and the pronunciation of the song text with the Hue dialect.

Table 4.2 provides summaries of the classification of songs outlined in this section:

Table 4.2. Classification of *chau van* songs according to the place, gender, and ethnicity of spirits

Song(s)	Spirit(s)	Associations and character of songs
"Xa" melodies	Female mountain spirits (some of which are ethnic minority spirits)	Mountains/ethnic minorities, lively, happy
"Con" melodies (+ "Van" and "Ham")	Female lowland spirits	Feminine, lyrical, smooth
"Phu" melodies (+ "Kieu Duong")	Adult male spirits (especially the high-status mandarin spirits)	Masculine, serious, strict
"Ho Hue" and "Con Hue"	Tenth Prince	Central Vietnam (the city of Hue)
"Cheo Do"	Third Lady	Water Palace

Let us now examine the musical features of songs that aurally construct the ethnicity of spirits. The musical construction of gender will be addressed further in the next chapter.

Mountain Songs

Musicians claimed that the "Xa" melodies have the "color," "identity," and "atmosphere" of the ethnic minorities and, by extension, the mountainous regions in Vietnam. The distinctive percussion of the "Xa" melodies was the main musical feature that musicians said evoked the ethnic minorities. For the "Xa" melodies, a small gong, called the *thanh la,* is placed on the face of a small two-headed drum. A bunch of keys is usually placed on top of the gong, producing a metallic rattle when it is struck. The gong is rarely used for other melodies and is never placed on the drum itself. Some band members said the gong was introduced by a musician about sixty or seventy years ago after he made visits to the mountainous regions, and that its use was inspired by the gong-chime ensembles of the Muong and Jarai. However, all "Xa" melodies employ the gong, so its use is not restricted to spirits designated as belonging to ethnic minority groups who play in gong-chime ensembles.

At some *len dong* I attended, the flautist Le Tu Cuong played a Hmong flute (*sao* Hmong) for some "Xa" melodies. This flute would seem to be an obvious and direct reference to Hmong music. However, Cuong learned to play the Hmong flute through studying neotraditional music at the Hanoi Music Conservatoire, and he does not perform Hmong melodies. Also, Cuong did not reserve the flute for Hmong spirits: he often played it during incarnations of the Muong spirit Lady Thac Bo. This illustrates once again that musicians imagine a pan-ethnic minority identity when they perform the "Xa" melodies.

Apart from the inclusion of the small gong and the Hmong flute, there are few other references to the musical cultures of ethnic minority groups in *chau van* performances. Indeed, the vocal ornamentation, song structure, and scales of the most popular "Xa" melodies—"Xa Thuong," "Xa Mua Moi," and "Xa Giay Lech"—do not stand out as particularly unique compared to other *chau van* songs. The lack of direct influences from ethnic minority music cultures indicates that the musical evocation of ethnicity in *chau van* is, to a great extent, *imagined*. This imagined relationship takes the form of evoking the atmosphere of the mountains and a pan-ethnic minority identity.

Most of the "Xa" melodies are associated with the mountains in a generalized way, but some regional distinctions are made within the "Xa" group. These distinctions are most evident in two melodies: "Xa Quang" (Track 11), also known as "Xa Bac" ("North Xa"), and "Xa Tay Nguyen" (Track 25). These two melodies are associated with the mountainous regions in northern and central Vietnam, respectively.

Figure 4.1. Le Tu Cuong playing the Hmong flute (2005)

"Xa Quang" is the only "Xa" melody that musicians claimed had links to a musical system from beyond Vietnam's borders. It was said to sound Chinese because it had been influenced by folk songs from the southern Chinese province of Guangdong, known in Vietnam as Quang Dong. "Xa Quang" is usually performed for the Little Lady; it is appropriate because the temple dedicated to her—Bac Le temple—is in northeast Vietnam near the Vietnamese–Chinese border. Yet even for "Xa Quang," musicians did not point out specific musical features as evidence of musical syncretism. The term "Quang" entered the Vietnamese musical lexicon in the 1920s, when it was used to refer to some songs of the music-theater genre *cai luong*, which drew on Chinese music (Pham Duy 1975:141–43). *Chau van* musicians thought that any Chinese influences on "Xa Quang" had probably occurred via the Quang melodies of *cai luong*, and this made it harder for them to specifically identify Chinese musical characteristics.

"Xa Tay Nguyen" was originally devised by *chau van* musicians in southern Vietnam, and Pham Van Ty learned it during a trip to Ho Chi Minh City in the early 1990s. The term "Tay Nguyen" refers to the central highlands, and Ty made his own innovations to the original song. These include the frequent use of vocables, such as *en ta na en trai ta na*, which have no meaning but imitate the languages of the ethnic groups living in central Vietnam; and the long phrases toward the end of the verse that start high and descend down an octave, using glissandi and a wide vibrato. The links between the central highlands and "Xa Tay Nguyen" are therefore based on generic imitation and mimicry of the musics and languages of ethnic minorities in the central highlands.

Although "Xa Quang" and "Xa Tay Nguyen" demonstrate how musical distinctions are sometimes made between the two main mountainous regions in northern and central Vietnam, all the songs in the "Xa" group have similar aesthetic connotations. Musicians characterized the "Xa" melodies as being happy and lively, and they maintained that these qualities suited the character of the mountain spirits. The "Xa" melodies are also considered to be the easiest and simplest to perform. It was noted above, in relation to the possession dances, that the one-beat rhythm is considered to be the most vibrant rhythm; the gong and keys placed on the drum make the sound of the percussion even livelier. Also, because all the "Xa" melodies are sung to the one-beat rhythm, the songscapes for the female mountain spirits are vivacious throughout. This contrasts with intermittent use of the one-beat rhythm for the songscapes of princes, young princes, and lowland female spirits.

The happy, lively, and simple character of the "Xa" melodies fits with the image portrayed by mediums when possessed by mountain spirits. For mountain spirits, mediums wear "ethnic minority" costume, dance energetically, and are generally vivacious. The ethnic costumes worn during *len dong* are a pan-ethnic hodgepodge of different items of clothing and jewelry from diverse groups. Female mountain spirits also distribute natural products to the disciples, such as fruit and areca nut, in contrast to the packaged food and drink distributed by other spirits, thereby emphasizing the connections between female mountain spirits and nature. The "Xa" melodies, then, along with the behavior and dress of the female mountain spirits, promote a feminized pan-ethnic minority stereotype of natural, happy, simple, colorful, and lively ethnic minorities.

Reflections on the "Xa" Melodies, National Discourse, and Ethnicity

Drawing on Homi Bhabha and others, Peter Wade has argued that a "nationalist project does not just try to deny, suppress, or even simply channel an unruly diversity; it actively reconstructs it" (1998:3). Wade tries to move beyond the idea of homogenizing elites against diversifying subalterns and suggests instead that diversity is part and parcel of nation building and is (re)constituted through it (1998:4; see also Wade 2000). It was noted above that nationalist discourse on ethnic minorities in Vietnam argues for the creation of a "higher Vietnamese community," yet it does so by implicitly acknowledging diversity. In this discourse, minorities are not characterized as a troublesome subaltern. Rather, diversity is a necessary prerequisite of, and mediated through, the project of nation building.

Understanding how diversity is embedded in national discourse opens up the way for examining how "a given style of music can be seen as a national unity and a diversity" (Wade 1998:16). Wade argues that Costeño music in Colombia can both "constitute the nation" and "constitute the Costeños as a regional group," depending on the "processes of imagining" by those engaged with the music (1998:16). The Colombian material illustrates the general point that music does not simply "represent" or "reflect" a particular social group. Instead, music is constitutive of identity and its "representational role" is flexible and contextual (see also Stokes 1994 and Frith 1996).

Processes of imagining that mediate unity and diversity are also at work in regard to the performances of the "Xa" melodies for female mountain spirits. The previous section discussed how musical representations of ethnic minority music in *chau van* are imagined and based on an idea of a generic, pan-ethnic minority identity that merges cultural difference. This implies unity with little diversity: *chau van* subsumes the diversity of ethnic minority musics within the frame of a Viet musical system. Such a position suggests that ethnic minority culture is subject to a process of homogenization by the Viet majority.

A different reading of the representation of ethnic minority groups during rituals maintains that ethnic diversity is celebrated, not homogenized. This argument is made in the book *Hat Van:*

> There are a number of spirits of the Muong, Tay, Nung, Dao and Cham ethnicities especially among the lady spirits . . . the dress and way of dancing of the lady spirits as well as the song texts and the *hat van* [i.e., *chau van*] melodies sung are characteristic of different ethnicities. . . . In feudal society the Viet majority, who had a higher social and economic level than the ethnic minorities, had an ideology that discriminated against other ethnic groups in all social relations. However, . . . in the religious beliefs of the four palaces we find the spirit of equality; there is no discrimination against any other nationalities. Because of this, the activities of *hat van* and *len dong* contribute to cultural exchange and increase understanding between different ethnicities. (Ngo Duc Thinh 1992:140)

According to this narrative, *len dong* is a vehicle for cultural exchange between different ethnic groups and contributes to national unity *through* diversity. Such arguments are strikingly similar to those used by nationalist discourse. However, it should be noted that the adoption of nationalist arguments by researchers at the Folk Culture Institute, who wrote the book *Hat Van*, is primarily motivated by a concern with providing a positive interpretation of mediumship in the light of it being condemned as superstition. Interpreting *len dong* and *chau van* as multiculturalist is part of the folk-culture scholars' attempts to legitimate *len dong* and their research. Publicly stated arguments suggesting that *len dong* contributes to national unity, whether by subsuming or celebrating ethnic differences, would have been inconceivable during the vigorous implementation of the antisuperstition campaign. Indeed, contemporary critics of mediumship still see those Viet people that participate in rituals as a troublesome diversity.

Discussion of the representation of ethnic minority music and identity during rituals would obviously benefit from consideration of the views of people who belong to so-called ethnic minority groups. Unfortunately, however, the voices of the "represented" will have to remain silent until further research is carried out. Nevertheless, I hope to have demonstrated that there are different possible readings of the representation of ethnic minority groups and their music. *Chau van* and *len dong* may therefore be said to involve differing and contested processes of imagining.

Sung Text: Place, Gender, and Recalling the Past

The poems dedicated to the spirits are the main "texts" through which the stories of spirits are transmitted. They tell of the legends, great deeds, and miraculous powers of the spirits. They praise their talents, virtue, and generosity. They describe their beauty, character, appearance, and gestures.

The song texts for the spirits are littered with references to and descriptions of the celestial palaces where they reside and the places they visited in the human world, many of which have become famous sites of pilgrimage. In this way, the human and spirit worlds are brought closer together. The journeys of spirits are depicted with poetic images celebrating the beauty of the natural world (rivers, lakes, waterfalls, mountains, forests, birds, flowers). These images fuse human with celestial landscapes. The Third Princess drifts down from the water palace in a rowing boat and goes up- and downstream saving her disciples from misery; the Tenth Prince returns to his native province of Nghe An and writes poems to bring peace to the world; the Third Mandarin is carried in a gold sedan chair by disciples to his temple in Lanh Giang in Ha Nam province; the Second Lady descends from the Mountains and Forests Palace to dance and sing joyously in the mountainous regions in northern Vietnam. The fulcrum of these journeys to the human world is the connection between spirits and their disciples. The texts implore followers to worship and make offerings to the spirits. Devotion to the spirits is reciprocated with divine protection and assistance. As a line of text for the Third Princess bluntly warns: "Worship skillfully and you will float, otherwise you will sink" (Video Extract 27).

Like the songscapes for male and female spirits, which display marked gender differences, texts are also highly gendered. The poems for mandarin and prince spirits, who are "warrior-scholars" (*van vo*), make frequent reference to their military strength, literary achievements, and heroic deeds, whereas those for female spirits tend to emphasize stereotypical feminine characteristics such as gracefulness and physical beauty. A comparison of the following extracts of poems for the Tenth Prince, the Fifth Mandarin, and the Second Lady are illustrative:

TENTH PRINCE:

In central Vietnam there are many famous rumors about the
    Tenth Prince.
He leads the army that defeats enemies; he keeps the precious
    rivers safe.
The Chinese enemies of the Thanh dynasty are defeated.
Wherever the prince goes, the people greet him warmly.
He has been worshipped with incense for thousands of years.
Kneel before the Tenth Prince, who has pity on people's misery.

FIFTH MANDARIN:

The Trieu Da enemy tried to invade;
The court ordered soldiers to be deployed.
The boats crossing the Tranh river filled the sky;
Suddenly a violent storm erupted.
The Tranh river! Oh, the Tranh river!
The reflection of the moon dances on the Tranh river.
For thousands of years the sacred spirit has been a glorious hero.
Whoever crosses the Tranh river, remember the brilliant warrior.

SECOND LADY:

She has ivory skin and the sparkling eyes of a phoenix,
A fresh face and youthful, silky hair.
She wears rouge and white powder,
Wrists like ivory, a head of plaited hair,
The princess of the heavens.

The texts of the Fifth Mandarin and the Tenth Prince link them to the
long history of resistance to Chinese domination. In some of the stories of
the Fifth Mandarin, the spirit appears in the form of a snake and destroys
Chinese military ships by creating a violent storm on the Tranh river in Hai
Hung province; "Trieu Da" is the name that was adopted by a Qin Chinese
general whose family ruled the northern Vietnamese area before it became
integrated as a province of China in 111 B.C. The Tenth Prince is thought to
have been a scholar and general in the Le dynasty (1428–1788), and in song
texts he is associated with the defeat of Chinese Thanh dynasty troops that
were sent to Vietnam in the late eighteenth century.

The references to the historical exploits of male spirits explicitly bring the
past into the ritual present. Musicians sing about the past as mediums bodily
reenact the meritorious acts of the spirits. The most direct evocation of his-

tory occurs when celebrated historical personages like General Tran Hung Dao, who famously defeated Mongolian invaders in the thirteenth century, are incarnated. But even when song texts do not pinpoint particular historical events, as is frequently the case especially for female spirits, they often recall a nonspecific sense of the past through the use of old terminology associated with feudal times. In short, the past is evoked as much by the rich, honorific language of song texts as by specific historical references.

Music and Spirit Possession

For spirits to descend and possess the medium, they must be aurally invited. Music makes possession possible by affecting the heart-soul of the possessee and inducing euphoric emotions: mediums feel the spirits and *chau van* in their heart and heart-soul. Once the spirit has been incarnated, music animates ritual action and incites dance; without "sweet playing and interesting singing," possession is short-lived. Songscapes structure time and entrain bodily movement. Sung text narrates ritual action and recalls the past.

The power of music to socialize possession is important, as *chau van* songs let all the ritual participants know which spirit has been incarnated. But *chau van* does not merely identify the spirits; it actively "makes" the presence of spirits. Just as possessed mediums must wear the spirits' clothes and carry out their work, so must the spirits be immersed in their music. Through sound and sung text, spirits are musically constructed and the past is vividly brought into the present.

Ritualizing enables mediums to make connections with spirits associated with different parts of Vietnam and with "ethnic minorities" in the remote northern and central mountainous regions. This mediation of places and people, which is made possible through music, is central to spirit possession. The place, gender, and ethnicity of the spirits are musically constructed through the performance of different songs for female mountain, female lowland, and male spirits. The "Xa" melodies for female mountain spirits, some of whom are ethnic minority spirits, convey the atmosphere of the mountains through evoking the music of the ethnic minorities in Vietnam. Yet the relationship between the "Xa" melodies and ethnic minority musics is, to a great extent, imagined.

The representation of ethnicity in *len dong* advances stereotypical notions of a pan-ethnic minority identity rendered female, natural, happy, simple, colorful, and lively. The processes of imagining ethnicity evident in *chau van* and *len dong* might be seen as promoting unhelpful stereotypes that hinder rather than enhance cultural understanding. However, Vietnamese folklore scholars have extolled the value of ritual practices, suggesting that they contribute to cultural exchange between the Viet majority and ethnic minority groups. These arguments should be understood within the context of scholars' attempts to legitimize *len dong*. Nevertheless, the interpretation of *len dong* as multiculturalist is complicit with nationalist discourse, which aims to incorporate the diversity of ethnic minority groups into a "community" dominated by the Viet majority.

In sum, music during *len dong* may be understood as being transformative: *chau van* songs enable mediums to cross between the human and spirit worlds, to traverse temporal, gender, and ethnicity boundaries. By constructing the identity of spirits—their contrasting histories, personalities, and places—music enforces the subject positions mediums assume during possession.

5

Musical Creativity and Change

Learning Chau Van

In October 1996, I started to study *chau van* with Pham Van Ty. In the first few lessons I learned instrumental phrases on the moon lute. The format of the lessons consisted of Ty demonstrating instrumental phrases (*luu khong*) for songs and me repeating the phrases as best I could. No notation was used, and Ty offered little verbal instruction. Ty would simply play a phrase in its entirety and expect me to repeat it. The *luu khong* were typically about thirty seconds in length, and, as I was struggling with the technique of playing the instrument and ornamentation as well as trying to remember the phrase, I could often play only the first part of a phrase before breaking down. The process of demonstration and imitation continued, and as I was having difficulty memorizing phrases in their entirety, I encouraged Ty to play short sections for me to copy. This went against the grain for Ty: he conceived of phrases in their entirety and sometimes found it difficult to repeat short sections out of context. But he obliged my requests, which made the learning process somewhat easier. To aid my memory, I also recorded all my lessons so I could listen to the phrases repeatedly and practice them again. As soon as Ty was happy that I could play one version of a *luu khong*, he would then play another. The more stock phrases I learned, the harder it became for me to remember specific versions and for Ty to repeat phrases in a fixed form. Like many orally trained musicians in other parts of the world (Nettl 1998), *chau van* musicians learn numerous stock phrases. This pool of stock phrases is a resource, which is drawn upon and recombined in performance.

Learning instrumental phrases was just the beginning. After several lessons on the moon lute, Ty introduced singing. The method of teaching songs also followed the demonstration and imitation approach. Ty would write down the text for several verses and then sing the verses. An important characteristic of Vietnamese singing is that the vocal melody changes for each verse. As a nonnative speaker, I found this bewildering. Although I could learn several verses of a song by rote, when Ty presented me with new words I found it difficult to adapt the vocal line to suit the new song text. I felt that however many verses I learned, I still did not "know" the song.

Musicians commonly explain the flexible vocal melody of songs in terms of poetic forms and speech tones. Song texts conform to certain poetic rules that enable them to be set to particular melodies. Vietnamese is a tonal language, so the vocal contour must reflect the linguistic tones; otherwise, the lyrics would sound strange and might be unintelligible. Ty pointed out how some speech tones affected the vocal melody. For example, he said the vocal melody must rise for syllables with the high-rising tone. But although I could hear the differences and similarities between different verses, knowledge of abstract rules did not make the practical task much easier. I had not yet acquired the musical framework necessary to spontaneously vary the vocal line according to the text. I did not have an instinctive "feel" for translating the tonal inflections of speech into melody.

While struggling with learning songs, I became interested in establishing their invariant features or identity. If I could comprehend the fundamental identity of songs, the elements that musicians always adhere to, I thought this would help me learn. At the beginning of 1997, I began to study with Dang Cong Hung as well as Ty. My lessons with Hung were similar in many respects to those with Ty: instrumental phrases and vocal melodies were transmitted orally without the use of notation. But Hung was more explicit about the melodic shape of the songs and concentrated more on their underlying characteristics. As I gradually found out, this approach was not used because of my curiosity about the identity of songs. Rather, it was part of the teaching method Hung had developed over many years.

I have begun with a brief sketch of my own learning experiences, as the issues addressed in this chapter arose largely from this learning. Michael Bakan (1999) has brought to the fore in his extended reflexive accounts of learning Balinese *beleganjur* drumming that "new understandings" are reached through musical relationships and dialogue, through learning from other musicians. In another Indonesian study, Rachel Swindells (2004) elucidates the differences between nonnative and native methods of learning in *gamelan degung* in Sunda and the transformative processes that inform musical competence. Through their own learning, both of these ethnomusicologists have explored cognitive models of musical competence that resonate with the issues addressed in this chapter.

It was mainly because of my learning experiences, which were challenging and intriguing, that questions arose about musical creativity in Vietnamese performance. It became clear through lessons and self-practice that the creation of vocal melodies is central to *chau van* performance and musical competence. Attention to vocal extemporization brings us closer to the creativity of *chau van* performance and enriches our understanding of Vietnamese music in general, as similar creative processes are also evident in most other types of traditional vocal music. The ways Ty and Hung conceptualize melodies offers insights into creative thinking and the relationship between musical thought and practical performance.

The insights I gained into the processes of musical change influencing the *chau van* tradition were also a result of my practical learning. After several months of learning and discussing *chau van* songs with musicians, I gained sufficient knowledge to recognize the songs performed during rituals and the conventions about when they should be performed. Yet each time I got to the point where I thought I was familiar with the entire repertoire, I would hear a song or a variation of a song that I had not come across before. It seemed that the more deeply I became immersed in the musical system, the more complex it became. Any feelings that I had gained a comprehensive familiarity with the genre were continually unsettled by new discoveries. Once I started exploring the less frequently performed songs, I began to realize the limitations of approaching the *chau van* musical system as a fixed entity with clearly defined boundaries. Instead, the issue of musical change came to the fore. It became apparent that there are variations in the songs different bands know and perform, and that performance practices and repertoire are continually evolving. The second half of this chapter examines the creative ways in which musicians have made changes to the *chau van* tradition since the mid-twentieth century and considers the relationships between musical, cultural, and political change.

The cultural landscape in reform-era Vietnam is being transformed by, among other things, increased cultural contact with the outside world. The growth in tourism and the influx of foreign cultural forms and products in the reform era have influenced cultural sensibilities and values. Greater accessibility to the many types of popular music circulating in Asia and the West is influencing musical tastes and the musical style of traditional musics.

At the same time, the pervasive presence of Western-influenced pop is being counteracted by a conscious return to tradition, which is being encouraged by state institutions and cultural cadres partly in response to fears about the negative cultural effects of globalization. Despite the cultural, economic, and political forces that have affected Vietnamese musical culture over the last few decades, musicians have to a great extent maintained and developed *chau van* within the limits of established processes of gradual change. Given Vietnam's war-torn history and the impact of the communist revolution and the Renovation policy, musicians have shown remarkable resilience in maintaining many aspects of musical form, style, and aesthetics.

Metaphors of Musical creativity: "Ways" and "Backbones"

Metaphorical thinking is a ubiquitous feature of musicians' conceptualizations of musical phenomena (Perlman 2004; Rice 1994; Feld 1990 [1982]). A pervasive "conceptual metaphor" (Perlman 2004:31) used by *chau van* musicians is the spatial concept of the "way." Songs are commonly referred to as "ways" (*loi* or *le loi*), rather than "melodies" (*giai dieu*) or "songs" (*bai hat*). The Vietnamese term *loi* has much the same meanings as "way" does in English. It can refer to (1) a path or track; (2) a course of movement or travel; (3) a manner or style of doing something. Despite the differences in the vocal contour each time a song is performed, every realization has the same direction or movement—a "way"—in common. Musicians consider every realization of a song to be the "same" because each performance conforms to the same "way." Nevertheless, the fluid nature of vocal melodies is evident at a number of different levels. First, there are differences between successive renditions of a "way" (with the same words) by a single musician. Second, renditions of the same "way" (with the same words) by different musicians differ. Third, the vocal line changes when the verse of a "way" is sung with different texts.

The metaphor of the "way" is also used in the context of Thai music. Francis Silkstone notes that Thai musicians make a distinction "between a particular 'composition' (*phleen*) and each of the many possible 'ways' (*thaan*) of playing that composition" (1993:16). The idea of *thaan* in Thai music refers to a number of different musical concepts: "It can refer to many specific 'ways,' such as the 'way' of playing (i.e. 'style') appropriate to each instrument . . . or the 'way' of playing (i.e. 'style') that characterizes one musician's performances on one instrument" (Silkstone 1993:16; see also Wong 2001:79–80).

The literal meanings of *loi* are the same as the Thai word *thaan,* but they have different musical meanings. *Loi* refers to songs themselves—for example, the "Phu Noi way" (*loi* Phu Noi)—rather than the different way of playing or method of realizing a composition. Also, *loi* does not apply to the style of particular musicians; the word *kieu* refers to musical style, as in the expression "each person [musician] has their own style" (*moi nguoi mot kieu*).

When *chau van* musicians talk about "grasping a way" (*nam vung loi*), they are referring to the internalization of the fundamental melodic shape of a song, not the particular performance style of individual musicians or their idiosyncratic realizations of songs. But what constitutes a "way"? What do musicians "grasp" and conform to when singing *chau van*? How is the "way" realized in performance, and what are the limits of variation?

Ty and Hung described the implicit melodies of "ways" in different terms. Ty said there was a "basic melody" (*giai dieu don gian*) or "general melody" (*giai dieu chung*) common to all verses of a song. To explain this, he demonstrated how the basic melody was made up of "axis notes" (*not truc*) or "main notes" (*not chinh*). Ty was not able to sing the basic melody, but he played the axis notes on the moon lute. In contrast to Ty, Hung thought of the identity of a "way" in terms of a "backbone" (*xuong song*). For Hung, the backbone was a "model in the mind" (*khuon mau trong dau minh*), a mental guide for performance. Although the backbone is subject to variation and is never actually realized in performance, Hung was able to make backbones explicit by humming them.

Although Ty and Hung used their own particular terms to refer to the implicit melody of "ways," other types of Vietnamese music employ their own distinctive conceptions of basic melody. In the southern chamber-music tradition *tai tu,* for instance, musicians refer to the basic melodic framework of pieces with various terms such as *long ban* (lit. "guts of the piece"), *suon* (lit. "ribs"), *cai can* ("the root"), or *chan phuong* ("the standard") (see Le Tuan Huong 1998:56; Hoang Dam 2003). This is not the place for a lengthy discussion of the differences between the melodic framework of *tai tu* pieces and the notion of implicit melodies in *chau van,* but it should be noted that these metaphors refer to related musical concepts.

The idea of songs being based on "backbones" has striking parallels with the implicit-melody concepts in Javanese music (see Sumarsam 1975 and 1995; Perlman 2004). The multipart music of Javanese gamelan is oriented around the melodic framework of the *balungan,* which is played on one of the gamelan instruments, the *saron.* The *balungan* is treated as a guide for the elaborating parts, yet as Marc Perlman demonstrates, "there are many situations in which the *balungan*'s guidance is obscure or nonexistent" (2004:115).

Irregularities and ambiguities in the guidance of the *balungan* have led some Javanese musicians "to postulate new musical entities, melodies neither played nor heard" (Perlman 2004:127). These "unplayed melodies" are "idealized guides" that have a greater degree of congruence with the elaborating parts than the sounded *balungan*. Perlman compares the concepts of unplayed melody proposed by three Javanese musicians: Suhardi, Sumarsam, and Supanggah. These three musicians conceptualized implicit melodies in slightly different ways, and they developed their ideas for different purposes. But Perlman argues that their implicit-melody concepts—Suhardi's "*lagu*" (melody), Sumarsam's "inner melody," and Supanggah's "essential *balungan*"—are all "creative responses to the irregularity of melodic guidance in Javanese music" (2004:170). Noticing the inconsistencies in the melodic guidance of the *balungan,* Javanese musicians have found creative ways to "articulate their implicit knowledge and give it a coherent and consistent form" (Perlman 2004:170).

There are important differences between the implicit melodies in the context of Javanese music and the idea of "backbones" or "basic melody" in *chau van*. Most obviously, unplayed melodies in Javanese music spring from the interpart relations of the musical texture, whereas backbones are a kind of synthesis of multiple versions of the vocal line.[1] Nevertheless, the construction of an idealized melodic guide by musicians in both traditions is a creative articulation of implicit musical knowledge involving similar processes of metaphorical thinking.

Few *chau van* musicians discussed the identity of songs or articulated variant and invariant elements in any detail. For most, knowledge of the "way" is implicit rather than explicit. Even Ty, who is the only *chau van* artist to my knowledge who has written academic articles on mediumship music, has not extensively theorized his idea of general melody. So what was Hung's motivation for formulating the idea of the backbone in such detail?

Hung's theorizing was not done in a vacuum. As Hung once remarked, musicians are instinctively aware of the melodic identity of songs but do not usually talk about it. Hung's father was one such musician: "My father, he sang and played differently all the time, but if you asked him why, he didn't know how to reply. I watched and listened to my father, and he taught me like that. But I couldn't study well, because he would just say, 'It is like that.' So how could I play and sing? He would take the instrument and say, 'It is like that, play!' But I couldn't play!" (Hung, pers. comm., January 2005). Faced with such complexity and variability, Hung tried to find regularities and coherence that would help his learning; he wanted to find "the key to open the way" (*chia khoa de mo di loi*). The idea of backbones came to Hung gradually. He said it took shape through a long process of learning, and it became more clear and detailed when he started to teach. He found it useful to introduce backbones to students, because it expedited their learning, and he attributed his own success at learning *chau van* and other music genres like *cheo* and *ca tru* to his explicit knowledge of backbones.

The reason why Hung articulated backbones is remarkably similar to Suhardi's motivation for postulating *lagu* ("melody"). Both musicians formulated implicit melodies to aid musical memorization and used them as teaching tools. Indeed, it is noteworthy that Hung and Suhardi both referred to their respective idealized melodies as "keys." For Hung, a backbone is a key that unlocks the way. For Suhardi, knowledge of the *lagu* is "a master key" that gives access to the performance practice of elaborating upon the *balungan,* known as *garap* (Perlman 2004:128).

In the following section, the creativity of *chau van* singing is addressed through comparison of performances by Ty and Hung of two songs, "Phu Noi" and "Phu Binh," and through analysis of the relationships between speech tones, vocal melody, and the melodic identity of songs.

Transcriptions, Backbones, and Abstracted Backbones

The Music Examples menu of the DVD includes multiple versions of "Phu Binh" and "Phu Noi." The renditions of "Phu Binh" consist of three verses sung by Ty (Track 12) and Hung (Track 13), a repeat performance of the first verse by Hung (Track 15), and Hung's backbone for "Phu Binh" (Track 14). For "Phu Noi," there are recordings of four verses performed by Ty (Track 16), two verses by Hung (Track 18), and Hung's backbone for "Phu Noi" (Track 17). All of these performances were conducted outside the ritual context at my request, and to facilitate comparison I asked Ty and Hung to use the same song texts. At some points, however, they use slightly different lyrics, which is a typical feature of *chau van* performance.

By listening to these tracks, the extent to which the vocal melody differs from verse to verse and between the renditions of the same verses by the two performers can be gauged. The vocal line of the first phrase of "Phu Binh" for all the recordings and the first phrase of Hung's "Phu Binh" backbone are transcribed and arranged vertically as a synoptic score in Figure 5.1 to enable direct visual comparison. The melodic contour common to every performance by each musician is also notated in Figure 5.1. These transcriptions are labeled as Ty's abstracted backbone and Hung's abstracted backbone. For each musician, the abstracted backbones consist of the pitches that occur in all of their renditions of the first phrase of "Phu Binh."[2] Pitches that occur in more than one verse, but not in every verse, are sometimes included in the abstracted backbones, because Ty and Hung indicated they were important structural pitches. To indicate that these pitches are not always realized in performance, they are placed in brackets. At the end of some phrases of songs, there are two alternative "end patterns," and this is the case for the first phrase of "Phu Binh." The abstracted-backbone scores include these two end patterns, which are indicated with a slur mark and labeled as "1" and "2." Rhythm is not notated in the abstracted backbones: the only rhythmic distinction made is the relative duration between long and short pitches, which is indicated by empty and filled-in note heads, respectively.

The transcriptions show that the vocal line of different verses by one performer varies a great deal, and the abstracted backbones illustrate the commonalities between verses. Much of the variation between verses is due to the speech tones of the text, and this is corroborated by Hung's repeat performance of the first verse of "Phu Binh." Hung's two versions of the first

Figure 5.1. Pham Van Ty's and Dang Cong Hung's backbones and verses of the first phrase of "Phu Binh"

Ty's abstracted backbone

Figure 5.1. Con't.

Hung's abstracted backbone

Hung's backbone

(i)

Hung verse 1

Mái thuyền nan nổi (i) dòng

Hung verse 1 (repeat performance)

Mái thuyền nan (i) nổi (i) dòng

Hung verse 2

Có phen dạo sông Giâu

Hung verse 3

Trấn (i) giang khê lên (i) ngàn

verse, which were recorded a year apart, have some rhythmic differences but much the same melody. Hung's backbone and abstracted backbone also have a similar melodic framework, and this close convergence confirms Hung's assertion that backbones guide his performances.[3]

Given that *chau van* is an orally transmitted genre and musicians are encouraged to develop their own singing style, it is not surprising that Ty and Hung realize "Phu Binh" differently. Ty and Hung's abstracted backbones demonstrate their different conceptions of the "basic melody" of songs, irrespective of the influence of speech tones. The abstracted backbones have many points of convergence: the initial rise from C to a long-held D, the descent to A in the middle of the phrase, followed by either end pattern 1, which descends to D, or end pattern 2, which resolves on A. However, there are also some points of divergence between the abstracted backbones: the end pattern 1 of the first phrase of "Phu Binh" has a different melodic contour in Ty and Hung's renditions. These differences are not influenced by the text or speech tones, because end pattern 1 is sung to nonsemantic vowels or vocables.

Speech Tones and Melodic Contour

Scholars have addressed the influence of speech tones on vocal melodies for several tonal languages, including Chinese (Yung 1989; Schimmelpenninck 1997; Stock 1999), Thai (Tanese-Ito 1988), and Ewe (Agawu 1988). Yet to date there has been no systematic study of how Vietnamese music vocal melodies are influenced by speech tones.[4] The following discussion refers to the northern Vietnamese dialect, which employs six speech tones. These tones can be graphically represented as follows:

High rising (*sac*)   Low rising (*hoi*)

Mid level (*khong dau*)   Low broken (*nang*)

High broken (*nga*)   Low falling (*huyen*)

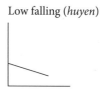

Figure 5.2. Vietnamese speech tones

Two effects of the speech tones on the melodic contour can be identified in *chau van* singing: tonal inflection and relative pitch level.[5] The tonal inflection refers to the melodic direction of each syllable of the text and the relative pitch level to whether the pitch goes up, goes down, or remains the same for each successive word of the text. Although complete transcriptions of all the recordings of "Phu Binh" and "Phu Noi" on the DVD are not included here, the following summary of the impact of speech tones on the vocal line is based on analysis of all these performances.[6]

TONAL INFLECTION

The melodic contours for each speech tone can be divided into four categories: falling (F), rising (R), level (L), or falling rising (FR).[7] Table 5.1 plots the pitch contour for the 271 syllables used during Ty and Hung's rendition of "Phu Binh" and Ty's rendition of "Phu Noi" (verses 3 and 4).

Table 5.1 shows a high correlation between tone and melodic contour for five out of the six tones. The only tone that does not show an obvious correlation is the high-broken tone, of which there are just five examples. For this tone, it is not just the melodic contour that enables it to be identified. The high-broken tone involves a glottal stop, which results in a short break followed by a resumption in sound. A glottal stop can clearly be heard when words are sung with the high-broken tone, so the tone can be recognized whether the melodic contour is rising or falling.

As with the high-broken tone, it is not just the melodic contour that identifies the low-broken tone. The low-broken tone is graphically represented as falling, but it is the tone's shortness that differentiates it from the low-falling tone. Either the sung syllables with the low-broken tone are short (and sometimes followed by a rest) or, when slightly longer in duration, there is a strong accent when the syllable is pronounced. Therefore, accent and duration—rather than the level melodic contour—indicates the low-broken tone.

For the other four tones—the high-rising, mid-level, low-rising, and low-

Table 5.1. Pitch contour of syllables

Tone	F	R	L	FR
High rising		55		
Mid-level	15	10	74	
High broken		3	2	
Low rising		1	1	20
Low broken	4		21	
Low falling	57	2	5	

falling tones—the melodic contour clearly reflects the inflection of the speech tone in the vast majority of cases. Most of the exceptions are due to musical factors that override the matching between tonal inflection and melodic contour. The mismatches are most numerous for syllables with a mid-level tone, which in twenty-five out of ninety-nine cases have either a rising or falling, rather than a level, melodic contour. Ty's explanation for many of these mismatches was that he varied the melodic contour for some words with mid-level tones to avoid "monotony" (*don dieu*) and to conform to the basic melody. An example of this appears at the end of the first phrase (second verse) of Ty's performance of "Phu Binh" on the words *song Giau* ("the Giau river"). Both of these syllables have a mid-level tone, but Ty avoids the monotony of reiterating pitch A by singing a short phrase to a vocable between the two syllables of the text and setting the syllable "Giau" to a rising melodic contour (G to A). Ty considered this rising melody at the end of the phrase to be a defining characteristic of end pattern 2 of the backbone (though Hung did not). Ty's end pattern 2 always contradicts the speech-tone contour, as it is used only when the last syllable of the text has a mid-level tone.

RELATIVE PITCH LEVEL

From the examination of the relations between speech-tone and relative-pitch-level succession for all the syllables sung during the verses of "Phu Noi" and "Phu Binh" included on the DVD, some rules can be posited. These are listed in Table 5.2.

The rules in Table 5.2 do not cover every possible speech-tone sequence. Although the performances from which these rules are formulated consist of a total of 324 relative pitch levels between successive pairs or dyads of pitches, the comprehensiveness of the sample is limited by the unequal use of the speech tones in the text and a low instance, or absence, of some

Table 5.2. Rules for the relative pitch level of successive syllables

1. High-rising tone	Higher relative pitch level than the low-broken, low-falling, and low-rising tones; relative pitch level is higher than or equal to the mid-level tone
2. Mid-level tone	Higher relative pitch level than the low-broken and low-falling tone; relative pitch level is equal to or lower than the high-rising tone
3. Low-broken tone	Lower relative pitch level than the high-rising and mid-level tones
4. Low-falling tone	Lower relative pitch level than the high-rising and mid-level tones
5. High-broken	Higher relative pitch level than the low-broken and low-falling tones
6. Low-rising	Lower relative pitch level than the high-rising and mid-level tones

speech-tone combinations. This is a fact of the Vietnamese language itself, because some tones are used less than others and some tones rarely appear consecutively (e.g., some combinations involving the low-broken and low-rising tones). The relative pitch level for successive syllables with the same speech tone also cannot be determined, as no consistent pattern was found. Despite these limitations, the rules outline the main ways in which vocal contour is influenced by the relative pitch level of successive syllables.

The rules outlined in table 5.2 are generally applicable, but there are some exceptions. In some cases, vocables between successive syllables of the text are a complicating factor.[8] In others, musical factors override the rules. As with the correlation between tonal inflection and melodic contour, the relative pitch level of successive syllables is sometimes determined by the invariant aspects of the implicit melody (especially at the ends of phrases), rather than the pitch hierarchy of the speech tones.

Finding the "Way": Music Theory and Modernization

> It is impossible to remember exactly how to sing one sentence of the text because there are too many texts. The texts, for example, of the Mother Spirit of the Water Palace are many pages long . . . so how can you remember exactly which notes you should sing? You can't remember exactly—there is a "way," that is all . . . Each time you sing is different, but the "way" must be correct.
>
> —Pers. comm., Dang Cong Hung, May 1998

In the above comments, Hung neatly sums up the practical challenge of *chau van* singing. In performance, musicians create vocal melodies that adapt to the speech tones of the song texts while preserving the "way," the fundamental melodic identity of the song. A similar creative process in Cantonese opera is described by Bell Yung: "The singer uses, within the constraints of the skeletal structure . . . the relatively less-defined pitches of the texts' linguistic tones as a guide in creating a series of well-defined musical pitches to form the melodic line" (1989:90).

Several studies of Chinese music have highlighted the impact of speech tones on vocal melody, yet they have tended to assume that the vocal line merely reflects the speech tones. Jonathan Stock's study of Beijing opera arias reassesses this assumption and concludes that "music-structural considerations may, sometimes, challenge the dictates of speech tone and lyric structure" (1999:184). Like the vocal line of Beijing opera arias, the contour of *chau van* vocal melodies is not always subordinate to the dictates of the song text. Much of the time, musicians skillfully accommodate both the implicit melody of the "way" and the speech tones. On occasions when there is a discrepancy between melody and text, the fixed melodic elements of "ways" usually take precedence over the tonal inflection and pitch hierarchy of syllables. This was confirmed by Hung when he remarked that the backbone is ultimately more important than the speech tones of the text: "You must respect the speech tones, but you must obey the backbone. The backbone is more fixed. Sometimes . . . it "forces" [i.e., goes against] the speech tones" (pers. comm., Hung, January 2005).

The metaphor of the "way" encapsulates the fluidity of *chau van* songs. It helps musicians make sense of the complex melodic diversity of performance. Yet *chau van* performers differ in the degree to which they articulate their implicit knowledge of "ways." As Marc Perlman (2004) has discussed, musicians engage in creative thinking and theorizing about music for different reasons, and the way concepts are formulated is dependent on historical context and the demands of the social situation. Theories of melodic guidance and implicit melody in Java have arisen in the context of increasing and changing verbalization about music during the twentieth century. Perlman links this "new inducement to discourse" to modernization, the spread of formal music training and written texts, and encounters with Western ethnomusicology (2004:117–26).

Chapter 1 outlined some of the effects of modernization on Vietnamese music culture: the nationalization and professionalization of artistic activity, the ideological transformation of musical expression, and the attempts to develop "scientific" pedagogical methods. In parallel with the modernization of practice, theorizing about music in Vietnam has increased substantially since the mid-twentieth century. Vietnamese theorists, many of whom were trained in the former Soviet Union and Eastern Europe, have sought to carry out "modern," "scientific" research, which has been strongly informed by Western music theory. Vietnamese scholars have described genres and styles and investigated musical characteristics such as modes and scales, yet they have paid surprisingly little attention to improvisation based on melodic frameworks, despite this being one of the fundamental features of musical practice.

Further research of a broad range of genres is required to establish a thorough genealogy of implicit melody concepts in Vietnam music. However, in the context of *chau van,* the notion of implicit melody does not seem to be a direct result of transnational dialogue or a response to Western music theory or ethnomusicology as it was in Java. Although Ty and Hung were both trained in Western music theory and notation at the Hanoi Music Conservatoire, they did not attribute their ideas about implicit melodies to their formal music training. Hung said he was "green" (*non*) as a young conservatoire student and did not conceive of backbones until years later. His theorizing developed from his experiences of learning music orally rather than from the notation-based teaching methods at the conservatoire. Hung was prompted to "find the way"—to formulate the notion of backbone as a blueprint in his mind—in order to develop a more effective method of learning and teaching music orally. While Hung and Ty's theorizing may not have been a direct result of their conservatoire training, musicians formally trained in music institutions showed a greater propensity for theorizing; spirit priests who learned *chau van* through the traditional "ethnopedagogy" of learning by imitation did not usually verbalize their implicit music knowledge of "ways."

Processes of modernization have not only affected theorizing about music and conceptualizations of implicit melody, they have also influenced other aspects of *chau van* performance. The rest of this chapter addresses the innovations made by musicians, which have given rise to musical changes to repertoire and performance practice.

Chau Van and Musical Change

Chau van musicians tend to assert continuity with the past, rather than change. They have a reverent attitude to tradition and argue that the genre has not fundamentally changed for generations. The prevailing view is that *chau van* as a form of traditional music established by the "elders" (*cac cu*) should be maintained and preserved. The respect for tradition has contributed to *chau van*'s resistance to communist ideology and to other social, cultural, and political changes. As discussed in Chapter 1, socialist ideology has not influenced the music played at *len dong*, despite attempts to sever *chau van* from spirit possession and to assign socialist meanings to songs. Alan Merriam put forward the hypothesis many years ago that religious music is less susceptible to change than other types of music because it "is so much a part of general religious practice that it cannot be altered without altering other aspects of ritual" (Merriam 1964:308). Thomas Turino's research on Zimbabwean music also leads him to a surmise that "indigenous religious beliefs perpetuate cultural conservatism as a basic tenet and mode of practice for maintaining a good relationship with the ancestors" (2000:36). Similarly, the intertwining of *chau van* and spirit possession perpetuates cultural conservatism because radical musical change would require fundamental changes to mediumship practices.

Even though the government did not succeed in its aim of eradicating ritual music and replacing it with a new musical culture consisting of revolutionary *chau van* and modern national music, the prohibition of mediumship music meant that it was rarely performed at rituals from the late 1950s to the late 1980s. It might be expected that the restrictions on the performance of *chau van* until the recent *len dong* boom would have led to an impoverishment of the repertoire. Yet unlike some other music genres that were severely affected by government restrictions and prohibitions (see Norton 2005), *chau van* music culture was not severely eroded or lost. Although some musicians criticize the competence of contemporary performers and argue that their level of skill is lower than found among the spirit priests of the past, most elderly musicians who were active in the 1940s were positive about the development of *chau van*. Rather than becoming impoverished, they said, *chau van* had become more "abundant" (*phong phu*), "rich" (*giau*), and "popular" (*pho bien*). Even when *chau van* was forced underground during the period when mediumship was vigorously prohibited by the government, new songs were added to the repertoire.

The presence of popular music culture has risen considerably since the early 1990s. Just as other aspects of work and social life have been adjusted and reconfigured in the new market economy, so have musical experiences been profoundly affected by market relations and globalization. The spread of karaoke, Internet technology, hi-fi equipment, and international music channels like MTV has increased exposure to a wide range of Western and Asian popular music idioms. The growing demand for popular music has spurred on the domestic music industry, which has blossomed in the last decade. As a genre embedded in religious practice, *chau van* has largely remained independent from the commercial production, promotion, and dissemination of popular music. However, some recent changes in musical style and performance practice bear the influence of changes in musical taste that have ensued from increasing exposure to Western-style pop, rock, and dance musics. The reverence for tradition has prohibited radical changes like, for example, the introduction of Western or electronic instruments or the Western-style harmonization of songs. But musicians are responding to the "modern" musical sensibilities of ritual participants. Cultural conservatism has not reified the *chau van* tradition. Rather, it has marked out the permitted boundaries of musical change.

The processes of musical change affecting *chau van* are now addressed in more detail. First, I outline the changes in repertoire and style that have resulted from the composition of new songs, innovations to existing songs, the incorporation of new songs from other genres, and songs falling into disuse. I then turn to performance practices, particularly concerning the use of amplification and the size of bands. The chapter concludes with further thoughts on musical change in relation to broader patterns of cultural, economic, and political change.

COMPOSITION

Like many so-called traditional genres in different parts of the world, *chau van* songs are not usually attributed to particular individuals. The repertoire consists of an anonymous corpus of songs, which have been created and modified over successive generations. To a great extent, contemporary musicians continue the anonymity of tradition. Individual and group creativity is acknowledged, but questions of authorship are not prioritized, partly because *chau van* has not yet been subject to intensive commercialization and commodification. The lack of strong copyright laws in Vietnam may also have acted as a disincentive for establishing the authorship of songs. Despite recent attempts to tighten copyright laws, the legal system in this area is in its infancy, and musicians rarely receive licensing royalties for their compositions.[9] As copyright law and intellectual property rights become more established, identifying the composers of "traditional" songs will likely become a more important issue for musicians.

In current usage, the Vietnamese term *sang tac,* which means "compose" or "write," is used for both music and literature and implies, as in the West, that an individual has full creative responsibility for composing or writing a prestructured "work" (*tac pham*). The concept of the composer in Vietnam, which can probably be traced to French colonial influence early in the twentieth century, was consolidated in the 1930s and 1940s with the emergence of Western-style popular songs or *ca khuc* composed by Vietnamese musicians (Jähnichen 1991; Gibbs 2004).

Despite the lack of commercial incentives for authorship, the individualistic notion of the composer has permeated some forms of traditional music. For instance, a composer is often credited for arranging new *cai luong, cheo,* and *tuong* plays even when traditional song forms constitute most of the musical material. In the case of *chau van,* composers are not commonly attributed to songs. Musicians indicated some songs that they thought had been recently composed, but they were not always sure of their origin. Two musicians, Pham Van Kiem (b. 1922) and Doan Duc Dan (1921–c.1994), however, were acknowledged by musicians who personally knew them as *chau van* composers. Kiem's song "Suoi Oi" (Mountain Stream) (Track 19) and

Dan's song "Cac Ban Tien" (The Fairies) (Track 21) have become standards, and another song by Kiem, called "Mua Dang" (Lit-Rope Dance) (Track 20), is sung less frequently and in more restricted circles. Pham Van Kiem wrote "Suoi Oi" and "Mua Dang" in the 1960s (pers. comm., Pham Van Kiem, June 1998), and Doan Duc Dan's song probably dates from the late 1970s.[10] All of these recently composed songs are upbeat and are performed for vibrant incarnations of the Little Lady (Chau Be), who belongs to the Mountains and Forest Palace. They all use the lively one-beat rhythm, and the texts are sung with a fast delivery, with a new word of text sung on almost every beat and half beat.

The fact that only a small number of songs have recently been composed, even bearing in mind the possibility that the composers of some songs have been forgotten, is consistent with the attitude of *chau van* musicians toward composition. In general, ritual musicians are reluctant to compose entirely new songs, and even when a new song is introduced, it is hard for it to be widely accepted as part of the standard repertoire. When I asked Hung about why he did not compose, he replied:

> I am frightened that people will laugh! . . . I have just inherited what the elders did . . . The elders were formidable, and I have not yet reached their level. Only when I reach a comparable level to the past masters will I dare to think about composing . . . What the elders have done is so interesting that I am hesitant and frightened to bring something of my own into *chau van*. (pers. comm., Hung, May 1998)

Hung's remarks demonstrate the respect for the musical achievements of previous generations, which daunts many contemporary musicians. When I raised the issue of composing new songs with the distinguished spirit priest Pham Quang Dat, he gave a one-syllable answer, "*Chiu.*" This pithy expression suggests that something is too difficult or irrelevant. Some *chau van* musicians are less deferential to the past than Hung and Dat, but most have a conservative attitude to tradition, which prevents them from introducing new songs to the repertoire.

INNOVATIONS

It is more common for musicians to make innovations to existing songs than to compose entirely new songs. Innovations can take various forms. A musician may change how the lines of verse are set to music for a particular song or make slight alterations to the rhythm or melody. Such innovations exceed the limits of "allowable variation" (Nettl 2006 [1983]). They go beyond the different realizations of the "backbone," the implicit melodic line, between successive performances by the same musician or between renditions of the same song by different musicians. To count as an innovation, songs must be noticeably different while still being recognizably related to the original. Like new compositions, not all innovations made by individuals are widely adopted by *chau van* bands, nor are new song titles always given to them. Whether or not an innovation is integrated into the repertoire depends on musicians' critical evaluation and the response it gets from other ritual participants.

Four examples of recent innovations are included on the DVD. These were made by three different musicians, Doan Duc Dan, Cao Mon, and Pham Van Ty. Three of the examples were referred to informally after the musicians who made them as "Doan Duc Dan's Don" (Track 23), "Cao Mon's Xa" (Track 24), and "Cao Mon's Melody" (see Video Extract 2). Also, as discussed in Chapter 4, Pham Van Ty has made his own distinctive alterations to "Xa Tay Nguyen" (Track 25). To illustrate the innovations made by musicians, I will briefly discuss two innovations: "Doan Duc Dan's Don" and "Cao Mon's Xa."

Comparison of the original "Don" melody (Track 22) and "Doan Duc Dan's Don" (Track 23), which are both performed by Hung, reveals that the two versions of "Don" have a different melodic shape but use the same basic scale. "Doan Duc Dan's Don" also exhibits the musical characteristics mentioned in relation to newly composed songs: it uses less melisma and has a faster delivery of text. According to Hung, who was a friend of Doan Duc Dan, the new version of "Don" was created to suit the musical tastes of ritual participants and to make it easier to listen to.

"Cao Mon's Xa" is based on a version of a "Xa" melody by Doan Duc Dan known as "Xa Lung." Cao Mon described the changes he made to "Xa Lung" in the following way: "The words [of the song] were already in existence, but I took the melody and made it a bit different to suit 'modern rhythms,' to make it happier and more animated . . . Doan Duc Dan used to sing a similar melody ["Xa Lung"]; I just reformed it some more." The song "Xa Lung" was itself the result of modifications to existing "Xa" melodies by Doan Duc Dan, so "Cao Mon's Xa" can therefore be thought of as a "second-order" innovation, that is, an innovation based on a previous innovation by another musician.

Innovation and change are the lifeblood of a living tradition. For *chau van* musicians, tradition is not static, and they do not expect the repertoire to be preserved in a fixed form. Through ongoing innovations to songs, the musical ideas of successive generations of musicians are absorbed into the current of tradition. The *chau van* tradition is sufficiently flexible to respond to changing musical tastes, while at the same time ensuring continuity with the musical heritage of the past.

SONG BORROWING

Cross-genre influence is an extremely common feature of Vietnamese music, and this often manifests itself through song borrowing. *Cheo* folk theater, for instance, routinely incorporates regional folk songs, and *chau van* also draws on songs from diverse sources. Indeed, Vietnamese folklore scholars contend that *chau van* is noteworthy for its eclecticism. As the book *Hat Van* states, "It is hard to find a type of folk music that has so many influences from many different types of folk song" (Ngo Duc Thinh 1992:57). Musicians, especially those proficient in several types of traditional music, often pointed out connections between genres. For example, Hung and Ty thought that "Ban Chim Thuoc" was related to the *cheo* song "Duong Truong Chim Thuoc," and that "Kieu Duong" and "Trong Chien" were influenced by *tuong* classical opera.

The crisscrossing threads of exchange and borrowing between genres are often hard to unravel because of a lack of reliable historical evidence, but the "*chau van*-ization" of songs from other genres can be substantiated in some instances. One of the best-known examples is "Luu Thuy," a melody taken from the court-music repertoire of *nhac cung dinh*. Less well known is the influence of *ca tru* on *chau van*. According to Le Ba Cao, a spirit priest called Pham Ngoc Lan modified several *ca tru* melodies in the early twentieth century to make them suitable for rituals. These include the *ca tru* pieces "Ty Ba Hanh" and "Bac Phan," which became part of the "Phu" group of songs and were known as "Phu Ty Ba" and "Phu Bac Phan," respectively. For the purposes of comparison, the DVD includes recordings of "Ty Ba Hanh" (Track 26) performed by the Ca Tru Thai Ha Ensemble and "Phu Ty Ba" (Track 27) performed by Le Ba Cao. Despite slight differences in text and melodic contour, "Ty Ba Hanh" and "Phu Ty Ba" clearly share the same melody. The most striking aspect of "*chau van*-ization" is the use of the three-beat rhythm for "Phu Ty Ba," in contrast to "Ty Ba Hanh," which does not follow a regular pulse. But even though a metrical framework is imposed, the vocal melody of "Phu Ty Ba" is highly syncopated and imitates the characteristic rhythmic flexibility and extensive vocal ornamentation of "Ty Ba Hanh."

The use of two "Ly" folk songs from southern Vietnam, "Ly Qua Cau" and "Ly My Hung" (Track 28), is a more recent example of song borrowing. In the early 1990s, Cao Mon set new words to these folk songs and has performed them for the Tenth Prince. "Ly Qua Cau" and "Ly My Hung" have not yet been widely adopted by bands, but they illustrate the continuing potential for songs from other genres to be incorporated into the *chau van* repertoire.

UNSUNG SONGS

Alongside the expansion of the repertoire through new compositions, innovations, and song borrowing, some melodies have fallen into disuse. Songs such as "Phu Ty Ba," "Phu Bac Phan," "Phu Ha," and "Thien Thai" are still occasionally performed by elderly spirit priests like Le Ba Cao, but most bands do not know them. The main reason why these melodies are out of favor is because mediums find them sad and "unfashionable" (*khong xin*). Le Ba Cao also thought that many young musicians lacked the skill and competence to perform these challenging songs, which are difficult to sing because of their long, melismatic melodies and the use of unusual poetic meters and word setting. Several melodies belonging to the "Phu" group, like "Phu Noi," "Phu Binh," "Phu Van Dan," and "Phu Chuoc Ruou," are regularly performed, but even these songs are unpopular with some mediums. This lack of popularity was evident from the comments made by Hang, the medium of Ritual 2, which were discussed in Chapter 3. On hearing "Phu Van Dan," Hang requested a happier song, and the band promptly changed to "Cao Mon's Melody."

NOISY RITUALS

During the 1990s, most bands in both rural and urban areas started to use amplification. Typically the sound system used by bands consists of two or three microphones plugged into a mixer/amplifier connected to a speaker or megaphone horn. Microphones are primarily used for the voice and for melodic instruments like the bamboo flute and the moon lute. In addition to adding amplification, bands have grown in size. According to elderly musicians, bands in the 1940s only had two members: a moon-lute player and a percussionist, both of whom usually doubled up as singers (see also Durand 1959:34). While some contemporary bands consist of two or three performers, larger bands with four or more members are now more common.

The use of amplification and larger instrumental forces has obviously increased the loudness of *chau van* performance. Le Ba Cao recalled that ritual participants were more attentive to the band when he played at rituals as a boy in the 1940s and 1950s, whereas now they were "noisy" (*on ao*) and less reverent. Because of this, Cao thought it was necessary to use amplification so that bands could be clearly heard. The Mulberry Temple—where I videotaped Ritual 2 in 1997—was one of the few temples in Hanoi at the time that had not installed a sound system. But when I visited the temple in 2004, the band had installed an amplification system. This decision was made because of pressure from ritual participants who wanted amplification and because singers had found it increasingly difficult to make themselves heard. Some band members had suffered from hoarse throats caused by singing loudly for long periods, and they said that the use of microphones helped lessen the strain on their voices.

The use of amplification during rituals relates to the increase in the mechanized reproduction of music in the 1990s. Until recently, stereo systems and television sets in households were a rarity in northern Vietnam. But higher incomes have enabled more people to buy electronic music equipment, such as hi-fi systems and karaoke machines. In the mid-1990s it seemed that the whole country had been taken over by a karaoke craze. Whether wandering in the backstreets of Hanoi or down little alleyways in remote villages, one was never far from a karaoke machine. The sound of amplified voices, with heavy reverb added, drifting above synthesized backing tracks of karaoke discs was a ubiquitous feature of the Vietnamese soundscape. The popularity of karaoke has decreased since its peak in the mid-1990s, but the use of amplification and electronic reverberation has affected aesthetic sensibilities. It is now the norm for performances of traditional music to be amplified. As if to underscore the influence of karaoke, some *chau van* bands use karaoke amplifiers and microphones for their performances. Sporadic feedback, crackle, and distortion were common features of these makeshift sound systems, and although ritual participants seemed to have high levels of tolerance for extraneous noise, bands found distortion from poor-quality equipment undesirable and tried to minimize it.

Thoughts on Musical Change

Tim Rice's classic book on Bulgarian folk music analyzes the "conflict between tradition and modernity" and issues of musical change after the communist revolution of 1944 (Rice 1994:18). By exploring the dynamics between systemic change (how music changes as economic and ideological systems change) and individual experience (how individuals experience, maintain, and challenge tradition in the face of modernity), Rice outlines the conflicting forces at work in processes of musical change. He points out that musical change is not merely a by-product of larger economic, ideological and cultural forces, it is also shaped by the musical experience of individuals and the meanings and values assigned to tradition (Rice 1994; see also Blacking 1995 [1977]). Also writing on Bulgaria, Donna Buchanan suggests the political transformation of music is a "dialectical and dynamic process that implicates the lives of individuals" within a complex of political, social, and cultural forces and should not be viewed merely as a result of "forced political domination by the socialist regime" (1995:383). Such a dialectical process is also evident in the case of *chau van*. Mediumship music was not in line with the new music culture promoted by the Party and state cultural organizations and institutions, and it was antithetical to the communist ideological and economic system. Some *chau van* musicians devised revolutionary *chau van* in an attempt to make the music conform to Party ideology, yet others managed to surreptitiously maintain and, to a certain extent, develop the tradition. The tradition was maintained because musicians considered themselves to be custodians of a valued musical heritage and ritual participants continued to demand that the spirits be praised in song. The experience of *chau van* and the values and meanings assigned to it—its power to invite the spirits, to construct the spirits' identities, to recall the past, to stimulate emotion, to entrain—have resisted communist transformation and control. This resistance highlights the agency of individuals operating within hegemonic discourses.

Chau van has not been taught or financially supported by state-run organizations and institutions, so the proliferation of *chau van* in the reform era has largely been independent of the state. Bands are instead supported by the network of temples and mediums, and the most popular bands demand quite high fees. Market forces are also fuelling changes in musical style and performance practice. The remarks of a spirit priest named Chen sum up the main changes in style and meaning:

> In the past *chau van* was leisurely, smooth, and graceful, sung sentence by sentence, word by word. Now, because Western [popular] music has come to Vietnam, *chau van* has become more noisy. Now that people are familiar with Western music, they find leisurely music sad. If people sing . . . word by word with ornamentation between each sentence, it drags, and people who are accustomed to lively music find it dull. (pers. comm., Chen, June 1998)

Mediums like Hang, who have "modern" musical tastes and prefer lively songs with new texts, are the motors of musical change. Yet changes in musical taste operate within clear limits: even Hang laughed at the prospect of introducing rock and pop songs or electronic instrumentation into rituals (see Chapter 3). *Chau van* as a sign of pastness, as textual and musical heritage with connections to prerevolutionary practice, is highly valued by ritual participants.

The interaction between popular music idioms and traditional musics is not entirely a one-way street. Some popular artists have sought inspiration in tradition. The use of national tradition has been a recurring feature in the modern history of Vietnamese music, but attempts to indigenize foreign influences in popular culture have intensified since the 1980s. Well-known songwriters like Pho Duc Phuong, Le Minh Son, Ngoc Dai, and Quoc Trung have in different ways combined "traditional" musical elements with Western-influenced song formats, harmonic progressions, and instrumentation. The work of these and other artists seeks to imbue foreign musical elements with a Vietnamese character and signals a move to indigenize foreign musical forms. Arrangements of classic songs like "Tren Dinh Phu Van" (On the Peak of Phu Van Mountain) and "Ve Que" (Returning to the Homeland) by Pho Duc Phuong often feature the sound of traditional instruments in combination with electronic keyboards and guitars and Western drum kits. Popular singers mainly use Western-influenced quasi-operatic vocal techniques and make little reference to indigenous vocal styles, except for the use of glissandi to reflect the linguistic tones of the lyrics. However, some singers, such as My Linh, Ngoc Khue, Tran Thu Ha, Khanh Linh, and Tung Duong, have strived to create unique styles by merging traditional ornamentation and vocal timbres with lighter, pop-oriented vocal styles. One of the best-known examples of such experimentation is Tran Thu Ha's singing on Ngoc Dai's album *Nhat Thuc* (Eclipse), released in 1999. Tran Thu Ha's singing combines jazz and pop styles with vocal ornamentation taken from traditional styles.

References to traditional genres in Vietnamese popular music culture are general rather than specific. The sounds of traditional instruments and vocal timbres in popular songs take on an aura of Vietnameseness, of generic national tradition; they rarely refer directly to specific performance traditions. The influence of Western-influenced popular musics on traditional musics has been equally generalized. In the case of *chau van,* some aspects of style have been affected by modern musical tastes, but musical practices have not been subject to radical change or syncretism. The meanings assigned to the performance of mediumship music by mediums and musicians emphasize continuity over change.

Continuity in *chau van* performance is partly due to the intimate inter-relationships between songs, ritual action, and the identities of spirits and mediums. An important aspect of these interrelationships is the musical performance of the gender identities mediums assume during possession, and this is addressed in the next chapter. As we shall see, the gender subjectivities of mediums are highly contentious and are the focus of public debate about gender and sexual identities in modern Vietnam.

6

Engendering Mediumship

Traversing gender is integral to *len dong*. When possessed by male spirits, female mediums become prestigious scholars, fierce warriors, playful princes, and naughty boys. They wear male tunics, perform vigorous military dances with swords and spears, speak in male idioms, smoke cigarettes, and drink rice wine (see Figure 6.1). When possessed by female spirits, male mediums become beautiful ladies, graceful unmarried princesses, and cheeky young girls. They wear dresses and colorful head scarves, speak in falsetto, dance elegantly with fans, jump vigorously while brandishing ropes set on fire, chew betel, and give out exotic fruit (see Figure 6.2). The cross-dressing practices of *len dong* draw on archetypal images of male and female and on cultural notions of masculinity and femininity.

The ability to perform the gender of male and female spirits beautifully is recognized by religious followers to be part of mediums' "destined aptitude." The adage *dong co bong cau*—literally, "'princess spirit' mediums, young prince spirits"—emphasizes that mediums may be possessed by spirits of the opposite gender, by both princesses and young princes. How convincingly mediums enact the transformation from male to female or female to male is a popular topic of discussion. Some ritual participants openly criticized the way mediums performed the actions of spirits of the opposite gender. Others remarked how successfully they traversed genders. Such comments brought home the importance of appropriate gendered behavior for successful possession and raised numerous related questions. For instance, how are gender identities successfully articulated through ritual acts and music? How do the male and female archetypes articulated during *len dong* relate to cultural ideas of gender? And how does transgendering possession relate to the gender/sex identities of participants? As I tried to find answers to such questions, it became evident that the gender implications of possession extend beyond the ritual domain. The gendered division of ritual roles and mediums' assumption of variant identities in their everyday lives reflect broader issues of gender and power in Vietnamese society.

Gender in Vietnam has often been understood historically in terms of a rigid binary of foreign Confucian codes and more flexible indigenous values (e.g., Ta Van Tai 1981; Jamieson 1993; Barry 1996). This construct has led to the claim that the customs and bilateral kinship system of indigenous Vietnamese culture afforded women a high status, whereas patriarchal Confucianism is held accountable for according women a low status. In this framework, the history of gender relations is seen as a dialectic between two poles. Confucian precepts like the "three obediences" (*tam tong*) and the "four virtues" (*tu duc*) are often cited as forces for oppression. The former outlines a system of women's subservience to male family members (fathers, husbands, and sons), and the latter is an idealized measure for women in the areas of labor (*cong*), physical appearance (*dung*), appropriate speech (*ngon*), and proper behavior (*hanh*). However, owing to the limited impact of the "patriarchal family system of China" on "upper-class Vietnamese" and the influence of

Figure 6.1. Doan possessed by General Tran Hung Dao, smoking a cigarette (2005)

Figure 6.2. Quyet possessed by the female spirit the Second Princess Cam Duong. Quyet is dressed in women's clothes and performs a graceful dance with a large hat (1998)

the more flexible elements of indigenous "pre-Chinese civilization" (Taylor 1983:298–300), it has been concluded that Vietnamese women have historically been granted a higher status than women in other East Asian societies influenced by Confucianism (Frenier and Mancini 1996). The yoke of Confucianism continues to be a prominent theme in feminist research projects in the reform period that focus on Vietnamese women and gender inequality. These projects have assessed the effects of political, social, and economic change on women's lives and on the relations between womanhood, sexuality, the state, work, the family, and the household (e.g., Werner and Bélanger 2002; Le Thi and Do Thi Binh 1997). This work provides an ethnographically grounded view of women's lives and the contradictions, tensions, and ironies women face in changing social and economic circumstances.

The wave of feminist scholarship on Vietnamese women has been supplemented by recent work on gender, ritual, and religion by anthropologists from outside Vietnam. Shaun Malarney (2002) has documented the changing ritual roles of women in rites held in communal houses (*dinh*) in northern villages. Communal house rites, which prior to the revolution were an exclusively male domain, have been revived in the reform period with the involvement of women. Malarney argues that the loss of elite male control over these rites is mainly due to government policies designed to desacralize communal houses in the revolutionary period. However, the reconfiguration of the communal house rites has not been universal: Kirsten Endres found that the gendered division of ritual space has largely been reinstated in the northern village of Dai Bai (2001). In regard to Buddhist practice, Alexander Soucy's research illustrates that participation in Buddhist activities in Hanoi is gender specific and that the different approaches men and women have toward religious practice relate to individual life experience and discourses of masculinity and femininity (1999). The intertwining of social life and religious experience is also a feature of Philip Taylor's theorizing on pilgrimage and goddess worship (2004). Taylor argues that one of the main reasons goddesses attract large numbers of female devotees is because they symbolize feminine concerns.

The only previous research on the gendered dimension of mediumship is Karen Fjelstad's work on the Four Palace Religion as transplanted in America. Women are the focus of Fjelstad's thesis because there was little male participation in rituals in the San Francisco Bay Area, where she conducted her research. Fjelstad's conclusion is that the religion "represents an alternate female view of the world" (1995:65), a yin-oriented system based on "compassion" (*nhan*), which gives "adherents an opportunity to bypass yang-oriented structures" (1995:67). In this interpretation, the religion is seen as a female system or a women's religion independent of the male, yang system of social values in the Vietnamese-American community. Following Neil Jamieson's model of Vietnamese history in terms of an opposition between yin and yang (1993), Fjelstad tags mediumship firmly to the yin pole.

Historical sources hint at a long-standing antipathy between male systems of feudal power rooted in Confucian orthodoxy and female spirit possession (see Chapter 1), and in this chapter I consider the challenges that the practices and divine utterances of female mediums pose to male authority and patriarchy. Yet the history of men's involvement in spirit possession and the issue of transgendering complicate readings of mediumship as an exclusively yin domain or female concern. Rather than thinking of male/female, yin/yang as mutually irreconcilable opposites, traversing gender during rituals encourages a performative approach. Transgendering possession depends on a dynamic flow between male and female, between stereotypical images and notions of masculinity and femininity, and mediums' subjectivities are in no small part forged through the ritual enactment of gender in song, speech, dress, and dance.

The writing of the gender theorists Tani Barlow and Angela Zito offers a fluid, dynamic conception of yin and yang, which is worth bearing in mind when considering much of the discourse on gender issues and the yin–yang binary in Vietnam. Based on writings from late imperial China, Barlow argues that "yin/yang is neither as totalistic nor as ontologically binaried a construct as the Western stereotype would have it . . . the dynamic forces of yin/yang do 'produce'—only not women and men but subject positions or hierarchical, relational subjectivities named mother and father, husband and wife, brother and sister, and so on" (1991:135). Extending Barlow's analysis, Zito identifies three different aspects of yin/yang: "their polarity, their relative positionality and their tendency to unequal encompassment" (1993:335). Polarity suggests yin and yang are "inter-implicated" and transform into each other, and relative positionality points out that men can occupy yin positions as well as yang and women may occupy yang positions as well as yin. Zito's third aspect, unequal encompassment, refers to the idea that "yang always somehow 'encompasses' yin" (1993:336). The idea of "relative positionality" applies well to Vietnamese mediumship as both male and female mediums occupy multiple gender positionalities. The authoritative male spirits might be seen as archetypes of yang characteristics, although these personae are in polarity with female spirits and aspects of ritual practice that might be designated as yin.

This study is rooted in fieldwork experience, and I begin by situating my gendered and erotic subjectivity in the field. This is followed by a consideration of the division of ritual roles along lines and issues of status, marginality, and male/female power asymmetries. I then discuss the musical performance of gender and the ways in which music constructs the gender of spirits. Scholarship on the Vietnamese performing arts has largely suffered from "gender blindness," so little is known about the influence of music, dance, and theater on gender ideologies. The analysis of the engendering of spirits through song moves toward understanding Vietnamese musical aesthetics and style from a gendered perspective. The final sections of the chapter explore how ritual practices relate to mediums' variant gender identities in their everyday lives and how these identities figure in discourse on sexuality and gender in modernizing Vietnam.

Gendered and Erotic Subjectivity in the Field

In the initial stages of planning my fieldwork on mediumship, I gave little thought to how my gender and sexuality would affect my research. I was more concerned about the political problems I might face than about gender issues. On arriving in Vietnam, I was keen to learn to perform *chau van* and spend time with musicians, but there were few official channels through which I could contact ritual musicians because of the lack of state support for and condemnation of mediumship and its music. So I first contacted *chau van* performers through the informal network of musicians I developed from two previous visits to Vietnam. In the first few months of my study of *chau van,* I came into contact with mediums and their disciples mainly through accompanying musicians to rituals. At the time, I did not think my approach was influenced by gender considerations, but in hindsight I realize that gendered cultural expectations were significant. It was culturally acceptable for me to meet male musicians for extended periods on my own, to travel with them to rituals, and to learn to play the moon lute and sing *chau van.* By being associated with male bands I think I also unwittingly assumed a gender subjectivity appropriate to my position as a "researcher." Musicians, especially those who are spirit priests, are respected within mediumship circles for their scholarly knowledge of song texts, Sino-Vietnamese characters, and specialist ritual practices, and it was expected that a male researcher would be interested in learning about these male scholarly traditions.

Female ritual participants were extremely open and talked frankly about their religious, social, and family lives and work and health issues. As I became more immersed in the world of mediumship, I developed acquaintances with religious devotees that were not reliant on introductions from musicians. In general, female mediums were happy to meet me, chat about mediumship, and invite me to rituals. They were proud of their religiosity and thought it had cultural value. Nonetheless, the shadow of Party condemnation of mediumship loomed large on some occasions when mediums were anxious about my presence and were reluctant to become too closely associated with me. Some mediums also had personal reasons, often relating to the concealment of activities from family members, why they did not want to draw outside attention to their ritualizing. Whenever awkward situations arose, I of course respected mediums' concerns and did not attend rituals.

A small circle of wealthy male mediums in Hanoi seemed wary of my presence and tended to be unavailable for any discussion. Although I was not always aware of the reasons for their reticence, some seemed to question the legitimacy of a foreigner's interest and the power dynamics of being "subjects" of research. This unwillingness to "cooperate" did not extend to all male mediums, as many were equally as welcoming as female devotees. However, there was often a flirtatious element to my interaction with male mediums, which went against the grain of "objective" inquiry. Male mediums are referred to as *dong co,* which evokes "effeminacy." Flirtation was often close to the surface when I was with male mediums, as they are known for behaving in an *ong eo* manner, that is, in an "affected" or "camp" way. They often made suggestive remarks about my appearance and asked questions about my sexuality. These remarks were usually playful, but on a few occasions I was propositioned for sex and groped. On one of these occasions, a male medium came to my room in the evening, uninvited. He brought with him a homosexual porn film and tried to caress and kiss me. I did not feel threatened by his behavior; I simply extricated myself from the situation. But instances like this prompted thoughts about how to avoid similar situations and at the same time maintain cordial relationships. One of the dilemmas I faced was that by raising the issue of gender and sexuality I seemed to be unwittingly encouraging sexual advances. But *ong eo* behavior was not just directed toward me: it was a well known aspect of male mediums' identity, and they often flirted with each other at *len dong.* Male mediums liked to tease and joke, and I once heard a male medium at the back of the temple making crude jokes about a woman's vagina being like "a huge fishing net" and about her husband's "small" penis.

As part of the reflexive turn in ethnography, some field researchers have written about their gender and sexual subjectivities (e.g., Whitehead and Conaway 1986; Kulick and Willson 1995). However, such reflexivity has not become a standard feature of ethnographic writing and has largely been consigned to the margins. As Carol Babiracki notes, "the paradigm of the ungendered scholar has been sustained almost uniformly in our models for the written ethnography" (1997:124). Babiracki recalls how this paradigm led her to suppress certain aspects of her fieldwork experience when translating it into a written form. It was only during a second research project a decade after her original fieldwork that she began to reflect on how her gender identities in the field and a romantic relationship with a traditional Nāgpuri musician in Bihar, India, shaped her field experience and her writing about it.

There are numerous reasons for ethnographers' reluctance to discuss their gendered subjectivity and erotic relations in the field. It is often considered overly confessional and may lead to fieldworkers prioritizing themselves and their own agendas irrespective of the views of their hosts. Ethnographers typically feel a deep sense of responsibility and indebtedness to the people involved in their research, and personal stories of sexual relationships may not conform to the way the community or group in question wants to be represented. It has taken me several years to write about the flirtatious behavior of some male mediums, mainly because I feared that recounting a few personal anecdotes would trivialize and give a distorted picture of the men involved in mediumship. I finally decided to note my erotic subjectivity, because I was not seen as an ungendered scholar by some ritual participants and because some of my research was affected by issues of sexuality.

Like many other fieldworkers, I felt in a largely unarticulated way that I would assume a position as a celibate, sexually neutral scholar in the field, but I found that this position was not always taken for granted by the communities among which I was working. In addition to male mediums' sexual advances, female religious followers did not assume I would not become romantically involved with Vietnamese women. It is a cliché that Vietnamese inquire about marital status on first meeting. I was repeatedly asked whether or not I was married, and when I answered in the negative, the response was invariably the imperative, "*Lay vo Viet Nam di!*"—"Marry a Vietnamese wife!" This was often said lightheartedly, yet when married women insisted they act as a matchmaker and introduce me to an unsuspecting daughter or friend, it sometimes seemed to have more serious intent. The perception was that being unmarried and alone, far away from my family and friends, was undesirable and needed to be rectified. I politely declined the matchmakers' offers, which was probably expected, but it made me aware of differing perceptions of my gender and erotic subjectivity.

Gender and Ritual Role

Despite the fluidity of mediums' gender traversing, rituals are characterized by a strong demarcation of ritual roles along lines of gender: the majority of mediums and ritual participants are female, and the majority of *chau van* musicians are male. However, followers of the Four Palace Religion were unwilling to see the matter in gendered terms; after all, both men and women attended rituals and became mediums and musicians. Ritual participants were generally resistant to the idea that the Mother Religion should be considered a "women's religion" or of interest only to women. Nonetheless, when I pressed them about the reasons why more women than men became mediums and participated in rituals, they gave a variety of responses, which may be summarized as follows: (1) the fate of women was such that they are "seized" by the spirits more than men; (2) women suffer "madness" more than men; (3) women are interested in "spiritual matters" (*duy tam*), whereas men are concerned with "material matters" (*duy vat*); (4) women, rather than men, are drawn to the mother spirits, in particular the most famous mother goddess, Lieu Hanh; (5) Women "carry the weight" of the family, so if anybody in the family needs the protection of spirits they must become a medium; (6) only "effeminate" men may become mediums, and because there are more women than "effeminate" men in society, it follows that there would be more female than male mediums; (7) it is the spirits who "choose" people to be initiated, so they are responsible for the ratio between male and female mediums.

The first four responses listed above do not so much provide reasons why women are drawn to mediumship as make the case that women have a natural propensity to be interested in the Mother Religion and thus to become mediums. The fifth and sixth responses edge toward sociological explanations, in terms of family responsibilities and the constitution of society at large, but still highlight cultural notions of gender. The seventh response emphasizes spiritual agency, rather than human volition, as the primary factor in determining whether men or women become mediums.

Predominantly female possession, as is the case in Vietnam, brings to mind Lewis's theory that oppressed groups in society, most notably women, establish marginal possession "cults" as a form of protest against established power asymmetries and that male ecstatics dominate the official institutionalized religions. Lewis interprets female possession as merely a strategy, either consciously or unconsciously employed, which gives "women an opportunity to gain ends (material and non-material)" (Lewis 1989 [1971]:77). Criticism of Lewis's interpretation has focused on the oppositions he sets up between male/female, marginal/institutionalized, center/periphery. Janice Boddy has argued that Lewis's emphasis on women's peripheral and subordinate status "is a classic but unhappily androcentric portrayal of women, who are forever seen as reacting to men rather than acting for themselves within a specific cultural context." (1989:140). Similarly, Laurel Kendall (1985) has argued that women's rituals are not peripheral to Korean society, and Karen Fjelstad

(1995) has suggested that Lewis's formulation promotes a male-centered view of female possession not shared by women. Work on how shamanism, official priesthoods, politics, and state power have intertwined in different historical contexts also makes it difficult to maintain rigid oppositions between marginal/institutionalized, and so forth (Thomas and Humphrey 1994).

Party ideologues and others opposed to spirit possession continue to brand mediumship as marginal and in need of eradication, but this was not the view of religious devotees or many Vietnamese I met who had never been to rituals. Indeed, to assert that mediumship is marginal seems untenable given the large number of followers of the Four Palace Religion in contemporary Vietnam. Mediumship is not institutionalized like Buddhism, but mediums are afforded varying degrees of status and prestige, which further problematizes the issue of marginality. It would also be inappropriate to describe temples as a predominantly female domain simply because the majority of ritual participants are women; public temples are often infused with male prestige.

It was apparent that male mediums have a disproportionate status and wealth compared with their number, as many of the most famous and opulent temples in the center of Hanoi and at the famous pilgrimage site of Phu Giay are run by men. Some public temples are presided over by women, yet these tend to be minor ones that are less popular with disciples. By contrast with the high percentage of male mediums at public temples, most female mediums construct private temples in their homes. The social differentiation between women's place in the domestic realm and men's authority in the public domain is therefore reflected within mediumship.

There is a common perception, which is most prevalent among male mediums and their disciples, that men are "better" than women at looking after large temples. To cite one example, a male temple medium in Hanoi told me men had more "talent," "ability," and "understanding" of religion than women, and he added that temples kept by men were "decorated more beautifully" and were "more magnificent" compared with those run by women. While such an assertion of male superiority was challenged by many of the female mediums with whom I raised the issue, it is indicative of a quite widely held attitude that has no doubt played a part in men assuming prominent positions at public temples.

A degree of male prestige is also accorded to *chau van* bands. Religious followers were respectful of the knowledge and expertise of musicians, and spirit priests are accorded particularly high status because of their specialist ritual skills. As discussed in Chapter 3, the "male" gender associations of the moon lute, the male–female dynamic between musicians and female mediums, and the historical exclusion of women from learning the scholarly skills of spirit priests have contributed to *chau van* often being perceived as a "male" genre.

Musically Engendering the Spirits

In her book *Engendering Song,* Jane Sugarman urges ethnomusicologists "to focus on the capacity of musical traditions not merely to reinforce gender relations within other domains but to actively *engender* those individuals who participate in them" (1997:32; emphasis in original). Sugarman's account of singing in Prespa Albanian weddings demonstrates how musical performance constructs the social and moral order and naturalizes differences between "females" and "males." Prespa weddings are characterized by marked gender segregation. Women and men sing different repertoires with different themes and musical styles: "While women sing softly and 'thinly' of courtship and marriage, sitting with great composure deep within the host family's house, men sing loudly and 'thickly' of heroism and romance, drinking and toasting boisterously in the family's *odë* or courtyard" (Sugarman 1997:252). According to Sugarman, such differences in the musical performances of Prespa women and men are consistent with, and construct, shared beliefs regarding gendered relations, so participants in wedding singing can be understood as engaging in "a process of 'engendering'" (1997:253).

Sugarman's examination of how musical performance engenders participants is part of a growing body of research on the musical construction or "making" of gender (e.g., Moisala and Diamond 2000; Magrini 2003). This work employs varieties of constructionism in which social and cultural practices are seen as making, shaping, and challenging gendered subjectivities (Ortner 1996). Within the context of a broader investigation of mediumship as a gendered activity, here I examine how *chau van* engenders possessed mediums. The performance of songs embodies and expresses notions of "femininity" and "masculinity" through differences in the musical characteristics and style of "male" and "female" songs.

As outlined in Chapter 4, the gender of spirits is musically distinguished through the performance of different songs for male and female spirits: the "Phu" group and "Kieu Duong" for male; the "Con" group and "Van" and "Ham" for female lowland; and the "Xa" group for female mountain spirits. The songs for male spirits sound masculine because they are heavy, authoritative, and serious; the songs for lowland female spirits sound feminine because they are soft, lyrical, and smooth; the songs for female mountain spirits evoke an "ethnic femininity" through largely imagined associations with the music of minority groups. But how do these aesthetic connotations relate to the musical characteristics of songs? What are the differences between these melodies, and are there masculine and feminine performance styles? These questions can be addressed through comparison of a Phu melody, "Phu Noi" (Track 16), a "Con" melody, "Con Giay Lech" (Track 7), and a "Xa" melody, "Xa Thuong" (Track 9). The musical examples on the DVD are performed by Pham Van Ty (moon lute and voice) and Pham Quang Dat (percussion).

Translation of the text in Figure 6.3:

> The boat floats on the Xich Bich river.
> The boat floats everywhere.
> Royally inspecting the Thuong river,
> Returning to the north to Luc Dau.

Translation of the text in Figure 6.4:

> Persist in understanding the political affairs of state,
> Help support the Le dynasty in destroying the Mac,[1]
> Make haste to go to the native place of Han Son.

Translation of the text in Figure 6.5:

> In the forest, the wind blows in the trees.
> In the valley, the fish jump and the birds fly back to the forest.
> Late at night, the moon wanes and the stars fade.

Although "Phu Noi," "Con Giay Lech," and "Xa Thuong" use different scales, the songs performed for the three categories of spirits—male, lowland female, and mountain female—are not clearly differentiated through the use of specific scales or ornamentation. However, "Phu Noi," "Con Giay Lech," and "Xa Thuong" do exhibit other distinguishing musical features, which are typical of the groups of songs performed for male spirits and for lowland and mountain female spirits. These musical features relate to melodic structure, rhythm, performance style, the instrumental accompaniment, the song text, and the way words are set to melody.

Each verse of "Phu Noi" consists of four long phrases, each separated by a short instrumental section. The words of the text are often extended through melisma, and the length of each phrase is prolonged with long sustained notes sung to vocables (*i* and *o*) between successive words. The four lines of text refer to the Third Mandarin traveling on the Xich Bich river in China, and

Figure 6.3. Transcription of a verse of "Phu Noi" for the Third Mandarin (Track 16)

Khang khang nam vung co tran phu Le diet Mac bao lan xong

pha Han Son chon ay que nha (i)

Figure 6.4. Transcription of a verse of Con Giay Lech for the Third Princess (Track 7)

Tren ngan (o) gio thoi rung cay duoi khe ca lan chim

bay ve ngan canh khuya (i) nguyet lan sao

tan (i)

Figure 6.5. Transcription of a verse of "Xa Thuong" for the Second Lady (Track 9)

he "inspects" the Thuong river, the implication being that he travels widely to protect and govern like a royal. The lyrics therefore confirm the mandarin's status as a powerful ruler.

Verses of "Con Giay Lech" are much shorter in length than those of "Phu Noi." Just three lines of text are sung, and there are no extended instrumental sections within the verse. Compared with "Phu Noi," the rate of delivery of the text is much faster; the "Con Giay Lech" melody is less melismatic and less syncopated and makes less use of vocables between successive words. These characteristics make the melody sound less "drawn out" (*e a*) than "Phu Noi." Each verse of "Con Giay Lech" concludes with a short, melodious "ending phrase" sung to the vowel "i." This type of ending phrase is a distinctive characteristic of all the female songs, which were said to make the songs more "lyrical" and therefore more feminine than the male songs.

The Third Princess is thought to have descended to earth from the heavens during the reign of King Le Thai To, and her songs refer to her support for the Le rulers. Other sections of the poems for the princess describe her beauty and grace and describe her traveling through the country by boat:

The princess parts her silky hair, which shimmers like the shadow of a
    willow tree.
Her perfect eyebrows are curved like a willow tree.
She has the sparkling eyes of a phoenix, which reflect like mirrors.
She has beautiful ivory skin, rosy cheeks, and lips like autumn moons.
With such fresh youth, she is in her prime.
Her three-colored head scarf is tied with a pin.

Shout out the rowing call,
So that the princess holds the oars.
Traveling everywhere,
The princess is drifting in all four directions.
The wind in the pine trees and the clouds,
The lady rescues mortals.

The songs performed for mountain female spirits have some features in common with those for lowland female spirits. Like "Con Giay Lech," the verses
of "Xa Thuong" are short compared with those of "Phu Noi," and the words
of the text are sung relatively quickly, without extensive use of melisma and
syncopation. The use of vocables is also primarily restricted to the ending
phrase. The text for the verse describes the Second Lady wandering happily
in the mountains and forests late at night. As is typical for female spirits, the
poems dedicated to the Second Lady also frequently describe her dazzling
beauty. Descriptions of the grace and beauty of female spirits are reminiscent of the Confucian "four virtues," which include idealized standards for
women's physical appearance and behavior.

Each of the three songs transcribed employs a different rhythm: the three-
beat, two-beat, and one-beat rhythm are used for "Phu Noi," "Con Giay Lech,"
and "Xa Thuong," respectively.[2] Each rhythm has a different associations and
a distinctive "feel." As discussed in Chapter 4, the lively percussion played
for the "Xa" melodies is associated with ethnic minority musics. Regarding
the other two rhythms, musicians considered the three-beat rhythm to be
less "tight" (chat che) than the two-beat rhythm because it does not include
the eighth-note upbeat. This lack of tightness permits greater scope for singing with rhythmic flexibility. The "Phu" melodies (and "Kieu Duong") are
rhythmically fluid, whereas the "Con" melodies (and "Ham" and "Van") are
subject to less rhythmic variation in performance. This difference in rhythmic flexibility also has an effect on the vocal forces used: the rhythmically
regular songs for female spirits are sometimes sung in unison by two or
more voices, but male songs are always sung solo, in part because they are

too rhythmically variable to sing in unison. It is tempting to relate the degree of rhythmic flexibility of songs to cultural notions of male and female: the greater independence, complexity, and fluidity of the vocal line for male songs resonates with ideas about male artistic prestige and individual authority, and the more lyrical, group-sung female songs are consistent with female gracefulness and communal, participatory values.

The instrumental sections and accompaniment to the vocal line also contribute to the musical construction of gender. The instrumental phrases played on the moon lute between verses of male songs are considered to be "strong" (*manh*), and those for female lowland songs are "light" (*nhe*) and "smooth" (*muot ma*). Also, the instrumental accompaniment to the voice tends to be more sparse for male songs than for the female lowland songs, which adds to their solemnity, and the lively instrumental parts of the "Xa" melodies are in keeping with the portrayal of mountain, ethnic, female spirits joyfully roaming in the natural world. Table 6.1 summarizes the musical characteristics of the songs for male and female spirits discussed so far.

Vocal quality also plays a part in the gendered aesthetics of songs. According to Pham Van Ty, male songs should be sung with a "strict," constrained vocal style compared with the more "feminine," relaxed style of female songs. Subtle differences in vocal timbre can be heard in Ty's performances of "Phu Noi," "Con Giay Lech," and "Xa Thuong" on the DVD. For "Phu Noi," he emphasizes the sharp contours of the speech tones and uses a tense, broken vibrato, whereas the other two songs are sung with a slightly softer timbre.

The vocal quality of singers is a hotly debated issue among musicians.

Table 6.1. Summary of the musical characteristics of "male" and "female" songs

Songs for female spirits	Songs for male spirits
Two-beat rhythm	Three-beat rhythm
Verses made up of short vocal phrases	Verses made up of long vocal phrases
Minimal melisma	Extended melisma
Little syncopation	Highly syncopated
Each verse of a song concludes with the same phrase sung to vocables	Verses do not usually end with a repeated phrase sung to vocables
Full instrumental accompaniment to the vocal line	Sparse instrumental accompaniment to the vocal line
May be sung in unison by more than one person	Solo voice

Genres of traditional music like *chau van, quan ho, cheo, tuong, cai luong,* and *nhac tai tu* are differentiated through the use of distinctive vocal styles, as well as other features like repertoire, performance context, and instrumentation. How melodies are sung—the vocal quality, ornamentation, use of vocables, setting and pronunciation of the text, and gender of the singer—is a crucial aspect of musical style. The expression *tron vanh ro chu,* literally "rounded [sound], clear words," encapsulates an ideal for vocal delivery that is applied across genres. Musicians further described the most appropriate vocal quality for *chau van* as being *kim pha tho,* literally "metal mixed with earth." This refers to singing that is "thin" and "clear" in the high register and more "earthy" in the lower register.

Vietnamese folklorists categorize *chau van* as sacred folk music, as an orally transmitted genre embedded in popular religious practices (Ngo Duc Thinh 1992). This "folk character" (*tinh dan gian*) and religiosity permeate the performance aesthetics of ritual music. *Chau van* texts, which are seen by many musicians as a rich source of folk wisdom and knowledge, are sung with a gravitas appropriate to *chau van*'s sacred role. The voices of *chau van* singers should ideally be "ripe" (*chin*), not "immature" (*suong*) or "unripe" (*non*). Ritual performances permit playfulness and jocularity at some points, but there is an underlying seriousness of intent that influences the musical aesthetics of *chau van.* Compared with singers of genres like *cheo,* whose primary purpose is to entertain paying audiences, the devotional singing of *chau van* singers tends to have a more serious quality. There are, however, signs that ritual participants are increasingly favoring "lighter" styles of singing, which are familiar to listeners of popular songs (*ca khuc*) and genres like *cheo.*[3]

"Effeminate" Men and "Hot-Tempered" Women

The perception of mediums in the public at large and within mediumship circles is strongly gendered. In different ways, male and female mediums do not conform to conventional gender identities: male mediums are effeminate and female mediums are difficult, hot-tempered women. These gendered subjectivities relate to ritual practices. As mentioned at the beginning of this chapter, the expression *dong co bong cau* refers to the traversing of gender during *len dong,* but the two components of the expression—*dong co* and *bong cau*—are used independently to describe male and female mediums, respectively.

Dong co as a term for effeminate male mediums was described by two mediums (one female and one male) in the following way:

> When a man has the "destined aptitude" of the Ninth Princess, then when that spirit is incarnated, the character of the man is naturally different: he has a sharp tongue, the voice of a woman and chews betel like a woman. He is still a man, but because of the aptitude of a princess, the female spirit helps his destiny and he becomes a *dong co* . . . who is very graceful . . . They [*dong co*] wear women's clothes on the outside and inside . . . Many people hug them and call them women.

> If male mediums have the destined aptitude of princess or lady spirits then they have a "strong femininity" . . . That is a natural phenomenon . . . They are men, but their appearance and mannerisms are "weak" and they speak like women.

Dong co is resonant with two meanings: it refers to the ability of male mediums to dress and behave like women while possessed and to their effeminacy. Apart from *dong co*, male mediums are also sometimes referred to as *ai nam ai nu* (lit. "love man, love woman) or *nua nam nua nu* (lit. "half man half woman"). These terms refer to transsexuals or hermaphrodites. None of the male mediums I met said they were hermaphrodites, but the terms are commonly used figuratively with a similar meaning to *dong co*. As one *chau van* musician remarked: "Male mediums are *ai nam ai nu:* their voice, bearing, and behavior are like a woman's."

The notion of *dong co* springs from mediumship, as it connotes possession by female spirits and cross-dressing during rituals, yet it has become part of the vernacular, with meanings beyond the ritual context. Men who are perceived to be effeminate in everyday life are called *dong co,* irrespective of whether they are mediums. In popular discourse, *dong co* is increasingly being conceived as synonymous with a modern, Western-influenced gay identity, but in mediumship circles *dong co* is understood as a gender identity, which does not determine sexual orientation. Religious followers, both male and female, did not presume male mediums were homosexual just because they were *dong co,* and I met many *dong co* who were involved in a variety of sexual relations with men and/or women. It is not uncommon for *dong co* to marry and have a family, although this did not necessarily mean they did not have homoerotic desires. Some *dong co* who were married said they had same-sex erotic relationships, and this was also acknowledged by other ritual participants. As one female medium commented, "[*dong co*] like relations with men . . . *Dong co* who have wives haven't made it public yet, but generally they have feelings for men." Other *dong co* said their involvement in mediumship precluded marriage, as the following comment by a male medium illustrates: "When I was possessed by the spirits . . . [the spirits] said I should not marry, and that if I did an ordinary job I would be taken back to the heavens, that if I went out on the road I would get run over by a car . . . So I had to become a religious person and do 'good work.'" Some unmarried mediums said they were celibate, whereas others were openly gay. But whatever sexual activities male mediums pursued, this did not affect their effeminate gender positionality. Cross-dressing possession experiences have been prone to Western interpretations as sexual (Kendall 2005), but mediums' performances were not understood to be sexual by most ritual participants. When I asked whether mediumship provided men with an opportunity to "express" or "show" their homosexuality, the response was invariably negative. The response of one female medium was typical: "You cannot combine *len dong* with homosexuality. Homosexuality is outside—you cannot enter it into *len dong;* they are separate." In general, religious devotees denied suggestions that ritual practices were related to sexuality.

Bong cau is not an equivalent category to *dong co.* When applied to female mediums, it emphasizes their ability to be possessed by male spirits; it does not connote a strong masculine gender identity, as *dong co* does femininity. Some female mediums are noted for their "strong masculinity" (*nang ve nam tinh*), yet they more commonly described themselves as having particular character traits such as being "hot-tempered" (*nong tinh*), "hot gutted" (*nong ruot*), or "difficult" (*kho chiu*). These traits were rarely linked to male spirits in the way that the behavior of male mediums was associated with female spirits. But they were considered part of a medium's unique character, and a female medium with a strong destined aptitude for a male spirit may be particularly hot-tempered. So even though female mediums are not usually thought of as being "masculine," they are "difficult" women and unfeminine in the sense that they do not conform to stereotypical women's roles or behavior.

Transgendering possession therefore affects the personal identities of male and female mediums in different ways. Cross-dressing for men opens up a third gender domain in which feminine mannerisms and demeanors are assumed outside of the ritual context, whereas there is no equivalent designation for female mediums. Unlike *dong co,* the term *bong cau* does not constitute a discrete identity; cross-dressing for women does not naturalize a variant gender identity as it does for men. Ritualizing enables female mediums to deal with unfeminine traits, but they do not automatically assume a default masculine identity. This suggests a degree of "unequal encompassment" (Zito 1993), as men encompass yin, whereas women's access to yang positionalities is more circumscribed.

Theories of performativity have been extremely influential in writing on gender and difference in recent years. Such theories conceive of gender identity as flexibly constructed through performative acts. In Judith Butler's formulation, "gender ought not to be construed as a stable identity or locus of agency from which various acts follow; rather gender is an identity tenuously constituted in time, instituted in an exterior space through a *stylized repetition of acts*" (1990:140; emphases in original). Butler offers drag as an example of performativity, and this has been employed by some gender theorists as a paradigm of transgressive practice that destabilizes or decenters gender categories. Rosalind Morris summarizes the appeal of gender performativity in the following terms: "By asserting that the body assumes its sex in culturally mandated practices of everyday life, the theory of gender performativity offers the possibility of restyling that same body in non-normative and occasionally subversive ways" (1995:573). Transgendering ritual practices have also been understood as offering possibilities for such nonnormative restylings (see Brettell and Sargent 2005). However, it is important to consider how gender transformation in rituals relates to personal subjectivities, as ritual play and parody may not translate into everyday forms of ironic resistance (Morris 1995).

Performance theory raises some interesting questions in relation to *len dong*. Does the repetition of ritual acts destabilize or subvert established gender categories? And to what extent do ritual acts constitute mediums' personal identity in their everyday lives? While possessed, women and men transgress gender identities: *len dong* is a site in which male mediums may assume feminine gender positions (as well as masculine ones) and in which female mediums can come to terms with unfeminine aspects of their personality, such as being hot-tempered (as well as displaying stereotypical feminine aspects, such as being graceful).

However, mediums' ritual acts should not be misconstrued as an example of identity being performatively constructed or deconstructed at will. In fact, Butler suggests in relation to drag that while gender performativity has the potential to subvert established categories by disrupting the relationship between anatomical sex and gender identity, it also reiterates ideal, normative corporeal styles. And in *Bodies That Matter,* Butler (1993) argues against the voluntaristic interpretations of gender performativity prompted by her previous book, *Gender Trouble*. Vietnamese mediums assume divergent gender positionalities, but only within the culturally prescribed limits established by the gender identity of spirits. In many ways, the spirits confirm normative gender identities (prestigious mandarins, graceful ladies, etc.). Mediums therefore construct their own gender identities with reference to pre-given stereotypes and assume identities that are also culturally sanctioned (e.g., being "effeminate," "unfeminine"). To assess the extent to which possession subverts normalized, societal gender categories, I now consider the intersections between ritual practice and gender/sex identity in everyday life.

Mediumship, Everyday Life, and "Family Happiness"

Mediumship practices are inextricably bound up with mediums' everyday lives. Mediums and disciples often call on the spirits to address practical concerns and personal issues, and during possession, aspects of mediums' characters find expression, negotiation, and (partial) resolution. Mediumship also affords religious followers with opportunities to alter the social and economic realities of their lives.

The interpenetration of ritual and everyday life is apparent for all ritual participants, but involvement in mediumship impacts upon the lives of male and female adepts in gender-specific ways. For female mediums, the exuberance of possession eases their "difficult" temperaments. Female devotees also linked worshipping the spirits with their concern for ensuring "family happiness" (*hanh phuc gia dinh*). Male mediums did not usually relate their activities to their family happiness as women did, but involvement in mediumship usually had a significant impact upon their domestic situation. Effeminacy is not just restricted to the ritual domain; *dong co* are perceived as behaving like women and assume a variant gender positionality in their everyday lives.

The economic realities of mediums are most radically affected if they support themselves financially through presiding over a public temple or through fortune-telling or healing. The tendency for men to preside over opulent temples means that mediumship becomes, in a sense, a profession. Most temple mediums, only a few of whom are female, devote themselves entirely to religious work, and they are supported through donations from devotees who worship at their temples. Female mediums who do not look after temples usually have regular jobs, though some earn a living through fortune-telling or healing.

Apart from the scope for becoming a "professional" medium, there are other practical ways in which the social realities of women are affected by their religious practices. The numerous *len dong* festivals that take place at temples all over Vietnam provide female religious followers with opportunities to frequently travel around the country and to enlarge their sphere of social interaction. The comments of one "husbandless" medium, called Khoat, who did not go to festivals, illustrate some of the constraints that are sometimes placed on women's movement:

> I don't go willy-nilly to many different festivals like other mediums. I am on my own, that is, I don't have a husband . . . so if I went out to different places, went on the back of someone's motorbike or did this or that, people would think this and that about me, and that I wasn't going to places to worship. So my parents don't allow me to go. I just worship at home.

Khoat's parents did not consent to their daughter traveling long distances because she was no longer with her husband and they were worried about gossip. But, as suggested by Khoat above, most mediums managed to overcome such obstacles and traveled freely.

The tendency for female mediums to construct their own temples, either in, or adjacent to, their homes, has been noted as a restriction to the domestic rather than the public sphere. However, private temples are separate from normal domestic life. Mediums are protective of their private temples, and other family members are not usually permitted to enter without their consent. Those mediums who hold fortune-telling and healing sessions also receive their clients in their temples. Often, clients are previously unknown to mediums, and some travel large distances for consultations. Interaction with clients therefore greatly expands female mediums' social sphere, and "private" temples are to a certain extent "public," as they are often visited by strangers. So, while it is the case that temples presided over by male and female mediums tend to be in the public and domestic spheres, respectively—which seemingly confirms gender-based power asymmetries—private temples are distinct from, and more public than, other domestic space.

"Family happiness" is a pervasive theme in discourse on gender in Vietnam. Maintaining good family relations is a preoccupation of Vietnamese women, and the ideal of a happy family is strongly propagated by government documents and popular culture (Gammeltoft 1999:72–76). Vietnamese women's-studies researchers have also promoted the notion of family happiness in order to improve gender equality within the family and to "overcome the vestiges of old and backward views and customs" (Barry 1996:12).

Many female mediums asserted that ritualizing ensured peace, harmony, and prosperity within their families. For instance, one woman said that the spirits "fulfilled the wishes" of her family and that she held *len dong* so that her family was safe and prosperous. Afflictions leading to initiation, such as the death of newborn babies, an inability to care for children, and illness, are instances of rupture in family well-being and breakdown in the prescribed role of women as procreators/nurturers. After initiation, these crises are resolved with the assistance of spirits. Although male mediums were not preoccupied with "family happiness," many shared the conviction that rituals helped bring prosperity, good health, and happiness.

Despite female mediums' desire for family happiness through seeking the benevolence of spirits, antagonism with their husbands is quite common. Some women concealed their ritual practices from their disapproving husbands, who objected because they thought *len dong* was superstitious or a waste of money, or because of fears that mediums often had "extramarital affairs" (*ngoai tinh*) with *chau van* musicians. So, contrary to women's expressed intention to maintain harmony within the family, many risk marital disputes as a result of participating in mediumship.

Antagonisms between female mediums and their husbands are not a recent phenomenon and so cannot be seen simply as a consequence of ritual revival and changes in marital and family relationships in the reform period. Recall the denigration of female mediums and their henpecked husbands by male nationalist intellectuals in the late colonial period and the satirical novels by Long Chuong and Nhat Lang in which disgruntled, skeptical husbands have to suffer the "humiliation" of their wives' ritualizing (see Chapter 1). Marital discord and threats to male authority within the family are prominent in both novels. Most dramatically, *Serving the Spirits* by Long Chuong concludes with family breakdown as Mrs. Hanh Sinh finds out her husband has an illegitimate child and she leaves her husband for a *chau van* musician who woos her with song. Rumors about female mediums being seduced by the flattery and charming voices of male musicians continue to have currency, and I occasionally heard gossip about affairs. There is little reason to believe that extramarital affairs are more prevalent within mediumship circles than in any other sector of society, but the specter of female sexual desire, liberated from the usual constraints of traditional family structures and Confucian imperatives of female subservience to male family members, is ever present. Female mediums' reputation for being difficult and hot-tempered in part stems from the challenges their practices pose to patriarchal power structures. Such challenges were evident during a ritual, held by Doan, to mark the end of the year.

Challenging Patriarchy: Doan's End-of-Year Ritual

Of all the mediums I met during fieldwork, Doan was one of the most charismatic, assertive, and outspoken. Always quick to express her opinions in frank terms, to admonish, tease, and joke, Doan had an authoritative presence and magnetic personality felt by everyone around her. I first met her on an unusually cold winter's day in December 1996. An elderly musician called Kha had taken me to Doan's home in a small village in Ha Tay province about fifty kilometers from Hanoi. Unfazed by the unexpected appearance of an ethnomusicologist from abroad, Doan warmly welcomed me into her home and urged me to film the "end-of-year ritual" (*le thuong nguyen*), which she was holding later in the day in her small private temple adjacent to her house. The day turned out to be full of incident and alerted me to the social importance of spirits' utterances.

After that first meeting in 1996, I became a frequent visitor to Doan's home and got to know her well. While I have spent much time with Doan and her friends and family over a period of nearly a decade, I hesitate to unproblematically use the word "friendship" to describe our relationship. As Tim Cooley comments in his discussion of the friendship model of fieldwork: "Friendship may be the most benign form of interpersonal human relationship, but . . . [it] risks obscuring subsurface and sometimes not fully formed or realized motivations and ideologies" (2003:10). My interactions with Doan were marked by occasional moments when tensions rose to the surface, as well as warmth, trust, and respect. Like many mediums, Doan was known for being *dong bong,* that is, tempestuous, changeable, or fickle, and she seemed to have stormy relationships with many of her friends and family. I have found knowing her extremely rewarding, from a personal as well as a research point of view, and Doan indicated she also valued our relationship. Indeed, she thought I had had a positive effect on her religious activities. She said that my interest in her and her appearance in the documentary *A Westerner Loves Our Music* had made her widely known and as a result more people came to consult her. Over the decade I have known Doan, she has grown more prosperous because of the donations given to her by disciples. In 2002, she had sufficient capital to enlarge her temple, and she now supports her family through her ritual activities. Doan's husband gave up work as a farmer, and he now assists her with her rituals and spends much of his time preparing and cooking meals for guests. Despite Doan's increased prosperity, she often remarked how wealthy I must be to spend long periods of time in Vietnam. Doan is a sharp, perceptive woman, and she was frank about the financial inequalities between us. In part because of my relative wealth, Doan insisted I film, photograph, and "sponsor" her rituals (see Chapter 4 and the Epilogue).

At Doan's end-of-year ritual, about twenty people from the village and the surrounding area crammed into her small temple. At Doan's request, I filmed the ritual and later transcribed the spirits' words. The meaning of these divine utterances was not always clear without additional explanation, because of the frequent use of opaque aphorisms, colloquial expressions, and specific references to disciples' circumstances. I was able to inquire more about the meaning of the spirits' words when I watched the video with Doan several weeks after the event.

The ritual began in the conventional way, with incarnations of several mandarins and General Tran Hung Dao, but then something unusual happened. While possessed by the Third Princess, Doan started to complain about being cold. Several minutes later, Doan stopped the ritual, saying the princess had made her so cold she could not continue. Interestingly, the moment when Doan temporarily stopped the ritual was preceded by critical remarks about the music. An angry mandarin, incarnated before the Third Princess, expressed his dissatisfaction with the following words: "The band sounds like cold rice—why should I praise them? Is the band not awake? My gifts are as abundant as the ocean, but the playing is like a sleeping dragon." The message is clear: *chau van* should be hot, not cold; it should warm up and energize the occasion.

When Doan terminated the ritual prematurely, she promptly left the temple, leaving everybody to wonder what would happen next. After a few minutes of confusion, some of Doan's disciples went to find her, and they eventually managed to persuade her to come back. On her return to the temple, Doan consulted the spirits about whether she should resume the ritual by tossing old yin-yang coins. On the second throw, the coins gave a positive response, so she continued with possessions by the Seventh, Ninth, and Little Princess, and finally the Third Young Prince.

When the Seventh Princess was incarnated, the spirit explained why the Third Princess had made Doan's body so cold. The spirit said the princess had punished her because her husband had criticized mediumship and because she had not worshipped the spirits properly. The utterances of the Seventh Princess were as follows:

> Today I "transmit" and then you [Doan] can tell the future . . . Your husband said the "tongues have no bones and there are many twisty roads," so the Third Princess scolded and punished [you].

> Why was nothing given to the Third Princess, yet [votive offerings] are pre-
> sented to me? For several days I have told everyone to concentrate "with one
> gut" [i.e., completely] on the spirits. Don't imitate stupid people of the mortal
> world, otherwise the Third Princess will scold and punish.

While watching the video, Doan said her husband had criticized her religious activities because he did not "believe" (*tin*) in the spirits. The phrase "the tongue has no bones and there are many twisty roads" is a reference to his criticisms. During possession by the Ninth Princess, Doan's mother-in-law, who was present at the ritual, was also told to reprimand her son to make him respect the spirits: "If that husband is still dishonest, why should I forgive [you]?" and "The relative (lit. "pink and red blood") who gave birth [to Doan's husband] must admonish him; only then will I forgive [you]."

These utterances are an example of how spiritual agency can influence family dynamics. The husband's position as the "head of the family" is flouted by the spirit's comments. The potential for mediumship to undermine the authority conventionally ascribed to husbands and to invert power asymmetries is highlighted by two popular proverbs: "Being a medium comes first; having a husband who is an emperor comes second." (*Thu nhat ngoi dong, thu hai chong vua.*) And "Marrying a wife who is a medium comes first; marrying a husband who is an emperor comes second." (*Thu nhat lay vo dong, thu nhi lay chong vua.*) These proverbs openly challenge patriarchal authority by asserting that female mediums are more important than patriarchal figures (husbands and emperors), and they overturn one of the three Confucian "obediences," namely a woman's subservience to her husband.

On one occasion when a medium called Van mentioned the first proverb above, she said that after *len dong* she was so happy she did not care about anything else, not even whether her husband became king. Van went on to suggest that women's traditional role of attending to every need of the family, especially the needs of the male members of the family, is reversed during rituals. To extend the two proverbs quoted above, *len dong* rituals provide a space where mediums are treated like husbands and kings.

Alongside direct challenges to patriarchal authority, ritualizing offers support for women in ways that do not rely on confrontation with troublesome husbands and sons. Spirits are attentive to the difficulties women face, and ritual gatherings allow female-oriented networks of support to flourish. This chimes with Fjelstad's interpretation that the Four Palace Religion represents an alternate female view of the world. Rituals are a site where women's worries are voiced and sympathy is expressed. Women's financial worries and concerns about physical ailments like headaches and tiredness, which Tine

Gammeltoft (1999) interprets as somatic expressions of women's distress, are often raised at rituals. During Doan's possession by the Ninth Princess, a disciple approached her saying she suffered from headaches. The princess said the headaches were due to worries about money, not the punishment of spirits: "I haven't tormented, [you] only have a headache because of money, here you go! [Doan gives the disciple money]. If you lack money, you will have a headache, that is all. I didn't punish!"

Airing concerns during rituals not only applies to women who are wives and mothers, but also to those who lie outside of conventional family structures, such as widows, divorcees, and childless and single women. When Dien, a widow who attended the end-of-year ritual, approached Doan with ritual offerings, she acknowledged the death of Dien's husband and reassured her that if she worshipped the spirits she would not have financial problems:

> Today the husband is in the heavens, not at the temple.

> The Pham lineage [i.e., Dien] has a difficult love match; there is only one "chopstick" [i.e., only one of the marital pair is still alive], but there will be lots of money if you persist with "one heart" [i.e., if you sincerely worship the spirits].

The "husbandless" medium Khoat, mentioned earlier, was also present at the ritual. When Khoat was twenty-seven she suffered repeated bouts of illness, split up with her husband, and returned to live at her parents' house. Having left her husband, Khoat tried to make a living from selling goods at markets (previously she had been working in the fields), but she was not successful as a market trader and did not like the work. A couple of years after the separation, Khoat was initiated and built a temple next door to her parents' house. Like Doan, Khoat tells fortunes and has a special relationship with the Ninth Princess. As a fortune-teller, Khoat receives "blessed gifts"—small amounts of money, fruit, packaged goods, and so forth—from her clients, so she no longer has to work as a farmer or market trader. To show her appreciation to the Ninth Princess, Khoat made an offering to the embodied spirit during the end-of-year ritual, and the princess confirmed she was responsible for her fortune-telling powers (Khoat is referred to by her family name, Van):

> The Van lineage! My people, my wealth!

> So today I say to the Van lineage disciples, the Van lineage enjoys my gift of fortune-telling.

Khoat has found living at home with her parents difficult, and she is prone to arguing with her mother. Such arguments were alluded to during Doan's incarnation of the Ninth Princess. Khoat's mother is referred to by her family name, Do:

> The Do lineage is insolent all the time. I swallow the bitter medicine and don't complain, but I will continue to let the Little Princess spirit seize the Van lineage. If the Van lineage do not behave properly, I will "rise up to the bank and go down to the fields" [i.e., create problems]—then you will know my magical powers!

According to Doan's explanation of these words, the Little Princess—who is known for her playful and truculent character—made Khoat's mother "insolent." The words "transmitted" by the Ninth Princess assert her power to stop the meddling of the Little Princess, but she threatens to make Khoat's life even more difficult if she does not worship.

Divine utterances mediated by women challenge patriarchy and comment on the personal circumstances and financial and health problems of participants. Incarnated spirits engage with devotees; they empathize and punish, reassure and chastise. In the ritual forum of *len dong,* women publicly voice their issues and worries within a largely supportive social network and call on the spirits for assistance and protection.

Modernity, Sexuality, and Gender

One evening in Hanoi in December 2004, I turned on Vietnamese television, VTV, and came across a drama called *A World without Women* (*The Gioi Khong Dan Ba*), a ten-part drama aired as part of the series *Criminal Police.* What was immediately striking was that the drama featured male gay characters in connection with a police murder investigation. The series was based on a best-selling, award-winning novel by Bui Anh Tan (2004 [2000]) of the same name, which was hailed in the press as the first Vietnamese novel about homosexuality.

Programming on Vietnamese state television is vetted and tightly controlled, which limits independent critical comment and the expression of contentious or subversive ideas. Nonetheless, within the boundaries of censorship, Vietnamese television directors and producers are striving to make programs that are relevant for contemporary audiences, and television is becoming an increasingly important medium for addressing cultural and social issues. Writing on Vietnamese television, Lisa Drummond illustrates how the soap-opera-style serial *12A and 4H* produced by VTV3 in the mid-1990s deals with issues such as "the fragmentation and conflict over social roles and behaviors" in urban society and the increasing rural-urban divide (2003:165).

The series *A World without Women* addresses equally pressing issues concerning homosexuality and family relationships. Two of the main characters in the drama are the police officer Lan and his younger brother Hoang. When Hoang told his family he was gay, his shocked father died upon hearing the news and Lan expelled him from their family home. In the course of investigating three murders of gay men between the ages of seventeen and twenty-five who were targeted by serial killers, Lan learns more about the difficulties and hatred faced by homosexuals and becomes more compassionate toward his brother. Toward the end of the serial, Lan and Hoang's mother dies, and Lan accepts his brother back home. Lan still hopes that Hoang will get married and lead a "normal" life, but he agrees to accept him regardless of his sexuality. The 2004 edition of the book has two endings. In the first, Hoang promises to put his homosexuality behind him and "to become a normal man." In the second, Hoang expresses his undying love for Trung, one of Lan's fellow police officers who posed as a homosexual while working undercover on the murder investigation, so he does not deny his sexuality. According to news reports, the Ministry of Public Security altered the book's original ending so that Hoang renounces his homosexuality, and the second ending was printed only in the third edition of the book. In the new edition, Bui Anh Tan offers the original, second ending as an alternative to the first and urges the reader to decide which to choose.

The novel *A World without Women* is a sincere attempt to raise issues about the discrimination against and hatred toward gay men in Vietnamese society. In the foreword to the book, Bui Anh Tan urges for an informed, scientific debate about homosexuality, for people's compassion and sympathy, and for acceptance of homosexuals in Vietnamese society. The author states that homosexuality has become a widespread phenomenon in Vietnam only in the last few years and associates it closely with the influence of Western culture (Bui Anh Tan 2004 [2000]:6). The book represents gay culture as a foreign import, with gay men wearing Armani shirts and Levi's jeans and hanging out in a bar called Saigon Boys to flirt, drink, and listen and sing along to recordings by Western rock and pop artists, Madonna and Richard Clayderman among them. The rift between this "underground" culture and more mainstream social values is dramatized in the novel. Lan is torn between traditional family values and his love for his brother as he struggles to overcome his objections to Hoang's sexual orientation and lifestyle. Like Lan, the television viewer is drawn into the "the world without women" as the investigation of the gruesome murders unfolds.

The novel maintains that homosexuality is a recent urban phenomenon most prevalent among artistic groups like dancers, musicians, and actors. It psychoanalyzes homosexuality and questions whether some men are "truly homosexual" or whether they are merely following a trend. The narrative is oriented around the ostentatious, trendy gay scenes in urban centers, and homosexuality is said to be uncommon in rural areas (Bui Anh Tan 2004 [2000]:238). It is the visibility and apparent newness of the Western-influenced gay culture in urban areas that draws attention. During my time in Hanoi, I came across a small gay scene and spent some time with young gay men in their twenties and thirties (one of whom was a medium) who were known to frequent certain bars and nightclubs. Such nightlife is rare outside of the main cities, yet this does not of course necessarily mean that homosexuality is uncommon in rural areas. Notably, *A World without Women* makes no mention of the category of *dong co* or mediumship. The novel largely denies the existence of same-sex relations in traditional, rural society, so it precludes historical understanding of sexual activities outside of the heterosexual matrix.

Although *A World without Women* does not mention mediumship, in some popular writing in newspapers and magazines the category of *dong co* is conflated with a modern homosexual identity. For instance, a feature article, "The World of Witchcraft of *Dong Co*" ("The Gioi Ma Thuat cua Dan Dong Co"), which appeared in the women's lifestyle magazine *Marketing and Family* (*Tiep Thi va Gia Dinh*) in December 2004, harshly satirizes *dong co* as "gay guys" (*ga gay*) obsessed with sex, money, and the latest fashions. *Dong co* are portrayed as playboys, addicted to drugs and gambling, who "change their lovers as often as they change clothes." They are seen as outcastes, living outside the law, who have been abandoned by their families. Ritual music and dance is also associated with illicit, "wild" behavior. One of the pictures of *dong co* has the caption "Wild dance to noisy music."

The article recycles a key argument of the antisuperstition campaign: mediums are portrayed as thieving con artists who extort large sums of money from helpless people, and their merciless trickery is said to drive families to financial ruin and to destroy the fabric of society. But a new, modern twist is added to the old accusation that mediums "sell the spirits." It is *dong co*, not female mediums, who are singled out for vilification as "devilish" (*ma manh*) gay men who con gullible female religious followers for their own financial gain. The blame for "social evils" is placed squarely on the shoulders of homosexual mediums.

Most French and Vietnamese sources dating from the late colonial period that discuss the "male cult" of General Tran Hung Dao do not mention the sexuality or gender identity of male mediums. An article by Trong Lang published in 1935 is a notable exception. Do Thien summarizes the content of Trong Lang's article, which states that male mediums "supposedly had heartbreaking experience in love, were eccentric, obsequious and emotionally highly strung" and were known for their "good looks and feminine manners" (Do Thien 2003:105; 254). Do Thien adds, "their [male mediums] celibacy, according to Trong Lang's informers, stemmed from the fact that they were hermaphroditic. They were therefore considered 'safe' around women" (2003:104–5). Although Do Thien does not provide the Vietnamese term Trong Lang used for "hermaphrodite," it was more than likely *nua nam nua nu, ai nam ai nu* or *dong co*. Certainly, Trong Lang's article makes clear that male mediums in the late colonial period, like their contemporary counterparts, were known for their effeminacy and for assuming a variant sexual identity. Crucially, however, it does not suggest that male mediums were conceived of as "*pe de*"—from the French word *pédéraste*. The language of homosexuality is predominantly foreign. The French loanword *pe de* was adopted in the colonial era and is still used, but it is now increasingly being replaced with the English words *gay* and *homo*. The official Vietnamese term for homosexuality, *dong tinh luyen ai* (lit. "same-sex love"), is more formal. The conflation of *dong co* with a Western-style homosexual identity seems to be as recent as the imported English term "gay" and must be understood within the context of changing conceptions about homosexuality.

As previously mentioned, many contemporary religious followers do not think the category of *dong co* determines sexual identity or activity, nor does it necessarily prohibit male mediums from fulfilling social or family obligations. Male mediums may be celibate, single, or married and may or may not engage in sexual relations with other men. It is only with the imposition of the binary of homosexuality and heterosexuality that *dong co* is configured as a public, homosexual identity incompatible with the structure of the family.

It is tempting to compare *dong co* with *kathoey* in Thailand. Rosalind Morris's account of the historical transformation of discourses on gender and sexuality in Thailand has some interesting parallels with Vietnam. In Thailand, Morris highlights a "dialogic confrontation" between a historically prior tripartite system—"the system of the three" consisting of *phuuchai* (male), *phuuying* (female), and *kathoey* (transvestite/transsexual/hermaphrodite)—

and a newly emergent sex/gender "system of four" in which a "biological located opposition between male and female grounds a secondary . . . opposition between heterosexuality and homosexuality" (1994:28). Based on a reading of ancient religious texts, Morris argues that all three sexes in the system of three are of "equal materiality," by which she means that *kathoey* is a third point in the triad with the same ontological status as male and female. The importance of this is that the category of *kathoey* has often been celebrated by Western gender theorists as an escape from the binarity of male and female and the dominant heterosexual matrix. However, Morris argues that *kathoey* has come to be construed in modern Thailand as only a "category of maleness," an identity available only to homosexual men, because of its appropriation by Thai and Western patriarchal institutions and the importation of gay and lesbian identities from the West. In the earlier system of three, *kathoey* is not a "point of articulation" mediating naturalized identities of maleness and femaleness or an identity based on the binary system of hetero- and homosexual identities. Instead, in the tripartite system, "sexual and gender identity is conceived as a repertoire of public appearances and behaviors that is quite independent of the various subject positions and sexual practices available within the private realm" (Morris 1994:20). This separation of public and private is dissolved in the newly emergent sex/gender system "by bringing homoerotic desire into the public domain as *identity*" (Morris 1994:32. emphasis in original). Morris also makes the Foucauldian point that the redefinition of public identity in terms of patterns of sexual consumption "legitimates the surveillance of the private on the grounds that it affects the public world" (1994:32).

Notwithstanding the uniqueness of Thai and Vietnamese history and the different ways modernization has progressed in the two countries, the similarities between *kathoey* and *dong co* are compelling. The traditional conception of *dong co* as a public demeanor independent of sexual practices in the private realm is comparable with *kathoey* in the system of three. The public debate about homosexuality in Vietnam at the turn of the twenty-first century has influenced the meanings of the term *dong co*. Increasingly, men who are *dong co* are being perceived as "gay guys" and effeminate male mediums are themselves identifying with Western homosexual identities defined by sexual practice. Gay men are popularly thought to be promiscuous, and some mediums boasted and joked about having numerous lovers.[4] From the moral outrage about *dong co* that is now being voiced in popular discourse, we can see that the externalization of homosexuality as an identity has the effect of subjecting homoeroticism to new forms of control.

The emergence of modern gay identities is gathering pace. In 2005, male mediums referred to themselves as "gay" or "homo" much more readily and openly than in the mid-1990s. Some female mediums also remarked on change, saying that homosexuality was currently more prevalent among male mediums than it had been in the past. In Thailand, Morris contends that the system of the three has not entirely given way to the system of the four and that the coexistence of the two systems is "a dimension of the total social fabric" (1994:38). In Vietnam, coexistence is in evidence, as modern sexual identities have not entirely replaced the notion of *dong co* as an effeminate public demeanor. Many ritual participants, including some male mediums, do not assume *dong co* refers to a particular sexual orientation, but rather to men who have the aptitude to be possessed by female spirits and to act like women.

Like *kathoey*, *dong co* is a category available only to men.[5] Although female mediums have faced accusations of sexual promiscuity since the colonial period, this pertains only to affairs with male musicians, not with women. Traditionally, heterosexuality for Vietnamese women has been naturalized to such an extent that it precluded any other forms of female sexual activity, at least publicly. But there are some signs that this is changing. In the wake of the success of *A World without Women*, Bui Anh Tan's follow-up novel—*Les: Vong Tay Khong Dan Ong* (*Lesbians: An Embrace without Men*) (2005)—raises the issue of "lesbians" in society. It is too early to tell how debates about Vietnamese lesbians will develop. However, within the world of mediumship, female transgendering has not yet been permitted to alter a woman's sexual identity. In my discussions with ritual participants, some said they knew female mediums who had sexual relations with other women but that this was uncommon and unconnected to spirit possession. In this respect, it is significant that *bong cau* is not a widely used, popular expression like *dong co* and has not become enmeshed in modern discourse on homosexuality.

The Performance of Music and Gender

Spirit possession demands that mediums transgress lines of gender. Established gender identities are, to a certain extent, destabilized through transgendering ritual acts: male mediums assume an effeminate gender identity, and female mediums deal with aspects of their personalities, such as being difficult and hot-tempered, that are, according to widely propagated stereotypes, unfeminine. Mediumship therefore enables—indeed, requires—men and women to behave in ways that are outside of conventionally prescribed gender roles. It provides female mediums with possibilities of challenging patriarchy. It affords a space for female empathy and for women to be treated like "husbands and kings." However, the gender positionality of mediums is still made in relation to stereotypical, normative gender boundaries: male spirits exhibit idealized masculine traits, such as being prestigious and serious, and female spirits present idealized versions of soft and graceful women.

Musical performance is crucial to the traversing of gender. The gender characteristics of spirits are articulated not only through the ritual dress, movement, and words, but also through the use of distinctive *chau van* melodies and song texts for male and female spirits, which embody masculine and feminine characteristics. Musical performance enables mediums to dance and carry out ritual actions appropriate to the gender identity of the spirit. Music is therefore constitutive of the gender identities performed during *len dong*. Male musicians sing with the distinctive quality of "metal mixed with earth" and are adept at flattering female mediums in song. *Chau van* is a gendered music culture, in that it elaborates gender values.

Vietnamese mediumship defies reduction to a single, unitary interpretation. Rather, it is complex and contradictory: the system of mutual support fostered at rituals has to be measured against subservience to the spirits and the hierarchical nature of the pantheon of spirits; female mediums' increased access to the public domain should be balanced with the fact that many of them preside over private temples in the domestic realm; and female mediums' concern with family happiness needs to be understood in the context of some of them going against their husbands' will by becoming mediums and presenting other challenges to male authority. Ritual acts therefore do not constitute a voluntaristic construction or destabilizing of gender identities; rather they afford mediums—within clearly defined limits—a degree of flexibility to negotiate the conventional gender identities ascribed to men and women. Such negotiation is not merely confined to the ritual domain: it also affects mediums' everyday lives and has implications for the conceptualization of gender relations in Vietnamese society.

Mediums' performative negotiation of alternate gender identities is an aspect of discourse on gender and sexual identity, which complicates conventional readings of Vietnamese gender relations in terms of a rigid yin–yang binary. The gender identities performed during *len dong* stem from historical archetypes of masculinity and femininity embodied by the spirits, yet cross-dressing mediums negotiate these archetypes as they dance to gendered music. Regarding sexuality, female mediums have long faced accusations of immorality, and in emergent discourse on homosexuality, male mediums are incriminated as "gay guys." This intertwining of spirit possession and sexuality looks set to intensify as processes of modernization continue to unfold. The next chapter concludes with an account of further dimensions of modernization that are challenging the religious meanings of mediumship and its music.

7

Ritual and Folklorization in Late Socialist Vietnam

Cultural change has been as dramatic as economic change in late socialist Vietnam. In the realm of mediumship, market capitalism and higher levels of prosperity have most noticeably impacted upon the material conditions of rituals. Contemporary rituals are often opulent, and I begin this chapter by assessing whether the extravagance of rituals has altered the devotional purpose of spirit possession. Displays of affluence during *len dong* are bound up with mediums' commercial success as traders and entrepreneurs and their infamous reputation for being involved in illicit economic activities like smuggling and gambling. Stories of mediums' commercial prowess have shaped prerevolutionary as well as postrevolutionary perceptions of them, and mediumship practices have long been implicated in struggles for financial security and material well-being. However, the recent boom in the popularity of mediumship raises questions about how religiosity relates to the spread of the market economy. While economic issues have not superseded spiritual efficacy in matters of health and love, divine responses to financial concerns and anxieties are highly prized by religious devotees. Transacting with the spirits with the aim of financial assistance is also noticeably gendered and dovetails in interesting ways with the gendered structure of the economy.

Following discussion of how economic change has affected religious practices, we return in the latter part of this chapter to the themes of cultural nationalism and folklorization first introduced at the end of Chapter 1. The creation of secular, staged reenactments of spirit possession in the early 1990s is a significant development, as it marks a substantive shift in the public acknowledgment of mediumship. Instead of performing revolutionary *chau van,* which erased all references to spirit possession, state-run *cheo* troupes are now re-presenting possession on the stage as a celebration of "ritual," "folklore," "tradition," and "national culture." The folklorization of *len dong* is still in its early stages, but the commodification of ritual practices as entertainment, as well as the transfiguring of religious devotion as folklore, threatens to blur the boundaries between theatrical and spiritual performance.

Extravagant Rituals and the Exchange of Blessed Gifts

In late 2004, I stayed for several weeks at the house of a friend, an expatriate who was living in Hanoi for several years. My friend employed a Vietnamese woman in her thirties, let us call her Hanh, as a domestic helper, to clean the house. One morning in November, I was chatting to Hanh about my interest in mediumship, and she began to talk enthusiastically about her wish to become a medium. Hanh had consulted a spirit priest who confirmed that she had the "destined aptitude" of a medium, but she had not yet been initiated because she did not have enough money to do so. Hanh estimated the cost for her initiation ritual would be five million Vietnamese *dong* (approx. U.S. $350). She would have to buy all the ritual clothes, donate money to the temple, and pay for all the expenses of the initiation. These expenses included the fees for the band and spirit priest, purchasing the votive objects and gifts, and paying for the feast after the ritual. Hanh had two jobs, working for my friend in the morning and doing a cleaning job for a foreign company in the afternoon. Her combined income was about U.S. $130, a relatively high income compared with others in her village in Ha Tay province, from where she commuted five days a week on her Japanese motorbike. As the main money earner in her family, she spent most of her income supporting her children and other family members. Hanh thought it would take her many years to save up the money for the initiation, yet she was determined to become a medium whatever the cost. If she held *len dong,* Hanh said she would receive the support and assistance of the spirits and this would bring good luck, health, and prosperity to her and her family.

The considerable expense of rituals was often remarked upon by mediums, and the conviction that financial investment in religious activities would be beneficial was frequently expressed. One male medium told me he had to borrow a large sum, equivalent to twice his monthly salary, from friends so that he could organize his initiation ritual. After initiation, he was able to pay off his debts as he received donations from clients who consulted him about their health. Such stories of financial gain have long been seen by critics as selling the spirits. But the portrayal of mediums in antisuperstition propaganda as scheming fraudsters who make money out of gullible, ignorant religious devotees fails to take account of the cultural matrix within which exchanges of money are made and the morality of gifts (Parry and Bloch 1989). Typically, mediums attribute positive developments in their financial fortunes to the benevolence of spirits. One female medium described how all the fruit on her stall at the market used to rot before she could sell it. However, she found that after she was initiated she was able to sell her fruit more quickly and she stopped suffering losses. In her view, this change in fortune was due to her spirit worship: the spirits were satisfied by her devotion, so they had stopped punishing her.

The distribution of *loc* is a conspicuous feature of *len dong*. For each spirit possession, gifts are carefully chosen to suit the character and identity of each spirit and are even coordinated with the color associated with the spirit's palace in the celestial world. Prestigious male spirits usually distribute "male" products such as packs of cigarettes and cans of beer. An example of this can be seen in the DVD video extracts. When possessed by the Third Mandarin, Lai and Hang give out large trays stacked with cans of the popular "333" beer. This beer has a white can and is the favored brand for the Third Mandarin because it matches the spirit's white tunic and the color white signifies the Water Palace. Beer is inappropriate for female spirits, so while possessed by the Third Princess, who also belongs to the Water Palace and wears white clothes, Lai and Hang distribute trays of bottled water, cans of soft drink, and packets of soap. These gifts suggest the refreshing, rejuvenating qualities of the Water Palace. In general, natural products, such as fruit and areca nut, are distributed by female spirits belonging to the Mountains and Forest Palace, and other food products, like various types of Vietnamese savory and sweet cakes and imported packets of instant noodles and biscuits, are blessed by lowland female spirits. Packets of sweets are reserved for child spirits. An array of ritual products can be seen in Figure 7.1, which shows a female medium in her shop in Hanoi, which specializes in selling ritual goods.

Gifts are distributed to disciples in two main ways. The first involves an assistant preparing a large tray of gifts, bought in advance by the medium, which are blessed and distributed by the possessee. The second type of exchange is prompted by the disciples. These offerings usually consist of a small plate of money with other small items, like some cigarettes or small pieces of fruit. To make the offering, the disciple kneels behind the possessee and makes a plea for blessed gifts. Mediums sometimes throw a pair of coins to check that the spirits approve, and once the offering is accepted, some of it

Figure 7.1. A medium in her shop in Hanoi (2004)

is placed on the altar. The plate is then replenished with new bills and other small gifts before being returned to the disciple with the spirit's sanctification as *loc*.

When disciples receive *loc,* they are getting more than just money or products to consume. *Loc* is charged with spiritual power and brings with it good fortune and happiness. Blessed gifts are tangible manifestations of spiritual efficacy and have the potential to generate wealth. Many devotees claimed that *loc* had positively affected their livelihoods and well-being.

The reciprocity of making offerings and receiving *loc* is an expression of religious devotion, and it also establishes "sentimental relations" or *tinh cam* between ritual participants. In relation to funerary ceremonies, Malarney (2002) has discussed how *tinh cam* relationships between non-kin groups are a moral ideal. Displays of sentiment and sympathy for others through the exchange of gifts and attendance at ceremonies are a strong moral obligation and play an important role in governing social relations. In a similar fashion to funerary ceremonies, *len dong* is a site where *tinh cam* relationships flourish. Through the interactions that occur during rituals—the intimate muttering of wishes, pleas, and prayers when disciples approach the possessee, the fun and jocularity of receiving the gifts of the spirits, the sharing of thoughts and gossip with friends—participants are able to express their solidarity and sympathy for one another. Sentimental relationships are developed and maintained through morally charged exchanges. Friends, family, and disciples who attend rituals are in debt to the medium when they receive blessed gifts, but they reciprocate with their presence and through making their own offerings to the spirits. This system of gift exchange sets up a network of interdependence, mutual support, and empathy and provides the opportunity for antagonisms to be worked through.

The manner in which blessed gifts are distributed depends on the spirit incarnated. For prestigious high-ranking spirits like General Tran Hung Dao and the mandarin spirits, *loc* is given out in a controlled and formal way. But as the ritual progresses through the pantheon to the lady, prince, princess, and young prince spirits, the atmosphere becomes more informal and relaxed. When possessed by mountain spirits like the Second Lady, the Little Lady, and the Little Princesses, mediums often toss fruit and large bundles of small-denomination bills around the temple, causing much excitement and laughter among the ritual participants as they clamber for the *loc* (see Figures 7.2 and 7.3).

There is a widely held perception in mediumship circles that rituals were less elaborate and expensive in the past: the spirit's costumes were less ornate, the gifts distributed to disciples and the ritual feasts more modest, and

Figure 7.2. A male medium throwing money to participants at a *len dong* (2005)

Figure 7.3. A female medium distributing crabapples at a *len dong* (2005)

so on. Religious followers attributed the increase in the quantities of gifts and modern packaged goods to higher levels of prosperity. The opulence of contemporary rituals was generally seen as positive development by devotees; it made rituals more, rather than less, enjoyable. But some mediums and musicians, especially of the older generation, expressed their view that *len dong* had lost some of its "spiritual" (*tam linh*) character as a result of increased affluence.

Critics in the media have ridiculed the ostentatious display of modern consumer products during rituals and accuse mediums of being greedy and obsessed with consumerism and fashion. Some ritual participants also accused some new initiates of being "racing mediums" (*dong dua*), who just wanted to compete with their friends by "showing off" their wealth at lavish rituals, However, others argued that receiving *loc* was equally important in the past, it was just that people did not previously have the means to buy an abundance of gifts. Accounts of mediumship in the first half of the twentieth century confirm that *loc* was a central feature of rituals and was esteemed in much the same way as it is today (Long Chuong 1990 [1942]; Durand 1959). So despite the recent increases in the quantities of *loc*, there would seem to be no neat division between "capitalist" rituals in the reform era and rituals in a mythic "precapitalist" past.

Mediumship and the Market Economy

Criticism of ritual extravagance is tied to the long history of condemnation of mediums' commercial activities. In the late nineteenth century, female mediums who gained economic power from trading commodity goods were disparaged by Confucian scholars, and toward the end of the colonial period, wealthy women who called upon the spirits for help in business pursuits were derided by modernist intellectuals. After the communists gained power in northern Vietnam and implemented a centralized command economy, mediums came to be associated with the black market and smuggling as private trade and commerce were prohibited. As one musician remarked, many of the secret rituals he went to in the 1970s and 1980s were funded from smuggling across the Vietnam–China border. As a result of economic reform, many forms of private trade have been authorized and encouraged, but mediums are still rumored to be involved in illegal commerce and gambling.

Anthropologists working on religion have noted the relationships between the rise in religiosity and the booming capitalist economies of East and Southeast Asia. Robert Weller (1994) has argued that the "amoral ghost cult" in Taiwan has arisen as a way to deal with the unpredictability, insecurity, and competition of the capitalist market, which emphasizes individualism and utilitarianism above community values and shared morals. Laurel Kendall (1996) gives an account of how shamans in South Korea are increasingly called upon by their clients to hold rituals for good fortune, *chesu kut,* with the hope of ensuring business success and exerting some control over the seemingly arbitrary and precarious economic environment. In Thailand, Shigeharu Tanabe discusses spirit mediumship as "an object of modern consumption," suggesting that "Khon Müang spirit mediumship responds flexibly to the insecurity and anxiety caused by recent capitalist transformation and the territorial rearrangements of the nation-state in the globalised milieu" (2002:63). In Vietnam, Philip Taylor (2004) has linked the increase in the worship of the female goddess the Lady of the Realm (Ba Chua Xu) and the expansion of pilgrimage to the goddess's sacred shrines on Vietnam's border with Cambodia in southern Vietnam to the spread of market relations in the country.

Economic reform in late socialist Vietnam has provided new opportunities and higher levels of prosperity. During the early and mid-1990s, Vietnam experienced growth rates of up to 8 percent of GDP per annum and significant reductions in poverty levels (Haughton et al. 2001). However, the effects of the liberalized economy have been uneven, the gap between rich and poor has increased, and anxieties have arisen as a result of the uncertainty of the market (Beresford and Tran 2004). Although Vietnam was not affected as severely as some other countries that were rocked by the 1997 Asian economic crisis, since the late 1990s, foreign investment in Vietnam has fallen, growth rates have decreased, unemployment and underemployment have increased, prostitution and drug addiction have become prevalent in some areas, and there have been sporadic incidences of social protest and unrest in rural areas (Drummond and Thomas 2003).

Philip Taylor (2004) relates the rise in the worship of female goddesses to concerns about the volatility and unpredictability of "market relations" and connects the engendered nature of commerce to goddess worship. The entrepreneurial dominance of Vietnamese women has long been noted (Luong 1998), and Taylor argues that commercial-oriented goddesses like the Lady of the Realm have gained unprecedented prominence in the reform era because they represent and celebrate women's informal economic initiatives and success. Counter to the marginalization of women's place in the economic sphere by the "patriarchal political economic order of the state," according to Taylor the goddesses "represent a popular reworking and telling of history, where women's activity is considered socially central, where commercial prowess is highly valued, where smugglers are the epitome of efficacy" (2004:107).

Compared with goddess worship in the south, northern mediumship has many points of convergence, but also some important differences. Like the pilgrims who propitiate the Lady of the Realm, the predominantly female devotees of the Four Palace Religion are typically involved in small- or medium-scale commerce. Many are petty traders who sell goods at the market or in small retail outlets, and others own or manage small and medium-sized businesses such as hotels or shops selling items like jewelry and clothes. Government economic policy has drastically affected the activities of small-scale traders. One elderly female medium recalled the financial difficulties she encountered in the 1970s when the government prohibited private commerce: "I went into the highland region to sell bamboo shoots, but all [private] trading was banned and I was arrested. I lost everything and I was extremely worried . . . I was being punished by the spirits, so I became a medium . . . I pleaded to make a living from trade like before. After that, I managed to sell noodle soup, but I still had to borrow money off people who sold ritual goods. Three years after I was initiated I felt more relaxed." Such tales of financial adversity followed by recourse to the spirits demonstrate how mediumship can mediate and ease financial anxieties. While private commerce is now permitted and economic conditions have been improving, people working in the private sector now face the unpredictable fluctuations of the market, and anxieties and worries about financial security have not disappeared. Here it is pertinent to recall Hanh, the would-be medium, whose primary income depends on an expatriate remaining in the country and being employed by a foreign organization. Hanh's livelihood is dependent on international variables over which she has little or no control. Increasing integration into the global economy and the spread of capitalism have provided new economic opportunities, but these can also lead to a feeling of powerlessness, as the individual has little control over the "globalized" macroeconomic environment. For people like Hanh, the financial protection the spirits bestow on their followers offers a measure of security in a rapidly changing and volatile labor market.

While female followers of the Four Palace Religion hold an important place in the informal, private spheres of trade and commerce, they do not necessarily show a preference for female spirits like women who propitiate the Lady of the Realm. In the case of mediumship, the gendered relationships among mediums, spirits, and commercial prowess are complex. The rank of lady spirits and other female deities are known for distributing abundant gifts to disciples and for their power to bring prosperity to their followers. Yet it is not just female spirits who are valued for their economic resourcefulness: male spirits are at least as well known for bestowing gifts and financial assistance as female spirits. Also, many of the wealthiest Hanoi-based mediums I met identified most strongly with mandarins and princes, rather than female spirits. As noted in Chapter 6, male mediums' close affinity for female divinities was understood in terms of effeminacy, rather than struggles over economic agency. In general, male mediums, some of whom were successful businessmen, are wealthier than their female counterparts, so they do not experience the same feelings of economic instability, vulnerability, and powerlessness as female petty traders and entrepreneurs. They often attributed their economic power, affluence, and success to their skill and proficiency at organizing temple affairs. This pragmatic approach contrasts with female devotees' emphasis on the economic potency of spirits. Let us now turn to the links female mediums made between male spirits and commerce.

Historically, the feudal elite in northern Vietnam stigmatized commerce (Malarney 1998), and because many of the prestigious male spirits like General Tran Hung Dao and the mandarin spirits are considered to be senior figures of the feudal order, they are not particularly renowned for their activities as traders. Like mandarin spirits, the princes are also warriors and scholars, but they are lower in the pantheon hierarchy and more closely associated with the commercial sphere. One of the most popular spirits among female mediums is the Tenth Prince, who was reputedly a civil mandarin in the Le dynasty. A key reason why the Tenth Prince is favored is because he is known, as one medium put it, for "opening the store and giving out money" (*mo kho cho tien*). Hang, featured in Ritual 2 on the DVD, explained her relationship with the Tenth Prince in the following terms:

> I have the destined aptitude of the Tenth Prince. Why? Because I have a propensity for commerce, and the Tenth Prince also made a living from trade. I've received an education, but I finished studying after high school. I work in the private sector, I don't do government work . . . The Tenth Prince is extremely talented; [during rituals] he gives us money and capital. It is exhilarating! He is a "state trader" (*thuong nhan cua nha nuoc*) (pers. comm., Hang, December 2004)

Hang is the owner of a hotel, and she used to run an import–export company and a jewelry shop. Prior to the reform era, Hang said, "the state appropriated everything," so "the state prospered and the people lost out." It was only with the introduction of market capitalism that Hang began to prosper. Given Hang's views about the communist state-run economy and her success as a businesswoman, her description of the Tenth Prince as a state trader is fascinating. For Hang, the Tenth Prince is a representative of male-dominated state enterprise, and her strong relationship with the prince enables her to gain access to the "money and capital" of the state. Through having the destined aptitude of the Tenth Prince, female mediums like Hang bring patriarchal power to the center of their religious domain. During possession by the Tenth Prince, male economic power is embodied and state resources are symbolically distributed. Female mediums, then, do not just celebrate female economic prowess with recourse to female goddesses, they also access and appropriate the male-dominated economic power of the state through the embodiment of male spirits like the Tenth Prince.

One of the other most popular prince spirits, the Seventh Prince, is also associated with financial matters. Officially, the prince is a prestigious official, known for protecting the mountainous border area with China in the northern provinces of Yen Bai and Lao Cai. Unofficially, he is famous for being involved in the illicit world of gambling and drugs. As one female medium put it, "People who are traders and gamblers like the Seventh Prince. He is addicted to opium, he gambles. He is 'reserved' for people who gamble, for people who bet on card games and do the illegal lottery and the football pools."

During an incarnation of the prince at a *len dong* I attended in Ha Tay province, a man called Tuan approached the female possessee with an offering of money and cigarettes. While receiving the offering, the medium spoke about Tuan's gambling addiction and urged him to stay devoted to the deity. When I spoke to Tuan after the ritual, he said he had the destined aptitude of the Seventh Prince and had recently become a medium. Tuan had serious debts because of gambling, but since his initiation he said the prince, who shared his problems, had helped him control his gambling. Apart from Tuan, I knew female mediums who were trying to overcome their "addiction" to illegal lotteries, and for these women the Seventh Prince was a figure who understood the risks and hazards of gambling and was responsive to their plight.

In quite different ways, the Seventh and Tenth princes are implicated in the financial fortunes of their devotees. The errant, addictive personality of the Seventh Prince points to irregularities and fissures within the patriarchal regulation of the economic order in the northern border regions, whereas the Tenth Prince is a more orthodox representative of male-dominated state power. The increasing popularity of these spirits, especially among female mediums, shows the potential for the personalities and attributes of historical personages to be adapted and molded to suit changing societal and economic circumstances. At a time when the restructuring of the state and private sectors of the economy is an ongoing project and social problems like drug addiction and gambling are on the rise, spirits like the Seventh and Tenth princes are especially valued for their compassion and responsiveness. Interactions with embodied spirits provide an opportunity for exchange and support as people grapple with economic and social change.

* * *

Vietnamese mediumship is a multifaceted and flexible system. One of its strengths is its capacity to accommodate the diverse concerns and aspirations of its followers. Its popularity relies on appealing to a broad spectrum of the populace. The largest contingent of people who attend mediumship rituals are women involved in private enterprise, from business entrepreneurs to black-market traders, from petty traders to service-sector workers, but this does not mean that those working in the state sector, in agriculture, or in other areas are excluded. The diversity of the spirit pantheon enables followers from a wide range of backgrounds to forge distinctive patterns of religious devotion within the overarching framework. The Four Palace Religion is founded on the attributes and characters of spirits, and by developing special relationships with individual spirits who can address specific concerns, devotees mark out their own pathways through the pantheon and the complex of religious beliefs.

The introduction of "market socialism" in Vietnam has thrown up distinctive problems as well as benefits. Some of the relationships that followers of the Four Palace Religion develop with the spirits can be related to people's attempts to exert control over crucial matters relating to their livelihoods. In the context of increased opportunities for gaining personal wealth in the market economy, it is not surprising that some contemporary mediums hold rituals in the hope of riches. For some who have experienced the pitfalls and instabilities of the market system, recourse to spirits' economic assistance and protection offers a form of financial security. The large amount of gifts distributed during rituals has led to accusations that mediumship has become increasingly about financial reward. Yet economic issues are not always predominant, and spiritual efficacy does not pertain just to the financial arena. Individuals participate in spirit worship for diverse reasons, including reasons concerning matters of love, family relations, and physical and emotional health. Furthermore, the interrelationship between the spirits and the economic concerns of ritual participants has a long history; it is not a new phenomenon that has arisen with the spread of capitalism. In different historical periods, participation in mediumship has been a means by which people have sought to address, imagine, and control the economic realities affecting their lives. Nonetheless, the unprecedented numbers of people who have been drawn to mediumship in late socialist Vietnam can be linked to the strong need to make sense of the changes that have occurred as a result of economic reform and the latest drives toward industrialization and modernization. That the spirits can respond to this need is a measure of the efficacy attributed to them and their capacity to adapt to changing social and economic circumstances.

Ritual as Folklore

THE LANH GIANG FESTIVAL AND THE THREE SPIRITS

Early in the morning on April 1, 1997, I boarded a bus with Pham Van Ty and a group of followers of the Four Palace Religion, the majority of whom were elderly women. Our destination was the Lanh Giang temple (Den Lanh Giang) in Ha Nam province south of Hanoi. Ty had invited me on the trip so I could experience the festival celebrating the Lanh Giang temple's recent renovation and official designation as a "historical-cultural vestige."

When we arrived at the temple, hundreds of people were already at the site, milling around the temple complex. Ty showed me around the main temple, pointing out the various spirit altars and translating the inscriptions written in Sino-Vietnamese characters. The temple was full of pilgrims paying their respects to the spirits. The pilgrims kowtowed in front of the effigies of spirits, muttered prayers, presented offerings of incense and money, and put money in the temple donation box. While we were in the temple, a band entered and performed *nhac le* ceremonial music in front of altar of the Three Mothers. The band played "Luu Thuy" and other stately melodies on the two-stringed fiddle (*dan nhi*), three-stringed lute (*dan tam*), moon lute (*dan nguyet*), and bamboo flute (*sao*). The rhythmic accompaniment was provided by four girls, who danced in a square formation while beating *senh tien,* wooden percussion sticks with metal coins attached.

When the *nhac le* band finished performing, we followed them outside to the temple yard, which was crowded with people preparing for the "procession" or *ruoc,* the main event that was to take place later in the day. An elaborately carved sedan chair, painted in rich gold and red, had been placed in the yard. The sedan chair, Ty informed me, was the carriage for an effigy of the Mother Goddess of the Water Palace and would head the procession between Lanh Giang and another nearby temple. As we walked through the crowds, we passed a group of *dong co,* dressed in the colorful clothes of lady and princess spirits, who were playfully dancing with fans. The cross-dressed dancers stimulated much interest and amusement among the festivalgoers; they were surrounded by a large group of onlookers, who clapped along to the rhythm of the dance.

At the perimeter of the temple yard, a performance space had been set up by the local *cheo* troupe from Ha Nam province. Before modern proscenium-arch theaters were built, *cheo* performances took place in temple yards and other outside spaces in villages and towns. Following this traditional practice, the *cheo* "stage" at the festival was marked out by several raffia mats placed on the ground. Behind the performance space, a curtain screen had been erected and in front of the screen a framed photo of Ho Chi Minh was prominently displayed on a table. An audience of several hundred children and adults, some sitting in rows of chairs, crammed around the performance space.

After the obligatory speeches by local officials that formally announced the opening of the festival, the audience stood in silence for the national anthem, which was played on a tape through the sound system. The *cheo* troupe then began their performance with some folk songs. I positioned myself near the musicians on one side of the stage and started to film the performance. After renditions of *quan ho* and *vi dam* folk songs, I was surprised by what happened next: the troupe began to reenact scenes of spirit possession. This was the first time I had come across a "theatricalized" version of *len dong.* The performance lasted about thirty minutes and consisted of the reenactment of the incarnations of three different spirits: the Third Princess, the Little Young Prince, and the Second Lady. After the performance, Ty introduced me to the head of the troupe, Luong Duyen, who had played the role of the medium, and some of the musicians, including Duyen's husband, who was one of the main singers. Duyen referred to the performance, which had been devised by the troupe only a few months earlier, as *The Three Spirits* (*Ba Gia Dong*).

Watching *The Three Spirits* for the first time, it was immediately evident that it was closely modeled on *len dong*. The sequence of actions was similar, though not identical, to those a medium would carry out when possessed, and Duyen was surrounded by four artists playing the role of the medium's assistants. The music consisted of *chau van* songs, but the ensemble of four singers and six instrumentalists was larger than normal *chau van* bands.

In order to compare *len dong* and *The Three Spirits* in more detail, Table 7.1 details the reenactment of the possession by the Little Young Prince by the Ha Nam Cheo Troupe (formally known as the Nam Ha Cheo Troupe) and the ritual actions carried out when Hoa, the medium who held Ritual 1, was possessed by the same spirit. The video recording of the Ha Nam Cheo Troupe's performance is included under the "Ritual as Theatre" menu of the DVD.

The Three Spirits retains many aspects of the ritual progression: (1) possession by the spirit; (2) dressing in the clothes of the spirit; (3) dancing; (4) drinking rice wine; (5) termination of possession. Within this framework, however, there are a number of differences. For example, the reenactment of possession includes dances like the "horse riding" dance, which do not feature in *len dong*, and the ritual action of presenting incense to the altar is omitted. The sequence of songs performed during *The Three Spirits* conforms for the most part to the conventions employed in the construction of songscapes, although the music deviates from ritual convention on a few occasions. The use of a larger ensemble, unison singing, and ornate vocal ornamentation characteristic of *cheo* also means that *The Three Spirits* is stylistically different from *chau van* performances during *len dong*.

Perhaps more significant than the structural differences between *The Three Spirits* and *len dong* are differences in context and the manner in which ritual actions are carried out. Whereas the ritual actions of mediums are orientated toward the temple altar, there is no altar on the *cheo* stage, and Duyen faces the audience and directs her performance toward them. The performative interactions between a medium and her disciples are also quite different from the staged performance. The disciples present at Hoa's *len dong* participate

Table 7.1. Comparison of possession by the Little Young Prince (Cau Be) at Ritual 1 and the reenactment of possession by the Little Young Prince during *The Three Spirits*. English glosses of song titles are placed in brackets.

Len Dong		The Three Spirits	
Description of the actions of the medium (M) and her assistants (MAs)	Names of the *chau van* songs performed	Description of the actions of the *cheo* artist playing the role of the medium (C) and her assistants (CAs)	Names of *chau van* songs performed
M sits facing toward the altar and does not turn her back on the altar. A scarf is placed over M's head (*phu dien*), and her head gyrates (*lac dau*)	"Thinh Bong" (Inviting the Spirits)	C sits facing toward the audience and continues to face the audience throughout the performance; there is no altar. A scarf is placed over C's head, and her head gyrates	"Thinh Bong" (Inviting the Spirits)
M throws the scarf off. M remains sitting and changes clothes (*thay doi le phuc*), helped by the MAs. MAs remain seated throughout the possession	"Doc"	C throws the scarf off and changes clothes while standing, helped by the assistants. CAs stand and kneel around the C and wave their fans	"Doc"
M presents incense to the altar (*le dang huong*)	"Luu Thuy" at a stately tempo	—	—
M dances with bell-sticks (*mua heo*). The dance consists of hopping on one foot and shaking bell-sticks or beating them together in time with the rhythm of the music	"Luu Thuy" at a fast tempo	C dances with bell-sticks. The dance includes lifting one or other foot off the ground and beating the bell-sticks together in time with the rhythm of the music. C also makes 360–degree rotations	"Luu Thuy" at a fast tempo
—	—	C dances with swords (*mua kiem*). The dance includes energetically waving the swords and playfully thrusting them toward the CAs	"Trong Chien" (War Drums)

Table 7.1. Con't.

Len Dong		The Three Spirits	
Description of the actions of the medium (M) and her assistants (MAs)	Names of the *chau van* songs performed	Description of the actions of the *cheo* artist playing the role of the medium (C) and her assistants (CAs)	Names of *chau van* songs performed
—	—	C dances as if imitating riding a horse. CAs wave their scarves in time with the drum rhythm	Drum beats start slow and gradually increase in speed
M sits down to drink three cups of rice wine (*chuoc ruou*). Each cup of rice wine is blessed with incense prior to drinking. M remains seated for the rest of the possession	"Bi Tho Chuoc Ruou" (Pouring Rice Wine Prelude) "Nhip Mot Chuoc Ruou" (Pouring Rice Wine Melody)	C sits down to drink three cups of rice wine CAs join in singing Nhip Mot Chuoc Ruou and wave fans in time with the rhythm of the music	"Bi Tho Chuoc Ruou" (Pouring Rice Prelude) "Nhip Mot Chuoc Ruou" (Pouring Rice Wine Melody)
M distributes gifts (*phat loc*), including money, cigarettes, and packets of sweets. A disciple approaches M offering gifts and exchanges words with M	"Nhip Mot"	C acts drunk by swaying, rolling eyes, etc. CAs wave their fans in time with the rhythm of the music. C stands and walks around the performance space making gestures including imitating writing a poem on a fan. CAs move in formation around the performance space waving their fans. C gives out flowers to the CAs, which they put into their hair	"Bi" (Prelude) "Ban Chim Thuoc" (Shooting the Magpie Melody)
Scarf is thrown over M's head (*phu dien*)	Musicians sing the phrase "The spirit's carriage returns to the palace" (*xe gia hoi cung*)	C sits down and the scarf is thrown over C's head	Musicians sing the phrase: "The spirit's carriage returns to the palace" (*xe gia hoi cung*)

and affect events through dialogue and gift exchange, whereas the audience at *The Three Spirits* is relatively passive. During the reenactment of possession, there was no direct physical or verbal exchange between the *cheo* artists and the audience. Rather, the interactive aspects of *len dong* were enacted between the performers. This was achieved by the performers playing the role of the assistants behaving as if they were disciples at *len dong*. For example, they called out honorific phrases, such as *lay cau* (lit. "kowtow to the Young Prince"), and were given flowers. The assistants' role during *len dong* is to help the medium carry out ritual actions and to facilitate interaction between the medium and disciples, but during *The Three Spirits* the assistants' movements are choreographed to intensify the performance.

The work of performance theorists such as Schechner (1983) and Turner (1986) has given considerable attention to identifying the principal differences between ritual and theater. These differences have been neatly summarized by Beesman as revolving around three "dimensions": "efficacy vs entertainment, participation vs observation in audience's role, and symbolic representation vs literal self-presentation in the performer's role" (1993:379). In many respects, *len dong* and *The Three Spirits* may be placed at opposite ends of these three dimensions and be considered as ritual and theater, respectively.[1] The manner of performance during *The Three Spirits* reflects—indeed, promotes—the audience's role as passive spectators. In an attempt to make *The Three Spirits* an exciting theatrical display, Duyen's gestures are exaggerated to make them more visually appealing to the audience. As Duyen is not possessed, there is no attempt to mediate between the human and spirit worlds. By contrast, *len dong* is a forum in which the disciples interact with the spirits and receive divine advice and blessed gifts.

The Creation of The Three Spirits

After witnessing the Ha Nam Cheo Troupe at the festival, I asked Ty and other musicians more about *The Three Spirits*. It transpired that the first troupe to devise folklorized *len dong* was the Hanoi-based Vietnam Cheo Theater (Nha Hat Cheo Viet Nam). The performance item was created by the company in preparation for a tour to France in 1993, and there were also performances in Hue and Ho Chi Minh City in the same year.

The main architects of *The Three Spirits* were Tran Minh, the head of the Vietnamese Dancers Association (Hoi Nghe Si Mua Viet Nam), and Hoang Kieu, the vice director of the Film and Theatre Institute (Truong San Khau Dien Anh).[2] Because Tran Minh and Hoang Kieu held prestigious artistic posts, they were in a strong position to persuade Party officials to approve the performance item. As Tran Minh explained when I interviewed him in 2004, *The Three Spirits* encountered opposition from the Department of Performing Arts and the Ministry of Culture because some critics adhered to the view that *len dong* was superstitious and was inappropriate for presentation on the stage.[3] However, the mood in elite cultural circles was in flux. Many intellectuals and prominent figures in the arts were coming around to the view that *len dong* should be understood as "folklore," and this paved the way for the folklorization of mediumship. Tran Minh and other supporters of *The Three Spirits* overcame objections by convincing opponents that it was a legitimate theatrical performance with a traditional Vietnamese character. This argument was persuasive because it incorporated mediumship into the fold of "culture" and reiterated the government's nationalist cultural policy. At a time of growing concern about the effects of globalization on Vietnamese culture and society, performances of folk culture were beginning to be viewed by the government as a way to bolster national identity and to counter disruptive foreign influences. According to Tran Minh, the fact that *The Three Spirits* was created for performance abroad was also advantageous for gaining the official stamp of approval. Officials in the Ministry of Culture thought it would be beneficial to international relations to present "national folk culture" to foreign audiences and saw it as something of an antidote to international criticism of cultural and religious repression in Vietnam.

Both Tran Minh and Hoang Kieu wanted to adapt *len dong* for the stage many years earlier, but it was only in the new cultural climate of the reform era that they dared to do it (pers. comm., Hoang Kieu, November 2004). The inspiration for the project was personal as much as professional. Both men came into contact with, and developed respect for, mediumship at a young age because of relatives who were mediums. Prior to directing *The Three Spirits,* they attended *len dong* to observe and collect "primitive" ritual actions, dances, and costumes, which they thought were ripe for use in a theatrical context. In Tran Minh's estimation, *len dong* "had the beautiful, noble and aspiring way of thinking of the folk," yet he wanted to "improve" it and make it "more intellectual" (pers. comm., Tran Minh, November 2004).

Tran Minh and Hoang Kieu directed the choreography and staging of *The Three Spirits,* but they had no musical training, so it was left to the musicians at the Vietnam Cheo Theater to arrange the music. Dang Cong Hung, the main moon-lute player at the theater company, took on this responsibility. Hung's expertise as a *chau van* musician ensured that the music of *The Three Spirits* conformed to the conventions of songscapes.

The first performances by the Vietnam Cheo Theater group in France were by all accounts very successful. Hoang Kieu thought the warm reception of *The Three Spirits* in France was due to it seeming traditional: "The aim of the French tour was for foreigners to understand traditional culture . . . I know that foreigners like 'the traditional' (*cai truyen thong*); they don't like 'the modern' (*cai hien dai*) . . . The music and dance [of mediumship] was presented on the stage, but it kept to tradition" (pers. comm., Hoang Kieu, December 2004). Some of the international tours by neotraditional song and dance troupes after the implementation of the Renovation policy in 1986 had received a disappointing response from audiences and commentators, as they were perceived as being too modernized and "inauthentic." Just as Western tourists in Vietnam have not responded with much enthusiasm to neotraditional music (see Chapter 1), the neotraditional song and dance troupes who performed Western melodies on Vietnamese traditional instruments and Western-sounding harmonized arrangement of folk tunes on modified traditional instruments did not appreciate the desire of foreign audiences for a glimpse of the "real," "ethnic," "traditional" Vietnam. The creation of *The Three Spirits,* which plays on exotic notions of spirit possession and ritual, demonstrates the growing awareness among the directors of music and theater troupes of the expectations of foreign audiences, as well as of the changing views about what constitutes Vietnamese identity. Theatricalized *len dong* has been a successful concert item internationally. After the tour to France in 1993, different versions of folklorized *len dong* have entertained audiences in several countries in Europe and Asia. These include two tours for which I was the programmer: the Asian Music Circuit (AMC) tour in the UK in 1998, noted in the Introduction, and a tour in Holland and Belgium in 2001 organized by the Utrecht-based arts organization RASA.

Developing and Debating Folklore: From Three to Five Spirits

The musical community in Vietnam is well connected, and news of successful performances spreads quickly through the nationwide network of music institutions and troupes. Following the Vietnam Cheo Theater's international and domestic performances of *The Three Spirits,* it was not long before other troupes began rehearsing their own versions of it. After the Lanh Giang festival, I observed the development of folklorized *len dong* by attending more live performances by *cheo* troupes in Hanoi and by watching versions broadcast on Vietnamese television. To investigate how *The Three Spirits* had developed in provincial areas, in December 2004 I arranged a trip with Pham Van Ty to return to Ha Nam and the neighboring province of Nam Dinh. In 2004, the Ha Nam Cheo Troupe was still performing the version of *The Three Spirits* I had witnessed at Lanh Giang. But the Nam Dinh Cheo Troupe had devised a new performance item called *The Five Spirits* (*Nam Gia Dong*), consisting, as the name suggests, of the reenactment of five spirits: Goddess Lieu Hanh, Tran Hung Dao, the Princess Cam Duong, the Tenth Prince, and the Young Princess. Video extracts of *The Five Spirits* from a performance at the *cheo* theater in the town of Nam Dinh is included in the "Ritual as Theatre Menu" on the DVD.

Compared with *The Three Spirits,* the staging of *The Five Spirits* takes the drama and excitement to a new level. The flashing multicolored lighting, the booming amplified music, the elaborate costumes, and the vivacious choreography seem more akin to a rock concert than to a conventional *cheo* performance. According to the director of the troupe, Do Ngoc Vuong, *The Five Spirits* used theatrical devices to help convey the "mystical atmosphere" (*khong khi huyen bi*) of spirit possession. For the onset of possession of spirits like General Tran Hung Dao and the Princess Cam Duong, the stage was shrouded in semidarkness, the presence of the performers discernable only in fractured moments illuminated by the rapid flashing of a white strobe. The jagged movements of the performers under the strobe were matched by loud, amplified drumming, which sounded like it was rebounding off the walls of the theater because of the added reverberation. The strobe and the undulating colored lighting reminded me of the swirling, psychedelic lighting I saw at a performance by the Sabri Brothers of the Sufi music qawwali at Peter Gabriel's WOMAD festival in the UK. Just as the performance context of qawwali at WOMAD is a world away from the devotional qawwali assemblies held at shrines in India and Pakistan (Qureshi 1995 [1986]), so, too, is the staging of *The Five Spirits* quite different from devotional ritual performance in temples.

One of the most striking innovations of *The Five Spirits* is the inclusion of Goddess Lieu Hanh. During rituals, Lieu Hanh, like all the mother spirits, is incarnated only fleetingly and does not perform ritual actions, so the reenactment of possession cannot draw on the practices of *len dong*. The songs performed for Lieu Hanh are an amalgam of different songs—including a "Phu" melody, "Con Giay Lech," and "Xa Giay Lech"— conventionally performed for different male and female spirits, and the goddess's dance, which makes use of lanterns, is reminiscent of a popular folk dance, the "light dance" (*mua den*). The only "traditional" element of the Lieu Hanh performance in *The Five Spirits* was the use of the poems dedicated to the goddess, poems that are traditionally performed prior to *len dong* at *hat tho* sessions.

The theatrical performance of the goddess Lieu Hanh is a kind of "invented tradition," in Hobsbawn's sense, as it reconfigures old and new materials in a way that self-consciously implies a "continuity with a suitable historic past" (Hobsbawn 1983:1). The Nam Dinh Cheo Troupe included the goddess Lieu Hanh in their performances in order to celebrate their local history and heritage (pers. comm., Do Ngoc Vuong, December 2004). Because the goddess is thought to have lived as a mortal in the region and because of her mausoleum at Phu Giay, she is officially considered to be an important figure in the cultural history of the province.

One of the other four personas reenacted in *The Five Spirits*, General Tran Hung Dao, is also tied to the promotion of regional identity, as Nam Dinh is thought to be the general's native province (the other three spirits are associated with different regions in Vietnam). Like the goddess Lieu Hanh, the general is one of the most revered and famous deities in Vietnam. Yet, as noted in Chapter 2, the general has been embraced by the state as a national hero to a far greater extent than female deities like Lieu Hanh. In Nam Dinh, the official commemoration of General Tran Hung Dao as a symbol of national resistance and military prowess is being vigorously pursued by the authorities through the construction and reconstruction of temples and monuments and through elaborate state ceremonies (Trinh Quang Khanh 2000). The Bao Loc temple, dedicated to the general, and his mausoleum, both of which are in Nam Dinh province, have recently been renovated. The most noticeable monument in the city of Nam Dinh is an imposing bronze statue of the general that is over ten meters high and positioned on a large plinth in the center of the city. Completed in 2000, the statue was unveiled with an elaborate opening ceremony. Such projects are prominent examples of the "commemorative fever," which, as Hue-Tam Ho Tai notes, "is threatening to blanket the Vietnamese landscape with monuments to the worship of the past" (Ho Tai 2001:1).

The physical embodiment of General Tran Hung Dao on the stage is, at least potentially, more contentious than building commemorative monuments and memorials, because it implicitly acknowledges condemned practices of spirit possession. Like *len dong* itself, the reenactment of spirit possession on the stage can be seen as a commemorative ritual, in which bodily practices convey and sustain images of the past and collective cultural memory (Connerton 1989). But what is remembered in *The Five Spirits*, what is "encoded in set postures, gestures and movements" (Connerton 1989:59), is a past in which military heroism is prioritized and ecstatic acts of possession involving self-mutilation, which were carried out by male mediums who were possessed by the general in the past, are erased. The carefully choreographed reenactment of cultural memory in *The Five Spirits* leaves no room for deviation from the rehearsed sequence. Dressed as the general, the performer transmits a reassuring sense of national security and military strength by waving the old Vietnamese national flag and a wooden spear. The celebration of national military heroism is evident in *len dong* as well as *The Five Spirits*. Yet there is an unpredictability about ritual behavior that is precluded from folklorized reenactments. Mediums are strong and authoritative, often aggressive, when possessed by General Tran Hung Dao, and demand the respect of other ritual participants with impulsive, impetuous acts and words. In contrast to *The Five Spirits*, the past recalled and conveyed is not limited to the official narrative of national resistance to foreign aggression.

The performance of *The Five Spirits* was arranged at my request, and when it came to an end, Do Ngoc Vuong encouraged discussion between the members of the troupe and the small invited audience. Once the performers had mingled with the audience in the seating area of the auditorium, Pham Van Ty took the microphone and made an impromptu speech. As a specialist *chau van* performer and researcher, who was born and grew up in Nam Dinh province, Ty felt he was well qualified to express his opinions. He was broadly supportive, but praise was balanced with suggestions for improvement. His reflections on the performance ranged widely, but he concentrated mainly on the style and "authenticity" (*nguyen si*) of the music and song texts. For Ty, the inclusion of non–*chau van* songs, like the use of a *vi dam* folk song for the Tenth Prince, was inappropriate and unnecessary. There was no need to borrow songs from other genres, Ty reasoned, because of the large repertoire of *chau van* songs; the implication being that the *cheo* performers had only a limited knowledge of the repertoire. Ty urged the performers to improve their performances by learning special *chau van* drumming patterns, by using less amplification, and by singing more interesting song texts with the distinctive vocal style of ritual music. Ty's frank reflections on *The Five Spirits* demonstrate his strong commitment to maintaining high musical standards and the authenticity of folk culture, and he offered to work with the troupe to implement his suggestions.

The critique of *The Five Spirits* offered by Ty resonates with the view of folklorized performances as being "*chau van* mixed with *cheo*" (*chau van lai cheo*). The Vietnamese term *lai*, which I have rendered as "mixed with," has the negative connotation of being corrupted, tainted, and so on. When referring to the mixing of genres, *chau van* musicians argued that *cheo* performers used ritual songs, rhythms, and song texts inappropriately because of their lack of knowledge and made unacceptable stylistic changes, like the use of the ornate vocal style distinctive to *cheo* and faster tempos. Such comments may be in part due to professional protectionism. Bemoaning the loss of distinctive musical characteristics through the mixing of styles is also a common trope: a nostalgic trope that evokes an age when musical genres were considered to be pure and untainted by crossgenre influence.

Spirit Possession and Folklorization

In *Divine Utterances,* Katherine Hagedorn explores the process of folklori-cization and the interplay between "sacred" and "secular" in Afro-Cuban performance, between spirit possession during Santería religious events and staged folkloric renditions of African-based religious performance. Written in a reflexive, autobiographical mode, Hagedorn's account describes how she learned about "the sacred outside-in," how she learned about the music of Santería by studying with Cuba's national folkloric troupe, the Conjunto Folklórico Nacional de Cuba, before coming into contact with the religious context of the Santería drumming ceremony or *toque de santo* (Hagedorn 2001:3). African-based Cuban religions like Santería have been considered as folklore by many Cuban scholars since the early twentieth century, so the staged performances by the Conjunto Folklórico are a folkloric version of a folklore tradition. Hagedorn employs the term *folkloricization,* rather than folklorization, to refer to the "process of making a folk tradition folkloric" evident in performances by Conjunto Folklórico (2001:12). In Hagedorn's view, the extent to which a religious or folkloric performance is sacred or secular is dependent on the intention of the performers, the "rules of engagement," and the knowledge and background of the audience. Religious and folkloric events are both performative, and their meaning ultimately depends on the performers' intentionality and the interpretations of the audience.

The intentionality of the performers in theatricalized performances of *len dong* was unequivocal. *Cheo* artists who play the role of the medium and her assistants typically have little or no experience of mediumship and do not envisage their performance as engaging with spiritual forces. In discussions with Pham Van Ty prior to the AMC tour to the UK, I raised the possibility of inviting a practicing medium instead of professional performers who are not adepts of mediumship. I suspected my suggestion would be rejected because of censorship, but I wanted to explore the issues of authenticity it raised. Ty and the other artists involved in the tour were receptive to my suggestion but argued that there would be insurmountable obstacles with the Vietnamese Ministry of Culture and Information and immigration officials. Although many ritual specialists from other parts of the world have adapted rituals for urban performances—as, for example, Korean shamans have done (see Howard 1998)—the possibility of *len dong* being conducted by mediums outside the conventional ritual context is inconceivable in the present political climate. Yet even if Party objections could be overcome, it is highly unlikely that mediums would participate in folklorized performances, because they were skeptical of the idea of conducting spirit possession on the stage. Without the correct temple context, without "sacred mediums and sacred spirits" (*linh dong linh bong*), they said, possession would not be possible. On the other side of the equation, directors of *The Three Spirits* thought that mediums did not have the necessary skills to perform on the stage because they were "not professional performers" (pers. comm., Hoang Kieu, November 2004).

Unlike mediums, some *chau van* musicians, notably my teachers Ty and Hung, have been intimately involved in the folklorization process. Ty and Hung have both tried to ensure that the music of *The Three Spirits* is "authentic" in the sense that it is as close as possible to the music of *len dong* rituals. Nonetheless, they were very clear about the differences in meaning and context of ritual and theatrical performances. Ty is supportive of *The Three Spirits* because he sees its potential for increasing respect and knowledge of the rich musical traditions of mediumship within Vietnam and internationally, but he does not see theatrical reenactments as having religious content. Hung was more damning. He complied with the requests to arrange and perform the music for the first performances of *The Three Spirits* by the Vietnam Cheo Theater, yet he said it "did not have any meaning" because it had no connection to the sacred (pers. comm., Hung, January 2005). Without the correct ritual practice, Hung thought there was no sincerity, truth, or sacred purpose to the ritual or the music. This illustrates that, even if the authenticity of *chau van* is preserved in the folklorization process, the musical meaning changes dramatically depending on the performance context and musicians' intentionality.

The audiences for *The Three Spirits* can be divided into three main groups: (1) "foreigners" who typically know little about Vietnamese cultural and religious traditions and who see folklorized mediumship either in tourist-oriented performances in Vietnam or in theaters in other parts of the world;

(2) religious devotees who attend *len dong*; (3) Vietnamese who are unfamiliar with mediumship and *len dong* rituals and who have varying levels of familiarity with *cheo*.

As discussed above, *The Three Spirits* was devised in order to appeal to foreign audiences hungry for the traditional and the exotic. The performances of theatricalized *chau van* that I was involved in organizing in the UK, Holland, and Belgium captivated and fascinated the audiences. After some of the concerts, I was inevitably asked whether the ritual was "real" by audience members, but any uncertainties about authenticity did not seem to diminish the aesthetic impact or enjoyment of the spectacle. In Vietnam, *The Three Spirits* is usually performed on the *cheo* stage, alongside short extracts of famous scenes from *cheo* plays, renditions of folk songs, and other miscellaneous song and dance items. Such *cheo* programs consisting of short, varied items rather than a single play are now regularly performed, as part of a concerted attempt to attract larger audiences, both foreign and domestic.[4] *Cheo* is a narrative genre, which relies heavily on the appreciation of the story of the play and the words of the spoken dialogue and song, so there are problems of accessibility for foreign tourists, and *cheo* theaters have been slow to devise translation or subtitle services for non-Vietnamese speakers. Unlike some other genres, most notably water puppetry, which has become very successful with tourists, *cheo* has had only limited success being marketed for foreign consumption. Despite the presentation of lighter *cheo* programs of short items, including *The Three Spirits*, these performances have yet to become a major tourist attraction.

The mediums I met who had seen *The Three Spirits* were distinctly unimpressed. Most were dismissive of theatrical versions of mediumship, thinking it "false" (*gia*), "lacking flavor" (*vo vi*), and "unspiritual" (*khong co tam linh*). Although religious devotees did not think *The Three Spirits* had any sacred content, some interpreted it positively as a sign of increasing respect for mediumship. However, others did not see *The Three Spirits* in such benign terms and were wary of the motives for and consequences of presenting "religious beliefs" as a "folk culture."

The casual discussions I had with audiences of *The Three Spirits* at festivals and theaters suggest that it has been well received by Vietnamese who were not part of mediumship circles. Audience members remarked that they found the performance "interesting" and "enjoyable" and thought it was "very traditional." Stories about the miraculous deeds and unusual behavior of mediums have fueled popular interest in mediumship. For those who have never been to a *len dong*, mediumship has an aura of mystery and intrigue, not least because it has been outlawed for decades. *Cheo* artists put the enthusiasm for their performances down to curiosity for something "strange" (*la*). Folklorized mediumship provides a window on the mysterious sights and sounds of mediumship.

The language used by ritual participants to distinguish ritual from theatrical performance was precise. *The Three Spirits* was described as a "theatrical performance" (*bieu dien san khau*) whose aim was "to entertain" (*cho giai tri*), whereas *len dong* was referred to as a "spiritual performance" (*bieu dien tam linh*) that "served" (*hau*) the spirits. Despite these clear differences in context and function, it should not be assumed that spiritual efficacy is the sole function of *len dong,* nor that entertainment plays no part in ritual. In the discussion in Chapter 1 of the antisuperstition campaign, it was noted that a medium called Thang denied the efficacy of the spirits to cure illnesses. Although few mediums challenged the power of spirits to affect people's lives, Thang's views suggest that participation in mediumship is not necessarily reliant on spiritual causality. Also, efficacy is not the only measure of the success of *len dong.* Disciples would often debate whether the medium danced "beautifully" and whether ritual action and speech were carried out "well." In other words, they judged possession in performative terms, and the presence of the spirits had to be sustained in a creative and convincing manner to ensure ritual success. Seen from a performative perspective, *The Three Spirits* and *len dong* show points of convergence, even though performativity is foreground in *The Three Spirits* through bolder, more dynamic gestures and different use of the performance space.

The similarities between mediumship and theater have been discussed in some of the writing published by Vietnamese folklore scholars. Ngo Duc Thinh states emphatically that "all the components of *hau bong* [*len dong*] make it a specific theater performance where the leading part is played by the medium and the spectators are the cult faithful" (1999:59). He compares *len dong* with folk performing arts and concludes that "*hau bong* [*len dong*] is closer to the popular opera (*cheo*)" than other Vietnamese music genres, such as *ca tru* and *hat xam,* because it combines music, dance, and the spoken word (Ngo Duc Thinh 1999:60). At some levels this comparison merely points out that *len dong* has several performative elements, but Ngo Duc Thinh's assertion that spirit possession can itself be understood as a "theater performance" has important ramifications. This interpretation goes much further than the work of performance theorists who have seen ritual in analogy to theatrical performance or those who have championed the performative analysis of ritual (e.g., Laderman and Roseman 1996). As mediumship becomes increasingly interwoven with a culturalist ideology and becomes increasingly interpreted as a folk performance art, it is conceivable that the differentiation ritual participants made between *The Three Spirits* as theatrical performance and *len dong* as spiritual performance will become less clear. If *len dong* becomes widely understood as "folklore," then the term *folkloricization* could be appropriately applied to the process of creating theatricalized performances of *len dong*. However, the sacred dimension of *len dong* is still emphasized by contemporary mediums, and they cannot envisage performing rituals on the stage. Most ritual participants also have different expectations and intentions than the performers and audiences of *The Three Spirits,* so the "rules of engagement" in Vietnamese folkloric and religious performance are still relatively distinct, at least compared to the Cuban performances described by Hagedorn.

It is possible that as the reenactment of mediumship on the stage becomes more established and reaches large numbers of people through regular performances and television broadcasts that the public perception of mediumship will increasingly veer toward an understanding of mediums' practices as theater with little religious content. This would suit critics of *len dong* who, rather than condemning it as superstition, are now dismissive of it as mere entertainment. Or it may have contradictory, unpredictable effects. Mediums commonly refute the idea that *len dong* is a form of entertainment, but they are not immune to the flurry of folklorization. There are signs of professionalism in mediumship circles evidenced by professional temple mediums and musicians, and I even heard rumors that a *cheo* performer had been employed to teach a group of mediums dance moves to use when they were possessed. The current emphasis on mediums' visual appeal—the fascination with elaborate dances, costumes and cosmetics—opens up numerous possibilities for further interaction and exchange between "ritual" and "theater" as mediums vie for attention with dramatic performers. Certainly, the interplay between theatrical and ritual performance looks set to become more prevalent as mediumship practices become transfigured as "national folk culture."

Thanking the Spirits

A few weeks before I was due to leave Vietnam, Doan insisted she hold a *hau ta* or "thanking ritual" on my behalf. *Hau ta* are usually held one hundred days after initiation. They can also be arranged at other times when the expression of thanks to the spirits is deemed necessary. In my case, Doan said I should organize a *hau ta* to thank the spirits for overseeing my time in Vietnam and to pray for their assistance when I returned to my homeland.

Doan made this assertion at a fortune-telling session one afternoon in December 2004. On that same morning, Doan had held a *len dong* and, at her request, I had taken photographs of the ritual and of her friends, family, and disciples. Shortly after lunch, several people from the surrounding area came for fortune-telling consultations. Sitting in front of the temple altar, Doan slowly began preparing the areca nut she used to fortune-tell; when seeing clients Doan slices areca nuts in half and reads fortunes from the patterns inside the nut. While removing the betel leaves from the bunch of areca nuts, Doan declared she was possessed by the goddess Nguyet Ho (Ba Chua Nguyet Ho), a regional fortune-telling spirit who does not belong to the Four Palace pantheon. In 1996, when I first met Doan, she said that the Ninth Princess had enabled her to become a fortune-telling medium, but during my visits in 2004 and 2005 she attributed much of her continued success at prophesy to the goddess Nguyet Ho.

As soon as she was possessed by the goddess, Doan seemed distracted and moody, smiling one moment and scowling the next. Her voice had also changed. She spoke using playful, colloquial, and religious expressions, yet there was a forcefulness and impatience behind her words. I was expecting

Doan to begin fortune-telling for her guests. Instead, she cut an areca nut in two, examined one half, and began speaking to me:

> . . . The woman who gave birth to you was not English! I know everything, everywhere, in the sky, and down on earth. You are from abroad, so how do I know about you? Mortals like you respect me, we respect each other. The guardian of this temple, my disciple of the Van lineage [Doan], lets you come here and video without asking for anything because I have compassion for you. Do you know how great my compassion is? If you do not understand this clearly, then you cannot do interviews.

The lengthy speech that followed touched on many topics, from comparisons between Christianity and Buddhism to personal comments about where I lived in my homeland and how many siblings I had. Initially, I was not sure exactly what was happening: I had not asked to have my fortune told, and this was not a conventional prophesy. The use of colloquial expressions and old language made Doan's words hard to follow, but it was soon evident that the goddess was challenging and reflecting upon my presence and behavior. At one point Doan got upset. Tears welled up in her eyes, and she declared, as the goddess, that she was not satisfied with the photographs I had taken that morning. Her dissatisfaction stemmed from a group photograph of all the ritual participants, which had not included the "head of the household," Doan's husband. She said it was disrespectful not to include him and that to rectify the error I must show respect by organizing a *hau ta*.

In her book on spirit possession in northeast Thailand, Rosalind Morris recounts an incident when a Thai medium demanded she take a photograph of him while possessed by the child spirit Kumaannoj. On the occasion in question, Morris did not have a camera and Kumaannoj ends up, in a parody of photograph-taking Westerners, "rushing around the room while sputtering guttural sounds to evoke the camera" and eventually falling on top of her, much to the amusement of the medium's assistants (2000:188). Morris discusses Kumaannooj's aggressive and joking mimicry within the context of a sustained examination of the "history of appearances" in Thailand and the affinity between mediumship and photography as a symptom of modernity. Over the last three decades or so, Thai mediums have documented their possession performances with photography, and images of mediumship have been widely circulated in the mass media. It is through this new emphasis on mass-reproduced images, which Morris argues is rooted in modernity's fetishism of appearances and discourse on the preservation of "culture," that mediumship has come to require traditionalism, particularly the costume of the traditional, and to signify pastness.

The entwining of photography and mediumship in Vietnam is more recent than in Thailand, because various forms of technology, including photographic equipment, have become more affordable and widespread only in the last decade. Since I first encountered *len dong* at Phu Giay in 1995, mediums' self-documentation of their practices with photography and video has risen considerably. Except for a small group of prosperous Hanoi-based mediums, in the mid-1990s it was not common for mediums to collect photographs of their spirit possession performances, and even rarer for rituals to be videotaped. By the time of my last trip to Vietnam in 2004–5, this had all changed. Mediums now treasure photographs and videos of spirit possession as *ky niem,* as "memories" or "souvenirs." *Ky niem* are decidedly personal; images of spirit possession are not circulated widely in the mass media, mainly because of censorship. Mediums love to discuss these "memories"; they use them to assess the success and beauty of rituals. While poring over images of ritual, mediums often commented on changes in their outward appearance brought about by possession. For instance, distinctive bodily movements, a piercing look in the eyes, or youthful flushed cheeks were cited as evidence of the embodiment of spirits. Through the "truth of appearances," to borrow Morris's phrase (2000:190), the coquettish gracefulness of princesses, the regal strength and authority of mandarins, and the playfulness of child spirits are made manifest and recalled.

Mediums also lavish attention on their costumes when viewing images of possession. This is particularly true for the most elaborate "ethnic" clothes worn by female mountain spirits that draw on and promote exoticized notions of the "ethnic minorities" in Vietnam. Reports of the large sums of money mediums spend on colorful and flamboyant costumes has led critics to remark that *len dong* has lost much of its sacred quality and has become more like a fashion show. Similarly, Morris notes a "certain historical 'fashionability' (marked by the emergence of what can only be called the costume of generic pastness)" in Thai mediums' performances in the contemporary era (2000:181). In tracing the history of attire and photography in Thailand, Morris argues that it is "through photography that fashion assumed its capacity to represent culture" (2000:205). A thorough history of fashion and photography in Vietnam has yet to be written, yet there is no doubt that mediums' interest in self-portraiture has enhanced the importance of costume as a signifier of the spirits' identities and the past.

Doan's repeated requests for me to act as her cameraman, and the comments made by the goddess Nguyet Ho, demonstrate the significance placed on *ky niem*. My failure to please Doan with appropriate photographs was the main reason why I was told to organize a *hau ta,* but it was not the only one.

She added that I owed a great deal to the spirits because I had secured a job at a university because of my research and that my attempts to write a book would not be successful if I did not worship. Faced with the goddess Nguyet Ho's emotionally charged comments, I agreed—indeed, I felt compelled—to hold a thanking ritual. Doan consulted the lunar calendar for an auspicious date shortly before I was to leave Vietnam. The date chosen was the twelfth day of the twelfth lunar month.

Writing on "new fieldwork" in ethnomusicology has emphasized the need for reciprocity in fieldwork relationships, which are often inherently based on power asymmetries (Barz and Cooley 1997). Reciprocity is central to the exchanges between the spirits and followers of the Mother Religion. From a transactionalist standpoint, disciples serve the spirits through participating in *len dong* and in return receive divine protection and blessed gifts. By offering to hold a *hau ta* on my behalf, Doan was treating me like one of her disciples. By agreeing to the sponsor the *hau ta,* I could publicly show my respect for the spirits and for Doan. It was expected that I would finance the ritual, and I agreed to contribute U.S. $40. Doan stressed she would not profit from my contribution. The money, she said, would be used to cover the expenses of the ritual: it was needed to buy gifts, food, and drink and to pay the musicians and the spirit priest.

When I told Vietnamese friends in Hanoi about the *hau ta,* they were quick to ask how much it cost, and some cynically suggested that the whole event was just a ruse for Doan to make money. The view of mediums as con artists, which was propagated in the antisuperstition campaign, has persisted to some extent in popular consciousness and continues to be confirmed by critical voices in the media. Although Doan is one of the minority of mediums who make a living from fortune-telling, the general perception that mediums make money out of mediumship is unfounded. Most actually spend a great deal of their own money on rituals.

On the twelfth day of the twelfth lunar month, I woke early and rode by motorbike from Hanoi to Doan's house in Ha Tay province. When I arrived at 8.30 a.m., the house was already full of people. The visitors included relatives, friends, and disciples from the area, two local *chau van* musicians, Lan and Vinh, and a spirit priest called Vuong. In the background, a VCD of one of Doan's *len dong* was playing on the television, and the sound of *chau van* filled the room. The VCD had been filmed by a Vietnamese video company during a visit Doan made to Bac Le temple in northeast Vietnam.

I sat down to drink tea next to Vuong, the spirit priest. He wanted to check some of my details—where I lived in England, my year of birth, and so on—for the spirit petition he was preparing for the ritual. In one corner of the room, a young woman from the nearest town, about eight kilometers away, was applying makeup for the women involved in the ritual. She also made up the male musician Vinh: that a man wanted to wear makeup provoked much joking and laughter. Doan, though, said she was not going to wear too much makeup, because she thought it made her look old. After about half an hour of chatting and drinking tea, we went to Doan's private temple, next door to her house.

In the temple, Doan kneeled in front of the altar and muttered an incantation asking for the spirits' permission to hold a *hau ta,* before preparing for possession. The first spirit incarnated was General Tran Hung Dao. Dressed in a red tunic, Doan carried out the usual ritual actions: she kowtowed before the altar three times to the stately "Luu Thuy" melody, waved incense over written petitions to the spirits to the vibrant rhythms of the "Sai" melody. The spirit was then invited in song to drink rice wine and to appreciate refined poetry. Seated on a small plastic chair, Doan with a gruff cry signaled to the band to stop and declared: "For what purpose have I, the great Tran Hung Dao, been invited to 'descend' to the temple?" On hearing the question, Vuong stepped forward and read the spirit petition he had prepared. The petition, written in Sino-Vietnamese characters, used old terminology appropriate for addressing a thirteenth-century general:

> *Amitabha!* This winter, on the twelfth day of the twelfth lunar month, the medium, Doan, is holding a ritual for the "faithful" from London, England, whose name is Barley. He was born in the year of the pig. This person of the human world is holding a thanking ritual, as he has finished his business in Vietnam. He prays for talent and gifts, and for good progress in his work when he returns to England. Witness the ritual of the faithful who has a destined affinity for the spirits. The people of the human world worship, the musician Bui Thi Lan and the possessee serve you here in this temple. They wait for you to return and witness the ritual. *Amitabha!*

Doan responded:

> I, the great king of the Tran dynasty, descend to the temple. I witness the heart and praise the disciple from afar. [One of the mediums assistants called out, "*Amitabha!*"]. Praise the lineage that today respectfully worships . . . Work with all one's heart and you will be successful. Pray with your heart for honor and wealth, for your wishes to be fulfilled.

Having transmitted the words of the spirit, Doan's assistants threw the scarf over her head and the general "returned." The goddess Nguyet Ho was the second spirit incarnated. As the band sang the cheerful song "Xa Thuong," the assistants dressed Doan in a deep red and green, flowery long skirt with matching waistcoat and arranged a pink tiara-like hat with a flowing light green veil on her head. Once dressed, Doan stood and danced to the heavily accented one-beat rhythm of "Xa Mua Moi," first with a blue fan and then with four sticks set on fire. She then returned to sit in front of the altar, and her assistants gave her a large plate covered with a bunch of areca nuts. Doan took one of the areca nuts, sliced it in half, and glanced at it before giving it to me, recalling the fortune-telling session several weeks earlier. She then took another areca nut, wrapped it in a betel leaf pasted with a lime paste (*voi*), and chewed it. The rest of the nuts were given out to other ritual participants.

Although this was a *hau ta* with a specific purpose, it was expected that other ritual participants would interact with the spirits. Several disciples kneeled before Doan to offer gifts to the goddess Nguyet Ho. An elderly woman called Nghiem Thi Dau approached Doan with a plate, on which she had placed a fan, some small-denomination bank notes, and one betel nut. On receiving the offering, Doan said:

> The goddess Nguyet Ho returns! I crossed to this world for the Nghiem lineage. Today give all your heart to the Four Palace spirits. Make offerings to the goddess everywhere. The spirits force you to become a medium, but the Nghiem lineage has avoided kneeling and carrying the weight on your shoulders. Sit on the spirits' throne and become a medium! Concentrate all your inner feelings on the spirits. I transmit words for the Nghiem lineage: you must serve through ritual and return to the palaces of the other world so that you have "a cool stomach and satisfied heart" [i.e., are relaxed and content]. Today I, the goddess, give you orders and you must follow them! I observe and praise!

Another disciple, a woman called Quy, approached the goddess with a plate of money to seek advice about a recurring illness. Doan diagnosed Quy's complaint as having a human rather than a spiritual cause. She said: "The yin, other world protects you; take medicine and pray. Your stomach complaint is a human illness. . . . Today, call out to the goddess who saves and protects you with all your heart. Take the human medicine and then you will be cured, okay!" Doan took the bank note off the plate, put it on the altar, and replaced it with other notes before giving it back to Quy.

The next spirit to be incarnated was the Second Mandarin, who is often referred to as "the mandarin who supervises" (*quan giam sat*) because of his reputed powers to control and oversee the human world. Doan was dressed by her assistants in a green tunic, densely embroidered with gold, red, and white thread, and a sparkling silver sash was tied around her waist. In a similar way to the incarnation of General Tran Hung Dao, Doan stood up and kowtowed before the altar three times, before waving a bunch of incense sticks over petitions presented by the assistants. Doan then took the top petition, and kneeling before the outstretched petition held by the assistants, she proceeded to imitate writing old Sino-Vietnamese characters with a pen. She then performed a sword dance, before sitting cross-legged in front of the altar to drink rice wine and smoke cigarettes. At this point, I approached Doan and presented her with an offering: a plate with two 50,000 *dong* bills (about U.S. $6) and two cigarettes placed on it. She took the plate and declared:

> Today the disciple from afar, from abroad, comes to "the gate" of the community of spirits, to pray for success in his work in Vietnam. Plead to the spirit palaces for a thanking ritual. At the Four Palace gate, first I inspect and then I supervise. I return to witness! Pray for spiritual gifts and talent . . . Only if you study in a modern, advanced way will you be able to educate the young!

After this pronouncement, Doan took one of the notes off the plate and replaced it with several smaller notes and more cigarettes, and returned it to me. The *hau ta* concluded with two further spirit possessions by the Fifth Mandarin and the Little Lady.

The *hau ta* demonstrates the versatility of mediumship. Spirits have retained their relevance in modern Vietnam because of their capacity to speak to diverse issues and concerns, even those that arose from the investigations of an ethnomusicologist. During the *hau ta,* Doan adroitly drew on the spirits' talents: scholarly male spirits commented on the studies of a foreigner; powerful female mountain spirits addressed the health, well-being, and ritual commitment of other disciples. The Second Mandarin's exhortation that my work should be "modern" and "advanced" has often haunted me during the writing of this book. While I do not claim to have lived up to divine expectations, the fact that a mandarin spirit refers to the notion of the modern is a reminder of the pervasive influence of ideologies of modernity.

The vitality of *len dong* and *chau van* in these modernizing times is testament to their cultural and religious significance. Mediumship says so much about Vietnamese society and the recurrent collisions between "modernity" and "tradition." *Len dong* reflects the maintenance of tradition, yet it continues to be a contested site entangled with wide-reaching debates about cultural change, modernization and traditional music, national identity, gender, and religion. As long as *chau van* retains the power to evoke the spirits and to collapse the boundaries between the human and spirit worlds, mediumship will continue to inform these debates and to profoundly affect the lives of ritual participants.

As I watched Doan dance joyously, brandishing two ropes set on fire, I was struck by the words of the song, "Xa Mua Moi," being performed by the band. The words neatly encapsulated Vietnamese hopes for a more peaceful and beautiful future. Without the "illumination" of music and dance, without the songs for the spirits, it is hard to imagine such a future:

> The light of the candles flickers on the mountain shack.
> The Little Lady dances with two lit ropes for the mother spirits.
> Make the nation and people prosperous and powerful.
> Illuminate Vietnam and make it peaceful.
> Spread light near and far.
> Illuminate the mountains, rivers and flowers.
> Illuminate the imperial city.
> Illuminate the country and make it more beautiful.

Appendix

The Pantheon of Spirits

The pantheon below includes the spirits incarnated at *len dong* I attended from 1996 to 2005. Many spirits are referred to by more than one name; two Vietnamese alternatives are given for some spirits. Asterisks indicate those spirits who possess mediums only in an unrevealed way; the scarf draped over the medium's head is not removed. For spirits who belong to one of the four palaces, the palace of the spirit is noted: Sky Palace (SP), Water Palace (WP), Mountains and Forests Palace (M&FP), Earth Palace (EP). In some cases, opinion differs about which palace a spirit belongs to; a spirit's palace is not noted in ambiguous cases.

The Mother Spirits (*Mau*)

The First Mother (Mau De Nhat/Mau Lieu Hanh)*—SP
The Second Mother (Mau De Nhi/Mau Dia)*—EP
The Third Mother (Mau De Tam/Mau Thuong)*—M&FP
The Fourth Mother (Mau De Tu/Mau Thoai)*—WP

The "Tran Family" Spirits

General Tran Hung Dao
The Second Princess (of the Tran dynasty) (Co Doi nha Tran)
The Little Princess (of the Tran Dynasty) (Co Bo nha Tran)*
The Little Young Prince (of the Tran dynasty) (Co Bo nha Tran)*

The Mandarin Spirits (*Quan*)

The First Mandarin (Quan De Nhat)—SP
The Second Mandarin (Quan De Nhi)—M&FP

The Third Mandarin (Quan De Tam)—WP
The Fourth Mandarin (Quan De Tu)—EP
The Fifth Mandarin (Quan De Ngu/Quan Tuan Tranh)—WP
The Mandarin Dieu That (Quan Dieu That)*
The Second Mandarin Hoang Trieu (Quan Doi Hoang Trieu)

The Lady Spirits (*Chau*)

The First Lady (Chau De Nhat)—SP
The Second Lady (Chau De Nhi) —M&FP
The Third Lady (Chau De Tam) —WP
The Lady of the Temple (Chau Thu Den)
The Lady Thac Bo (Chau Thac Bo)
The Fourth Lady (Chau De Tu)*
The Fifth Lady (Chau De Ngu)*
The Sixth Lady (Chau Luc) —M&FP
The Seventh Lady (Chau Bay)*
The Eighth Lady (Chau Tam)*
The Ninth Lady (Chau Cuu)*
The Tenth Lady (Chau Muoi)—EP
The Little Lady (Chau Be) —M&FP

The Prince Spirits (*Ong Hoang*)

The First Prince (Ong Hoang De Nhat)* —SP
The Second Prince (Ong Hoang De Nhi)* —M&FP
The Third Prince (Ong Hoang Bo) —WP
The Seventh Prince (Ong Hoang Bay) —M&FP
The Tenth Prince (Ong Hoang Muoi) —EP

The Princess Spirits (*Co*)

The First Princess (Co De Nhat)—SP
The Second Princess of the Mountains (Co Doi Thuong)—M&FP
The Second Princess Cam Duong (Co Doi Cam Duong)
The Third Princess (Co Bo)—WP
The Fourth Princess (Co De Tu)—EP
The Fifth Princess (Co De Ngu)*
The Sixth Princess (Co Sau)—M&FP
The Seventh Princess (Co Bay)*
The Eighth Princess (Co Tam)*
The Ninth Princess (Co Chin)—EP
The Tenth Princess (Co Muoi)*

The Little Princess of the Mountains (Co Be Thuong)—M&FP
The Little Princess Dong Cuong (Co Be Dong Cuong)
The Little Princess Bac Le (Co Be Bac Le)—M&FP

The Young Prince Spirits (*Cau*)

The First Young Prince (Cau De Nhat)—SP
The Second Young Prince (Cau De Nhi)—M&FP
The Third Young Prince (Cau Bo)—WP
The Little Young Prince (Cau Be)—M&FP

Notes

Introduction

1. There are a number of Vietnamese terms used to refer to mediumship rituals and its music. Throughout this book I employ the most commonly used terms, *len dong* (lit. "mount the medium") and *chau van* (lit. "serving literature"). Mediumship rituals are also referred to as *hau bong* (lit. "serving the shadows [spirits]") or *dong bong* (lit. "medium and shadows [spirits]").

2. Maurice Durand's classic book, which documents the practice of mediumship at the end of the colonial era, is the only substantial work by a non-Vietnamese scholar that concerns mediumship in Vietnam (Durand 1959). Two other studies provide accounts of mediumship as practiced by the Vietnamese diaspora in France (Simon and Simon-Barouh 1976) and America (Fjelstad 1995). See also Fjelstad and Nguyen's (2006) edited volume for recent contributions to scholarship on mediumship by several Vietnamese and non-Vietnamese researchers. For further essays on religious revival in contemporary Vietnam, see Taylor (2007).

3. The lack of attention paid to *chau van* by Vietnamese scholars is evident in the fact that a seven-volume compendium of articles written in the twentieth century on Vietnamese music does not include any that focus on *chau van* (Vietnamese Institute for Musicology 2003). Thanh Ha is one of the few scholars who published articles on *chau van* music that focus on the analysis of scales and musical structure, before the reform era (e.g., Thanh Ha 1976).

4. There is a distinctive style of chau van in central Vietnam, and an examination of the differences between the northern and central styles of mediumship music would be an interesting topic for a future research project. Mediumship practices in central Vietnam also have many differences from *len dong* in the north. For instance, instead of the goddess Lieu Hanh, one of the main spirits worshipped in central Vietnam is

the Cham goddess Thien Ya Na (see Ngo Duc Thinh 1996a). In southern Vietnam, spirit possession is much less common, and when rituals are held the style of *chau van* music performed is similar to that heard in the northern tradition. In the south, *len dong* are known as *roi bong* (lit. "purification ritual of the spirits").

5. Trinh T. Minh-Ha, for instance, offers the following critique of "giving voice" in relation to documentary filmmakers' discourse: "For despite their denial of conventional notions of objectivity and contempt for romantic naturalism, they continue to ask: how can we be more objective?, better *capture the essence?*, 'see them as they see each other?' and '*let them* speak for themselves?' Among the validated strategies that reflect such a yearning and state of mind are: the long take, hand-held camera, sync-sound (authentic sound) overlaid with omniscient commentary (the *human science* rationale), wide angle lens, and anti-aestheticism (the natural versus the beautiful, or the real/native versus the fictional/foreign)" (1991:56–57, emphases in original).

6. This track appears on the two-CD compilation *Further East–Westercisms* (Law & Auder Records 1998, LA 4CD).

Chapter 1: Mediumship, Modernity, and Cultural Identity

1. Various terms are used for male and female mediums. The word *dong,* meaning "medium," can be preceded with personal pronouns indicating the sex, age, and status. Female mediums are usually referred to as *ba dong* or *co dong* (for older and younger women, respectively), and male mediums are usually referred to as *ong dong* or *cau dong* (for older and younger men, respectively). See Nguyen Khac Kham (1983) for further discussion of the terminology of Vietnamese mediumship.

2. Based on a police report from 1933, Do Thien notes the wide range of social backgrounds of females and especially the involvement of Vietnamese women married to Europeans (2003:98).

3. From Section 5 of Directive 56–CP of the Party Committee on the elimination of superstition, 13.3.1975.

4. "Que Ta" is frequently performed and broadcast and was one of the pieces in a concert I attended at the Youth Culture Palace (Cung Thieu Nhi) in November 1996, which commemorated forty years since the founding of the Hanoi Music Conservatoire. Another neotraditional composition influenced by *chau van* as well as the music of Hue is Thao Giang's "Du Thuyen Tren Song Huong" (Drifting in a Boat on the Perfume River), written in 1991.

5. The use of the term *hat van* (lit. "singing literature") is significant, as it is a more neutral term than *chau van* (lit. "praising literature"), which is closely associated with mediumship.

6. The Land Reform Campaign from 1953 to 1956 was followed by a Campaign for the Correction of Errors (1956–58), which tried to rectify some of the severe problems that resulted from collectivization. When I asked Xuan Khai if he had thought about writing a composition that reflected the problems of collectivization, he said

he wanted to write music that portrayed the beautiful and interesting aspects of Vietnam and he did not see it as the composer's role to critique society or the state (pers. comm., Xuan Khai, January 2005).

7. Le Loi expelled the Ming dynasty Chinese administrators who had control over Vietnam from 1407, and he established the Le dynasty in 1428.

Chapter 2: Experiencing Spirit Possession

1. One medium in Hanoi has been known to incarnate the female bodhisattva Quan Am in a ritual known as *hau Phat* ("serving the Buddha") (pers. comm., Katie Dyt). Quan Am is not incarnated during *len dong*, although there are similarities between *hau Phat* and *len dong*.

2. Rare instances of possession by snake and tiger spirits are briefly discussed in other scholars' accounts (e.g., Simon and Simon-Barouh 1973:57 and Nguyen Thi Hien 2002).

3. The policy of recognizing historical-cultural sites was a change from previous Party policy toward sacred places. In the years following 1954, many temples, pagodas, and village communal houses were destroyed, disused, or used for nonritual purposes such as storing farm produce (see Endres 2001; Malarney 2002).

4. The terms *can* and *can so* are difficult to translate. The literal meaning of *can* is "root" or "basis," and *so* means "fate" or "destiny." Some scholars have translated *can* as "spirit root" (e.g., Nguyen Thi Hien 2002). However, I translate *can/can so* as "destined aptitude," as mediums described *can/can so* as a kind of natural, fated ability or aptitude for mediumship, analogous to "talent" (*nang khieu*) for music. *Can* forms the first syllable in several compound expressions, such as *can dong* (where *dong* means "medium") and *can soi/can boi* (where *soi* and *boi* refer to "fortune-telling"). *Can dong* may be translated more fully as the "destined aptitude for mediumship" and *can soi/can boi* as "the destined aptitude for fortune-telling." The expressions *can mang* and *can menh* were also used as synonyms for *can so* (like the word *so, mang* and *menh* mean "fate" or "destiny").

5. The problem of "knotted hair" can lead to a rite of "combing out the hair" (*chai toc*), which takes place prior to initiation. See Nguyen Thi Hien (2002:82–83).

6. Although the vast majority of mediums carry out initiation rituals, some devotees who have a particularly "high aptitude and heavy fate" (*can cao so nang*) become mediums without a formal initiation.

7. The Renaissance meaning of *obsession* persisted into the nineteenth century. The *obsession* entry in the *Shorter Oxford English Dictionary* (Third Edition, Vol. 2), for instance, gives the following citation from 1871: "These cases belong rather to obsession than possession, the spirits not actually inhabiting the bodies, but hanging or hovering about them."

8. The term *me* is used in the title the VTV documentary about my research where I translate it as "love" to make the English translation more smooth: *A Westerner Loves*

Our Music (*Nguoi Tay Me Nhac Ta*). Here *me* refers to "infatuation" for Vietnamese music.

9. *Me* possession might be described as a "crisis." However, *obsession* is preferable because the term *crisis* has often been applied to many different states that do not involve possession. The afflictions Vietnamese mediums experience prior to initiation do not always involve involuntary possession.

10. See, for example, Nguyen Thi Hien (2002) and Nguyen Kim Hien (1996). Durand states that mediums "attempt to enter trance" (*tentatives d'entrer en transes*) (1959:15), although he is cautious about asserting that a trance state is always achieved. In Durand's interpretation, *len dong* is a vestige "of the ancient magic of the technique of trance" (*de l'ancienne magie la technique de la transe*) (1959:47).

11. Csordas's consideration of the body as a subject, rather than an object, is informed by Merleau-Ponty's phenomenology of perception and his concept of the preobjective (Merleau-Ponty 1962).

12. When quoting mediums' comments, I have translated *dau, oc,* and *dau oc* as "head," "brain," and "mind," respectively, but the distinctions between these terms did not seem to be important for mediums, as they used them interchangeably.

13. When mediums talked about possession, they used the compound words that I have rendered as "heart-soul." However, it should be noted that there are other words meaning "soul"—*hon, linh, linh hon*—that do not include *tam* or "heart."

Chapter 3: Songs for the Spirits

1. The idea of a songscape as a sonic environment has some similarities with R. Murray Schafer's term *soundscape* (Schafer 1977). However, *songscape* refers specifically to the sequences of songs performed for spirits during *len dong,* and I do not share the premises, aims, or methods of Schafer's analyses of acoustic environments.

2. *Chau van* bands are generally referred to as *cung van* and resident bands as *cung van truong. Cung* means "offer to," and *van* means "literature"; therefore, Durand renders *cung van* as "texts offered to the spirits" (1959:29). *Truong* means "head" or "principal."

3. The placement of bar lines and the choice of meter are often arbitrary in oral musical traditions that are not notated. Although my *chau van* teachers were familiar with Western staff notation, they did not conceive of the one-, two- and three-beat rhythms in terms of "bars" and so did not consider the rhythms to have a "downbeat." The transcriptions of the rhythms are arranged here so that the accented beat of each rhythm falls on the first beat of the bar. Bar lines are included in the transcriptions in this book because it makes the scores easier to read; they do not represent an emic view of metrical organization.

4. The Vietnamese government recognizes the achievement of individual artists through two official titles. The highest accolade is "People's Artist" (Nghe Si Nhan Dan), and this is followed by "Artist of Merit" (Nghe Si Uu Tu).

5. These "linking phrases" are known as *xuyen tam* in *cheo* theater pieces (Hoang Kieu 1974), although *chau van* musicians did not often use this term.

6. The ranks of spirits not represented are the mother, the young prince, and the "Tran family" spirits. Possession by a mother spirit has not been included because they are never fully incarnated: they "descend" only for a short period, and the scarf draped over the medium's head is not removed. Possession by a young prince or by one of the Tran family spirits is not included because there are many similarities between the music and ritual actions of these ranks of spirits and other ranks: the incarnations of the young princes are similar to those of the princes, while those of the Tran family spirits are similar to those of the mandarins and ladies.

7. "Don" is conventionally performed as an exciting conclusion before the spirit leaves the medium's body. In Video Extract 4, Hung changes from "Phu Noi" to "Don" because he anticipates the incarnation of the Third Mandarin will shortly come to a close. In fact, Hung turns out to be mistaken, because the possession continues for some time. After playing the "Don" melody for nearly five minutes, Hung realizes the possession is not about to finish, so he suggests to Cao Mon to change to the "Cao Mons Melody" (Video Extract 5).

8. This is not to say that all the songs performed after the medium's dance are un-affected by her movements. Exceptions include the melodies performed when the Tenth Prince is drinking rice wine; changes in melody prompted by the spirit's im-minent "return"; and cases when the medium actually asks the musicians to change songs. However, most of the songs performed after the medium stops dancing are not prompted by a particular ritual action, unlike the earlier songs.

Chapter 4: The Musical Construction of the Spirits

1. The only exception to this distinction is when, on rare occasions, a "Xa" melody is included in songscapes for the Seventh Prince. However, the songscapes for the Seventh Prince always include many non-"Xa" melodies. This is in contrast to the songscapes for female mountain spirits, which consist entirely of "Xa" melodies.

2. There are a few exceptions to this rule. Three "Phu" melodies, "Phu Dau," "Phu Ha," and "Phu Van Dan (Nu Than)," may be sung for female spirits during *len dong*. However, these melodies are very rarely performed and have been adopted from the *hat tho* repertoire. Furthermore, they are not typical "Phu" melodies (e.g., they are sung to the two-beat instead of the three-beat rhythm). Also, "Con Hue" is performed during possession by the Tenth Prince, but this is because of its associations with music in central Vietnam.

Chapter 5: Musical Creativity and Change

1. In *chau van*, the vocal line is predominant and the use of pitched instruments, apart from the moon lute, is optional. Although I do not consider here how the backbone of songs influences the instrumental accompaniment to the voice, my

discussions with *chau van* musicians indicate that the vocal melody acts like a guide for all the instrumentalists.

2. Abstracted backbones might have been called "abstracted melodies," a term employed by Giovanni Giuriati in his study of Khmer music (1988). Giuriati's abstracted melodies are similar to implicit melody concepts in Javanese gamelan, in that they are not actually performed but are the foundation for group improvisation (1988:244). I use the term *abstracted backbone* in the context of *chau van* because it is an extension of Hung's concept of backbone and to avoid confusion with Giuriati's term. Abstracted backbones are derived from multiple performances of songs, whereas abstracted melodies are abstracted from the multipart texture of Khmer ensemble music.

3. Hung's backbone for phrase 1 of "Phu Binh" includes two additional notes that do not appear in his abstracted backbone: the use of G as a "passing note" on two occasions in bar 3. It is likely that these "passing notes," which ensure the melody proceeds in stepwise motion, are included to make the melody more fluent and memorable. The version of the backbone Hung performed uses end pattern 1 rather than end pattern 2.

4. Numerous papers in Vietnamese have delineated how poems are set to songs, but the influence of speech tones on melody is mentioned only briefly by scholars (e.g., Tran Van Khe 1975).

5. In *chau van,* speech tones are not represented by a system of melodic formulas as they are in Thai court song (see Tanese-Ito 1988). Also, the use of certain pitches for certain speech tones, what Bell Yung (1989) calls "pitch matching," does not occur in *chau van* singing.

6. For a more detailed analysis, see Norton (2000).

7. The division of the melodic contours into four categories is adopted from Schimmelpenninck (1997). This classification, which is based on speech tones of Wu dialects in China, works well for Vietnamese speech tones, as all follow one of the four melodic contours.

8. Vocables were not taken into account when determining the relative pitch level of syllables. Usually pitch succession is unaffected by vocables, which suggests that relative pitch level is still usually significant even when vocables are used. However, it should be noted that sometimes the use of vocables did obscure the relative pitch level between syllables, and this accounts for some of the exceptions to the rules outlined in Table 5.2.

9. Although copyright law is still virtually nonexistent in Vietnam, some first steps have recently been taken. In 2002 the Vietnam Music Copyright Protection Agency was established under the directorship of the composer Pho Duc Phuong, and in 2004 Vietnam became a signatory of the Berne Convention for the Protection of Literary and Artistic Works, which establishes the right of the creator of a work of music or text to some kind of remuneration.

10. Dan died before my fieldwork. The changes he initiated were reported to me

by musicians who knew him, especially my teacher Dang Cong Hung and Dan's son-in-law, Ho Viet Chi.

Chapter 6: Engendering Mediumship

1. "Mac" refers to the general Mac Dang Dung, who overthrew the Le dynasty and briefly became king in the sixteenth century.

2. The songs that are *exclusively* performed for male and female lowland spirits use different rhythms: the "serious" songs for male spirits, the "lyrical" songs for female lowland spirits, and all the songs for female mountain spirits make use of the three-beat, two-beat, and one-beat rhythms, respectively. However, it should be noted that the percussion rhythms do not always neatly correlate with gender, as some songs associated with particular ritual actions are performed for both male and female lowland spirits.

3. Xuan Hinh—one of the most famous contemporary *cheo* singers, best known for his performances of the clown character (*he*)—released *chau van* recordings during the 1990s, and he sings *chau van* with his characteristic light and comic style. Although *chau van* musicians criticized Xuan Hinh for singing ritual music with a *cheo* singing style, some mediums said they preferred his voice to the less "polished," more "nasal" singing of some *chau van* musicians.

4. The filmmaker Nguyen Trinh Thi has recently produced an excellent feature documentary, *Love Man Love Woman,* which profiles Duc, a Hanoian male medium. The film shows Duc's romantic antics with other men on the phone and on the Internet and offers reflection on the status of gay men in Vietnamese society.

5. Morris (1994) suggests that in the past the category *kathoey* was not open only to men. Further historical research is needed to establish whether this is the case for *dong co.*

Chapter 7: Ritual and Folklorization in Late Socialist Vietnam

1. While a distinction between "theater" and "ritual" is useful for comparing *The Three Spirits* and *len dong,* it should be emphasized that the designation of *len dong* as "ritual" (*le hoi*) is itself a feature of the nationalist discourse on "national culture" and "tradition."

2. Although the Vietnam Cheo Theater gave the first public performances of *The Three Spirits,* Pham Van Ty said he was the first person to organize a theatricalized performance of spirit possession when in 1991 he performed a program of *chau van* for other artists at the Musicians' Association (Hoi Nhac Si) with members of the Vietnam Cheo Theater acting the scenes of spirit possession. According to Ty, Tran Minh attended this performance and it inspired him to develop the idea further.

3. One point of contention, Tran Minh recalled, was the name given to the performance. Tran Minh initially referred to it during meetings with official bodies as

"A Worship and Praise Ceremony" (Le Chau Le Bai) or as "Singing Praise to Three Spirits" (Ba Gia Hat Chau), rather than *Ba Gia Dong*, literally "*The Three Spirits of the Medium*," which I translate simply as *The Three Spirits*. Tran Minh was very conscious of avoiding the term *dong*, meaning "medium," so as not to sully the performance with superstitious connotations. *Ba Gia Hat Chau* is still sometimes used, but *Ba Gia Dong* emerged as the predominant name.

4. There has been much debate in academic and artistic circles about the direction, popularity, and standards of *cheo;* see, for example, Theatre Publishing House (1995).

Bibliography

Agawu, Kofi. 1988. "Tone and Tune: The Evidence of Northern Ewe Music." *Africa* 58: 127–46.

Arana, Miranda. 1999. *Neotraditional Music in Vietnam.* Kent, Ohio: Nhac Viet.

Atkinson, Jane M. 1992. "Shamanisms Today." *Annual Review of Anthropology* 21: 307–30.

Baily, John. 1989. "Filmmaking as Musical Ethnography." *World of Music* 31(3): 3–20.

Bakan, Michael B. 1999. *Music of Death and New Creation: Experiences in the World of Balinese Gamelan Beleganjur.* Chicago and London: University of Chicago Press.

Barbiracki, Carol. 1997. "What's the Difference? Reflections on Gender and Research in Village India." In G. F. Barz and T. J. Cooley (eds.), *Shadows in the Field: New Perspectives for Fieldwork in Ethnomusicology,* pp. 121–36. New York and Oxford: Oxford University Press.

Barlow, Tani. 1991. "Theorizing Woman: Funu, Guojia, Jiating [Chinese Women, Chinese State, Chinese Family]," *Genders* 10: 132–60.

Barry, Kathleen. 1996. "Introduction." In K. Barry (ed.), *Vietnam's Women in Transition,* pp. 1–18. Basingstoke, UK: Macmillan.

Barz, Gregory E., and Timothy J. Cooley (eds.). 1997. *Shadows in the Field: New Perspectives for Fieldwork in Ethnomusicology.* New York and Oxford: Oxford University Press.

Becker, Judith. 2004. *Deep Listeners: Music, Emotion and Trancing.* Bloomington: Indiana University Press.

Beeman, William O. 1993. "The Anthropology of Theatre and Spectacle." *Annual Review of Anthropology* 22: 369–93.

Beresford, Melanie, and Tran Ngoc Angie (eds.). 2004. *Reaching for the Dream: Challenges of Sustainable Development in Vietnam.* Copenhagen: NIAS Press.

Blacking, John. 1973. *How Musical Is Man?* Seattle: University of Washington Press.

Blacking, John. 1995 [1977]. "The Study of Musical Change." In R. Byron (ed.), *Music, Culture and Experience: Selected Papers of John Blacking*, pp. 148–73. Chicago and London: University of Chicago Press.

Boddy, Janice. 1989. *Wombs and Alien Spirits: Women, Men and the Zar Cult in Northern Sudan*. Madison: University of Wisconsin Press.

Boddy, Janice. 1994. "Spirit Possession Revisited: Beyond Instrumentality." *Annual Review of Anthropology* 23: 407–34.

Bohlman, Philip V. 2002. *World Music: A Very Short Introduction*. New York: Oxford University Press.

Brettell, Caroline B., and Carolyn F. Sargent (eds.). 2005. *Gender in Cross-Cultural Perspective*. Upper Saddle River, N.J.: Pearson Prentice Hall.

Brinner, Benjamin. 1995. *Knowing Music, Making Music: Javanese Gamelan and the Theory of Musical Competence and Interaction*. Chicago and London: University of Chicago Press.

Buchanan, Donna A. 1995. "Metaphors of Power, Metaphors of Truth: The Politics of Music Professionalism in Bulgarian Folk Orchestras." *Ethnomusicology* 39(3): 381–416.

Bui Anh Tan. 2004 [2000]. *Mot the Gioi Khong Co Dan Ba* (*A World without Women*). Ho Chi Minh City: Nha Xuat Ban Cong An Nhan Dan.

Bui Anh Tan. 2005. *Les—Vong Tay Khong Dan Ong* (*Lesbians—An Embrace without Men*). Ho Chi Minh City: Nha Xuat Ban Tre.

Bui Dinh Thao and Nguyen Quang Hai. 1996. *Hat Chau Van*. Ha Noi Nha Xuat Ban Am Nhac.

Butler, Judith. 1990. *Gender Trouble: Feminism and the Subversion of Identity*. New York and London: Routledge.

Butler, Judith. 1993. *Bodies That Matter*. New York and London: Routledge.

Cadière, Leopold. 1992 [1955]. *Croyances et Pratiques Religieuses des Viêtnamiens*. Paris: École Français d'Extrême-Orient.

Clifford, James, and George E. Marcus (eds.). 1986. *Writing Culture: The Poetics and Politics of Ethnography*. Berkeley, Los Angeles, and London: University of California Press.

Comaroff, Jean, and Comaroff, John (eds.). 1993. *Modernity and Its Malcontents: Ritual and Power in Postcolonial Africa*. Chicago and London: University of Chicago Press.

Connerton, Paul. 1989. *How Societies Remember*. Cambridge, UK: Cambridge University Press.

Cooley, Timothy J. 2003. "Theorizing Fieldwork Impact: Malinowski, Peasant-Love and Friendship." *British Journal of Ethnomusicology* 12(1): 1–18.

Csordas, Thomas J. 1994. "Introduction: The Body as Representation and Being-in-the-World." In T. J. Csordas (ed.), *Embodiment and Experience: The Existential Ground of Culture and Self*, pp. 1–24. Cambridge, UK: Cambridge University Press.

Csordas, Thomas J. 1999. "Embodiment and Cultural Phenomenology." In G. Weiss and H. F. Haber (eds.), *Perspectives on Embodiment: The Intersections of Nature and Culture*, pp. 143–62. New York and London: Routledge.

Csordas, Thomas J. 2002. *Body/Meaning/Healing*. Basingstoke and New York: Palgrave Macmillan.

Dang Nghiem Van et al. 1984. *The Ethnic Minorities in Vietnam*. Hanoi: Foreign Languages Publishing House.

Dao Trong Tu. 1984. "Renaissance of Vietnamese Music." In Dao Trong Tu, Huy Tran and Tu Ngoc (eds.), *Essays on Vietnamese Music*, pp. 96–161. Hanoi: Foreign Languages Publishing House.

DeNora, Tia. 2000. *Music in Everyday Life*. Cambridge, UK: Cambridge University Press.

Diguet, Ernest. 1906. *Les Annamites: Société, Coutumes, Religions*. Paris: Augustin Challamel.

Do Thien. 2003. *Vietnamese Supernaturalism: Views from the Southern Region*. London and New York: RoutledgeCurzon.

Dong Vinh. 1999. "The Cult of Holy Mothers in Central Vietnam." *Vietnamese Studies* 131: 73–88.

Dror, Olga. 2002. "Doan Thi Diem's 'Story of the Van Cat Goddess' as a Story of Emancipation." *Journal of Southeast Asian Studies* 33(1): 63–76.

Drummond, Lisa B. W. 2003. "Popular Television and Images of Urban Life." In L. B. W. Drummond and M. Thomas (eds.), *Consuming Urban Culture in Contemporary Vietnam*, pp. 155–69. London and New York: RoutledgeCurzon.

Drummond, Lisa B. W., and Mandy Thomas (eds.). 2003. *Consuming Urban Culture in Contemporary Vietnam*. London and New York: RoutledgeCurzon.

Dumoutier, Georges. 1908. *Essais sur les Tonkinois*. Hanoi-Hai Phong: Imprimerie d'Extrême-Orient.

Durand, Maurice. 1959. *Technique et Panthéon des Médiums Viêtnamiens*. Paris: École Français d'Extrême-Orient.

Emoff, Ron. 2002. *Recollecting from the Past: Musical Practice and Spirit Possession on the East Coast of Madagascar*. Middletown, Conn.: Wesleyan University Press.

Endres, Kirsten W. 2001. "Local Dynamics of Renegotiating Ritual Space in Northern Vietnam: The Case of the *Dinh*." *Sojourn: Journal of Social Issues in Southeast Asia* 16(1): 70–101.

Erlmann, Veit. 1982. "Trance and Music in the Hausa Bòorii Spirit Possession Cult in Niger." *Ethnomusicology* 26(1): 49–58.

Fabian, Johannes. 1990. *Power and Performance: Ethnographic Explorations through Proverbial Wisdom and Theatre in Shaba, Zaire*. Madison: University of Wisconsin Press.

Feld, Steven. 1990 [1982]. *Sound and Sentiment: Birds, Weeping, Poetics, and Song in Kaluli Expression*. Philadelphia: University of Pennsylvania Press.

Fjelstad, Karen. 1995. "Tu Phu Cong Dong: Vietnamese Women and Spirit Possession in the San Francisco Bay Area." PhD dissertation: University of Hawai'i.

Fjelstad, Karen, and Hien Thi Nguyen (eds.). 2006. *Possessed by the Spirits: Mediumship in Contemporary Vietnamese Communities*. Ithaca, N.Y.: Cornell Southeast Asia Program.

Frenier, Mariam Darce, and Kimberly Mancini. 1996. "Vietnamese Women in a Confucian Setting: The Causes of the Initial Decline in the Status of East Asian Women." In K. Barry (ed.), *Vietnam's Women in Transition*, pp. 21–37. Basingstoke, UK: Macmillan.

Friedson, Steven M. 1996. *Dancing Prophets: Musical Experience in Tumbuka Healing*. Chicago and London: University of Chicago Press.

Frith, Simon. 1996. "Music and Identity." In S. Hall and P. du Gay (eds.), *Questions of Cultural Identity*, pp. 108–27. London: Sage.

Gammeltoft, Tine. 1999. *Women's Bodies, Women's Worries: Health and Family Planning in a Vietnamese Rural Community*. Richmond, Va.: Curzon.

Gibbs, Jason. 2004. "The West's Songs, Our Songs: The Introduction and Adaptation of Western Popular Song in Vietnam before 1940." *Asian Music* 35(1): 57–83.

Giran, Paul. 1912. *Magie et Religion Annamites: Introduction à une Philosophie de la Civilisation du Peuple d'Annam*. Paris: Augustin Challamel.

Giuriati, Giovanni. 1988. "Khmer Traditional Music in Washington." PhD dissertation: University of Maryland–Baltimore County.

Ha Huy Giap 1972. "Nam Vung Von Dan Toc, Hoc Tap Tinh Hoa the Gioi De Xay Dung Mot Nen Am Nhac Hien Thuc Xa Hoi Chu Nghia Viet Nam" ("Grasp the National Heritage and Study the Best Elements of the World to Build the Socialist Music of Vietnam"). In *Ve Tinh Dan Toc Trong Am Nhac Viet Nam* (*On National Character in Vietnamese Music*), pp. 5–20. Ha Noi: Nha Xuat Ban Van Hoa.

Ha Nam Ninh Cultural Service. 1976. *Day! Thuc Chat Hoi Phu Giay* (*Here! The Real Essence of the Phu Giay Festival*). Ha Nam Ninh: Ty Van Hoa Ha Nam Ninh.

Hagedorn, Katherine. 2001. *Divine Utterances: The Performance of Afro-Cuban Santería*. Washington and London: Smithsonian Institution Press.

Hamayon, Roberte N. 1995. "A Three-Step History of a Long Scholarship on Shamanism: Devilization, Medicalization, Idealization." *Louis H. Jordan Lectures in Comparative Religion*, SOAS.

Haughton, Dominique et al. (eds.) 2001. *Living Standards during an Economic Boom: The Case of Vietnam*. Hanoi: Statistical Publishing House.

Ho Chi Minh. 1976 [1958]. "Bai Noi Chuyen Tai Hoi Nghi Can Bo Van Hoa" ("Speech at the Conference of Cultural Cadres"). In Ho Chi Minh et al. (eds.), *Ve Van Hoa Van Nghe* (*On Culture and Art*), pp. 83–86. Ha Noi: Nha Xuat Ban Van Hoa.

Ho Chi Minh et al. 1976. *Ve Van Hoa Van Nghe* (*On Culture and Art*). Ha Noi: Nha Xuat Ban Van Hoa.

Ho Tai, Hue-Tam. 2001. "Introduction: Situating Memory." In Hue-Tam Ho Tai (ed.), *The Country of Memory: Remaking the Past in Late Socialist Vietnam*, pp. 1–17. Berkeley and Los Angeles: University of California Press.

Hoang Dam. 2003. *Hoa Tau Bien Hoa Long Ban: Am Nhac Co Truyen Nguoi Viet* (*Performing Heterophony: Traditional Vietnamese Music*). Ha Noi: Vien Am Nhac.

Hoang Kieu. 1974. *Su Dung Lan Dieu Cheo* (*The Use of Cheo Melodies*). Ha Noi: Nha Xuat Ban Van Hoa.

Hobsbawn, Eric. 1983. "Introduction: Inventing Traditions." In E. Hobsbawn and T. Ranger (eds.), *The Invention of Tradition*, pp. 1–14. Cambridge, UK: Cambridge University Press.

Howard, Keith. 1998. "Preserving the Spirits? Rituals, State Sponsorship and Performance." In Keith Howard (ed.), *Korean Shamanism: Revivals, Survivals and Change*, pp. 187–207. Seoul: Royal Asiatic Society Korea Branch.

Hughes-Freeland, Felicia. 1992. "Representation by the Other: Indonesian Cultural Documentation." In P. I. Crawford and D. Turton (eds.), *Film as Ethnography*, 242–56. Manchester, UK: Manchester University Press.

Jackson, Michael. 1989. *Paths toward a Clearing*. Gainesville: University of Florida Press.

Jähnichen, Gisa. 1991. "On the History of Composition in Vietnamese Musical Culture." In Jürgen Elsner and Gisa Jähnichen (eds.), *Studies in Ethnomusicology 1: Oriental Music*, pp. 85–97. Berlin: Humbolt-Universität zu Berlin/Institut für Musikwissenschaft and Musikerzeihung.

Jamieson, Neil L. 1993. *Understanding Vietnam*. Berkeley and Los Angeles: University of California Press.

Jones, Stephen. 1999. "Chinese Ritual Music under Mao and Deng." *British Journal of Ethnomusicology* 35(1): 27–66.

Kapferer, Bruce. 1991 [1983]. *A Celebration of Demons: Exorcism and the Aesthetics of Healing in Sri Lanka*. Oxford and Washington: Berg and Smithsonian Institution Press.

Kendall, Laurel. 1985. *Shamans, Housewives, and Other Restless Spirits: Women in Korean Ritual Life*. Honolulu: University of Hawai'i Press.

Kendall, Laurel. 1996. "Korean Shamans and the Spirits of Capitalism." *American Anthropologist* 98(3): 512–27.

Kendall, Laurel. 2005. "Shamans, Bodies, and Sex: Misreading a Korean Ritual." In C. B. Brettell and C. F. Sargent (eds.), *Gender in Cross-Cultural Perspective*, 430–42. Upper Saddle River, N.J.: Pearson Prentice Hall.

Keyes, Charles, Laurel Kendall, and Helen Hardacre (eds.) 1994. *Asian Visions of Authority: Religion and the Modern States of East and Southeast Asia*. Honolulu: University of Hawai'i Press.

Kleinen, John. 1999. *Facing the Future, Reviving the Past: A Study of Social Change in a Northern Vietnamese Village*. Singapore: Institute of Southeast Asian Studies.

Kulick, Don, and Margaret Willson (eds.) 1995. *Taboo: Sex, Identity and Erotic Subjectivity in Anthropological Fieldwork*. New York and London: Routledge.

Laderman, Carol, and Marina Roseman (eds.). 1996. *The Performance of Healing*. New York and London: Routledge.

Lambek, Michael. 1998. "Body and Mind in Mind, Body and Mind in Body." In M. Lambek and A. Strathern (eds.), *Bodies and Persons: Comparative Perspectives from Africa and Melanesia*, pp. 103–26. Cambridge, UK: Cambridge University Press.

Lao Cai Cultural and Information Service. 1964. *Cai Tao Phong Tuc Tap Quan* (*Reforming Customs*). Lao Cai: Ty Van Hoa Thong Tin Lao-Cai.

Le, Chan Ngoc. 2002. "Quan Ho Singing in North Vietnam: A Yearning for Resolution." PhD dissertation: University of California, Berkeley.

Le Thi and Do Thi Binh. 1997. *Ten Years of Progress of Vietnamese Women, from 1985 to 1995*. Hanoi: Phunu Publishing House.

Le Tuan Hung. 1998. *Dan Tranh Music in Vietnam: Traditions and Innovations*. Melbourne: Australian Asia Foundation.

Levin, Theodore. 1996. *The Hundred Thousand Fools of God: Musical Travels in Central Asia*. Bloomington and Indianapolis: Indiana University Press.

Lewis, I. M. 1989 [1971]. *Ecstatic Religion: A Study of Shamanism and Spirit Possession*. London: Routledge.

Long Chuong. 1990 [1942]. *Hau Thanh* (*Serving the Spirits*). Ha Noi: Nha Xuat Ban Ha Noi.

Luong, Hy Van. 1998. "Engendering Entrepreneurship: Ideologies and Political-Economic Transformation in a Northern Vietnaemse Center of Ceramics Production." In Robert Hefner (ed.), *Market Cultures: Society and Morality in the New Asian Capitalisms,* pp. 290–314. St Leonards, Australia: Allen and Unwin.

Magrini, Tullia (ed.). 2003. *Music and Gender: Perspectives from the Mediterranean*. Chicago and London: University of Chicago Press.

Malarney, Shaun Kingsley. 1998. "State Stigma, Family Prestige and the Development of Commerce in the Red River Delta of Vietnam." In Robert Hefner (ed.), *Market Cultures: Society and Morality in the New Asian Capitalisms,* pp. 268–89. St Leonards, Australia: Allen and Unwin.

Malarney, Shaun Kingsley. 2002. *Culture, Ritual and Revolution in Vietnam*. London: RoutledgeCurzon.

Malarney, Shaun Kingsley. 2003. "Returning to the Past? The Dynamics of Contemporary Religious and Ritual Transformation." In H. V. Luong (ed.), *Postwar Vietnam: Dynamics of a Transforming Society*, pp, 225–56. Singapore: Institute for Southeast Asian Studies.

Manuel, Peter. 2002. "Modernity and Musical Structure: Neo-Marxist Perspectives on Song Form and Its Successors." In R. B. Qureshi (ed.), *Music and Marx: Ideas, Practice, Politics,* pp. 45–62. New York and London: Routledge.

McLeod, Norma, and Herndon, Marcia (eds.) 1980. *The Ethnography of Musical Performance*. Norwood, Pa.: Norwood Editions.

Merleau-Ponty, Maurice. 1962. *Phenomenology of Perception*. Evanston, Ill.: Northwestern University Press.

Merriam, Alan P. 1964. *The Anthropology of Music*. Evanston, Ill.: Northwestern University Press.

Moisala, Pirkko, and Diamond, Beverley (eds.). 2000. *Music and Gender*. Urbana and Chicago: University of Illinois Press.

Morris, Rosalind C. 1994. "Three Sexes and Four Sexualities: Redressing the Discourses on Gender and Sexuality in Contemporary Thailand." *Positions* 2(1): 15–43.

Morris, Rosalind C. 1995. "All Made Up: Performance Theory and the New Anthropology of Sex and Gender." *Annual Review of Anthropology* 24: 567–92.

Morris, Rosalind C. 2000. *In the Place of Origins: Modernity and Its Mediums in Northern Thailand*. Durham, N.C.: Duke University Press.

Neher, Andrew. 1962. "A Physiological Explanation of Unusual Behavior in Ceremonies Involving Drums." *Human Biology* 34: 151–60.

Nettl, Bruno (ed.). 1998. *In the Course of Performance: Studies in the World of Musical Improvisation*. Chicago and London: University of Chicago Press.

Nettl, Bruno. 2006 [1983]. *The Study of Ethnomusicology: Thirty-One Issues and Concepts*. Urbana and Chicago: University of Illinois Press.

Ngo Duc Thinh (ed.). 1992. *Hat Van*. Ha Noi: Nha Xuat Ban Van Hoa Dan Toc.

Ngo Duc Thinh (ed.). 1996a. *Dao Mau O Viet Nam, Tap 1 (Mother Religion in Vietnam, Vol. 1)*. Ha Noi: Nha Xuat Ban Van Hoa–Thong Tin.

Ngo Duc Thinh (ed.). 1996b. *Dao Mau O Viet Nam, Tap 2 (Mother Religion in Vietnam, Vol 2)*. Ha Noi: Nha Xuat Ban Van Hoa–Thong Tin.

Ngo Duc Thinh. 1999. "Hau Bong as Viewed from the Angle of the Performing Arts." *Vietnamese Studies* 131: 56–60.

Ngo Duc Thinh (ed.) 2004. *Dao Mau Va Cac Hinh Thuc Shaman Trong Cac Toc Nguoi O Viet Nam Va Chau a (The Mother Religion and Forms of Shamanism among Ethnic Groups in Vietnam and Asia)*. Ha Noi: Nha Xuat Ban Khoa Hoc Xa Hoi.

Nguyen Khac Kham. 1983. "Vietnamese Spirit Mediumship: A Tentative Reinterpretation of Its Basic Terminology." *Vietnam Forum* 1(1): 24–30.

Nguyen Kim Hien. 1996. "Le Phénomène de Transe Mystique (*Len Dong*) dans la Société Vietnamienne." Master's dissertation: École Pratique des Hautes Études.

Nguyen Minh San. 1996. *Nhung Thanh Nu Danh Tieng Trong Van Hoa Tin Nguong Viet Nam (Famous Goddesses in Vietnamese Cultural Belief)*. Ha Noi: Nha Xuat Ban Phu Nu.

Nguyen The Anh. 1995. "The Vietnamization of the Cham Deity Po Nagar." In K. W. Taylor and J. Whitmore (eds.). *Essays into Vietnamese Pasts*. Ithaca, N.Y.: Southeast Asia Program, Cornell University.

Nguyen Thi Hien. 2002. "The Religion of the Four Palaces: Mediumship and Therapy in Viet Culture." PhD dissertation: Indiana University.

Nguyen Thuyet Phong. 1986. "Restructuring the Fixed Pitches of the Vietnamese *Dan Nguyet* Lute: A Modification Necessitated by the Modal System." *Asian Music* 18(1): 56–70.

Nguyen Thuyet Phong. 1998. "Vietnam." In T. Miller and S. Williams (eds.), *Garland Encyclopedia of World Music, Vol. 4: Southeast Asia*, pp. 444–517. New York: Garland.

Nguyen Xuan Kinh. 1992. *Thi Phap Ca Dao (Folk Poetry)*. Ha Noi: Nha Xuat Ban Khoa Hoc Xa Hoi.

Nhat Lang. 1952. *Dong Bong*. Ha Noi: Nha In Le Cuong.

Ninh, Kim N. B. 2002. *A World Transformed: The Politics of Culture in Revolutionary Vietnam, 1945–65.* Ann Arbor: University of Michigan Press.

Norton, Barley, 2000. "Music and Possession in Vietnam." PhD dissertation: School of Oriental and African Studies, University of London.

Norton, Barley, 2005. "Singing the Past: Vietnamese Ca Tru, Memory, and Mode." *Asian Music* 36(2): 27–56.

Obeyesekere, Gananath. 1977. "Psychocultural Exegesis of a Case of Spirit Possession in Sri Lanka." In V. Crapanzano and V. Garrison (eds.), *Case Studies in Spirit Possession*, pp. 235–95. New York: Wiley.

Ortner, Sherry, 1996. *Making Gender: The Politics and Erotics of Culture.* Boston: Beacon Press.

Ots, Thomas, 1994. "The Silenced Body—the Expressive Leib: On the Dialectic of Mind and Life in Chinese Cathartic Healing." In T. J. Csordas (ed.), *Embodiment and Experience: The Existential Ground of Culture and Self.* Cambridge, UK: Cambridge University Press.

Parry, Jonathan, and Bloch, Maurice (eds.). 1989. *Money and the Morality of Exchange.* Cambridge, UK: Cambridge University Press.

Pelley, Patricia M. 2002. *Postcolonial Vietnam: New Histories of the National Past.* Durham and London: Duke University Press.

Perlman, Marc. 2004. *Unplayed Melodies: Javanese Gamelan and the Genesis of Music Theory.* Berkeley: University of California Press.

Pham Duy. 1975. *Musics of Vietnam.* Carbondale and Edwardsville: Southern Illinois University Press.

Pham Quynh Phuong. 2006. "Tran Hung Dao and the Mother Goddess Religion." In Karen Fjelstad and Nguyen Thi Hien (eds.), *Possessed by the Spirits: Mediumship in Contemporary Vietnamese Communities*, pp. 31–54. Ithaca, N.Y.: Cornell Southeast Asia Program.

Pham Van Ty. 1992. "Buoc Dau Tim Hieu Am Nhac Chau Van Trong Tin Nguong Tho Mau Lieu" (Toward an Understanding of the Music of Chau Van in the Religious Beliefs of the Mother Spirit Lieu [Hanh]"), *Tap chi van hoc* 5: 63–65.

Phan Ke Binh. 1987 [1913/1914]. *Viet-Nam Phong-Tuc* (*Vietnamese Customs*). Los Alamitos, Calif.: Xuan Thu.

Qureshi, Regula Burckhardt 1995 [1986]. *Sufi Music of India and Pakistan: Sound, Context and Meaning in Qawwali.* Chicago and London: University of Chicago Press.

Rees, Helen. 2000. *Echoes of History: Naxi Music in Modern China.* New York: Oxford University Press.

Reyes, Adelaida. 1999. *Songs of the Caged, Songs of the Free: Music and the Vietnamese Refugee Experience.* Philadelphia: Temple University Press.

Rice, Timothy. 1994. *May It Fill Your Soul: Experiencing Bulgarian Music.* Chicago and London: University of Chicago Press.

Roseman, Marina. 1991. *Healing Sounds from the Malaysian Rainforest: Temiar Music and Medicine*. Berkeley, Los Angeles, and London: University of California Press.

Rosenthal, Mila, 2002. "'Everyone Was Equal': Nostalgia and Anxiety among Women Workers in a Vietnamese Textile Factory." In Rainer Klump and Gerd Mutz (eds.), *Doi Moi in Wirtschaft und Gesellschaft: Soziale und Ökonomische Transformation in Vietnam*, pp. 207–31. Marburg, Germany: Metropolis-Verlag.

Rouget, Gilbert. 1985 [1980]. *Music and Trance: A Theory of the Relations between Music and Possession*. Chicago and London: University of Chicago Press.

Schafer, John C. 2007. "The Trinh Cong Son Phenomenon." *The Journal of Asian Studies* 66(3): 597–643.

Schafer, R. Murray. 1977. *The Tuning of the World*. Toronto: McClelland and Stewart.

Schechner, Richard. 1983. *Performative Circumstances: From the Avant Garde to Ramlila*. Calcutta: Seagull Books.

Schimmelpenninck, Antoinet. 1997. *Chinese Folk Songs and Folk Singers: Shan'ge Traditions in Southern Jiangsu*. Leiden: Chime Foundation.

Schutz, Alfred. 1977. "Making Music Together: A Study in Social Relationship." in J. Dolgin, D. Kemnitzer, and D. Schneider (eds.), *Symbolic Anthropology*, pp. 106–19. New York: Columbia University Press.

Silkstone, Francis. 1993. "Learning Thai Classical Music: Memorisation and Improvisation." PhD dissertation: School of Oriental and African Studies, University of London.

Simon, Pierre J., and Ida Simon-Barouh. 1973. *Hau Bong: Un Culte Viêtnamien de Possession Transplanté en France*. Paris: Mouton.

Soucy, Alexander D. 1999. "The Buddha's Blessing: Gender and Buddhist Practice in Hanoi." PhD dissertation: Australian National University.

Stock, Jonathan P. J. 1996. *Musical Creativity in Twentieth-Century China: Abing, His Music, and Its Changing Meanings*. Rochester, N.Y.: University of Rochester Press.

Stock, Jonathan P. J. 1999. "A Reassessment of the Relationship between Text, Speech Tone, Melody, and Aria Structure in Beijing Opera." *Journal of Musicological Research* 18: 183–206.

Stokes, Martin. 1994. "Introduction: Ethnicity, Identity and Music." in M. Stokes (ed.), *Ethnicity, Identity and Music: The Musical Construction of Place*, pp. 1–27. Oxford, UK: Berg.

Stoller, Paul. 1995. *Embodying Colonial Memories: Spirit Possession, Power and the Hauka in West Africa*. New York and London: Routledge.

Sugarman, Jane C. 1997. *Engendering Song: Singing and Subjectivity at Prespa Albanian Weddings*. Chicago and London: University of Chicago Press.

Sumarsam. 1975. "Inner Melody in Javanese Gamelan Music." *Asian Music* 7(1): 3–13.

Sumarsam. 1995. *Gamelan: Cultural Interaction and Musical Development in Central Java*. Chicago and London: University of Chicago Press.

Swindells, Rachel. 2004. "Klasik, Kawih, Kreasi: Musical Transformation and the Gamelan Degung of Bandung, West Java, Indonesia." PhD dissertation: London: City University.

Ta Van Tai. 1981. "The Status of Women in Traditional Vietnam." *The Journal of Vietnamese History* 15: 97–145.

Tambiah, Stanley J. 1985. *Culture, Thought and Social Action: An Anthropological Perspective*. Cambridge, Mass.: Harvard University Press.

Tanabe, Shigeharu. 2002. "The Person in Transformation: Body, Mind and Cultural Appropriation." In S. Tanabe and C. F. Keyes (eds.), *Cultural Crisis and Social Memory: Modernity and Identity in Thailand and Laos*, pp. 43–67. London and New York: RoutledgeCurzon.

Tanese-Ito, Yoko. 1988. "The Relationship between Speech-Tones and Vocal Melody in Thai Court Song." *Musica Asiatica* 5: 109–39.

Taylor, Keith Wellor. 1983. *The Birth of Vietnam*. Berkeley and Los Angeles: University of California Press.

Taylor, Philip. 2001. *Fragments of the Present: Searching for Modernity in Vietnam's South*. Honolulu: University of Hawai'i Press.

Taylor, Philip. 2004. *Goddess on the Rise: Pilgrimage and Popular Religion in Vietnam*. Honolulu: University of Hawai'i Press.

Taylor, Philip (ed.). 2007. *Modernity and Re-enchantment: Religion in Post-revolutionary Vietnam*. Singapore: Institute of Southeast Asian Studies.

Thanh Ha. 1976. "Cau Truc Loai Am Nhac Mot Doan Trong Hat Van" ("The Structure of the Musics of Hat Van"), *Tap Chi Nghien Cuu Nghe Thuat* (10): 42–52.

Thanh Ha. 1996. *Am Nhac Hat Van* (*The Music of Hat Van*). Ha Noi: Nha Xuat Ban Am Nhac.

Thanh Ngoc Pho. 1992. "Buc Tranh Van Hoa Dan Gian: Le Hoi Phu Giay" (A Picture of Folk Culture: The Phu Giay Festival"). *Tap Chi Van Hoc* 257: 59–62.

Theatre Publishing House. 1995. *Thuc Trang Cheo Hom Nay* (*The State of Cheo Today*). Ha Noi: Nha Xuat Ban San Khau.

Thomas, Nicholas, and Caroline Humphrey, 1994. *Shamanism, History, and the State*. Ann Arbor: University of Michigan Press.

Titon, Jeff Todd. 1997. "Knowing Fieldwork." In G. E. Barz and T. J. Cooley (eds.), *Shadows in the Field: New Perspectives for Fieldwork in Ethnomusicology*. New York and Oxford: Oxford University Press.

To Ngoc Thanh et al. (ed.). 2004. *Hue Court Music*. Hue: Hue Monuments Conservation Centre.

Tran Van Khe. 1962. *La Musique Viêtnamienne Traditionnelle*. Paris: Presses Universitaires de France.

Tran Van Khe. 1975. "Vietnamese Music." *Selected Reports in Ethnomusicology* 2(2): 35–47.

Trinh Quang Khanh. 2000. *Hung Dao Dai Vuong Tran Quoc Tuan* [*The Great Tran Hung Dao*]. Nam Dinh: So Van Hoa Thong Tin Nam Dinh.

Trinh T. Minh-Ha. 1989. "Surname Viet Given Name Nam." New York: Women Making Movies.

Trinh T. Minh-Ha. 1991. *When the Moon Waxes Red: Representation, Gender and Cultural Politics*. New York and London: Routledge.

Trinh T. Minh-Ha. 1992. *Framer Framed*. New York and London: Routledge.

Truong Chinh. 1985. "Dien Van Nhan Dip Ky Niem Lan Thu 40 Ngay Ra Doi Cua De Cuong Ve Cach Mang Van Hoa Viet Nam" ("Speech to Commemorate Forty Years since the Cultural Thesis on Vietnamese Revolutionary Culture"). *Bon Muoi Nam De Cuong Van Hoa Viet Nam* (*Forty Years of the Vietnamese Cultural Thesis*). Ha Noi: Nha Xuat Ban Su That.

Truth Publishing House. 1982. *Bai Tru Me Tin Di Doan* (*The Elimination of Superstitions*). Ha Noi: Nha Xuat Ban Su That.

Truth Publishing House. 1985. *Bon Muoi Nam De Cuong Van Hoa Viet Nam* (*Forty Years of the Vietnamese Cultural Thesis*). Ha Noi: Nha Xuat Ban Su That.

Tu Ngoc et al. 2000. *Am Nhac Moi Viet Nam: Tien Trinh Va Thanh Tuu* (*New Vietnamese Music: Processes and Achievements*). Ha Noi: Vien Am Nhac.

Turino, Thomas. 2000. *Nationalists, Cosmopolitans, and Popular Music*. Chicago and London: University of Chicago Press.

Turner, Victor. 1986. *From Ritual to Theatre and Back*. New York: Performing Arts Journal Publication.

Vander, Judith. 1996 [1988]. *Songprints: The Musical Experience of Five Shoshone Women*. Urbana and Chicago: University of Illinois Press.

Vietnam Government. 1962. *Dau Tranh Chong Doi Phong Bai Tuc Cai Tao Thoi Quen Cu Xay Dung Nep Song Moi* (*Struggle against Bad Practices and Corrupt Customs, Reform Old Habits and Build the New Ways*). N.p.

Vietnamese Institute for Musicology. 2003. *Hop Tuyen Tai Lieu Nghien Cuu Ly Luan Phe Binh Am Nhac The Ky XX* (*Anthology of Researches, Theories and Critiques on the 20th-Century Vietnamese Music*). Ha Noi: Vien Am Nhac.

Vietnamese Institute for Musicology. 2004. *Am Nhac Dan Toc Co Truyen Trong Boi Canh Toan Cau Hoa* (*Traditional Music in Globalization Context*). Hanoi: Vietnamese Institute for Musicology.

Vu Ngoc Khanh and Pham Van Ty (eds.). 1990. *Van Cat Than Nu* (*The Van Cat Goddess*). Ha Noi: Nha Xuat Ban Van Hoa Dan Toc.

Wade, Peter. 1998. "Music, Blackness and National Identity: Three Moments in Colombian History." *Popular Music* 17(1): 1–20.

Wade, Peter. 2000. *Music, Race, and Nation: Música Tropical in Colombia*. Chicago and London: University of Chicago Press.

Waterman, Christopher. 1990. *Jùjú: A Social History and Ethnography of a West African Popular Music*. Chicago and London: University of Chicago Press.

Weller, Robert. 1994. "Capitalism, Community and the Rise of Amoral Cults in Taiwan." In Charles Keyes et al. (eds.), *Asian Visions of Authority: Religion and the Modern States of East and Southeast Asia*, pp. 141–64. Honolulu: University of Hawai'i Press.

Werner, Jane, and Bélanger, Danièle (eds.). 2002. *Gender, Household, State: Doi Moi in Viet Nam*. Ithaca, N.Y.: Cornell Southeast Asia Program Publications.

Whitehead, Tony Larry, and Mary Ellen Conaway (eds.). 1986. *Self, Sex and Gender in Cross-Cultural Fieldwork*. Urbana and Chicago: University of Illinois Press.

Wong, Deborah. 2001. *Sounding the Center: History and Aesthetics in Thai Buddhist Performance*. Chicago and London: University of Chicago Press.

Xuan Khai. 1994. *Sach Hoc Dan Nguyet* (*Moon-Lute Text Book*). Ha Noi: Nhac Vien Ha Noi–Nha Xuat Ban Am Nhac.

Yung, Bell. 1989. *Cantonese Opera: Performance as Creative Process*. Cambridge, UK: Cambridge University Press.

Yung, Bell. 1996. "The Nature of Chinese Ritual Sound." In B. Yung, Evelyn S. Rawski, and Rubie S. Watson (eds.), *Harmony and Counterpoint: Ritual Music in Chinese Context*, pp. 13–31. Stanford, Calif.: Stanford University Press.

Zito, Angela. 1993. "Ritualizing Li: Implications for the Study of Power and Gender." *Positions* 1(2): 321–47.

Index

Note: Page numbers in *italics* represent illustrations; page numbers followed by "*t*" represent tables or charts.

amplification, 151–52
animal spirits, 58
An Pho temple, 94–95
antisuperstition policy, 5–6, 28–32, 126–27
Arana, Miranda, 8, 40
Asian Music Circuit (AMC), 15, 208
"asking rite" (*le khat*), 3, 69
aware possession, 73–76, 78

Babiracki, Carol, 161–62
"backbone" metaphor, 135–40
Bakan, Michael, 132
bamboo flute (*sao*), 12, 202
bands, 81–84, 232n2
Barlow, Tani, 159
bat am (ceremonial music), 33
Becker, Judith, 75, 111–12
Binh (medium), 67, 68, 76, 77
Blacking, John, 113
Boddy, Janice, 54, 163
Bodies That Matter (Butler), 174
Bohlman, Philip, 4
bong cau (term for female mediums), 173
Brinner, Benjamin, 80, 99
Buchanan, Donna, 152–53
Buddhism: Four Palace Religion relationship, 57; gender-specific practices, 158; institutionalization, 164; mediumship relationship, 30–31, 72
Bui Anh Tan, 182, 187
Butler, Judith, 174

Cadière, Leopold, 24
cai cach (renovated or new music), 27
cai luong (reformed opera), 27
Cambodia, 196
Cao Mon, 95, 149
ca tru (chamber music), 8, 33
Ca Tru Thai Ha Ensemble, 15
censorship, 14, 182. *See also* Ministry of Culture and Information; Vietnamese Television (VTV)
ceremonial music (*bat am*), 33
chau van: amplification, 151–52; antisuperstition campaign, 30; backbone notation, *138–39*; bands, 81–84, 232n2; books treating, 8; borrowing of songs, 150–51; characteristics, 2; classification by place, gender, and ethnicity, *122*; composition, 147–48; continuity v. change, 154; cultural nationalism, 51–53; flexibility, 149–50; folklorization process, 213; form, 48; gesture and rhythm, 115–16; history relationship, 128–29; individual interpretation and notations, 137–40; innovations, 148–50; instruments, 83; interrelationships overview, 106–7; invocation of spirits, 110–12; *len dong* interrelationship, 79–81, 93; linkages

of place, gender, and ethnicity, 119–21; male gender, 82; medium-band interaction, 105–6; melodic relationships and visual cues, 102–4; metaphorical thinking, 134–37; modernization processes, 143–45; musical change effect overview, 145–47; musicians, 81–82, 84–90, 102, 160; notation, *138, 139*, 234n3; as optional, 126; poetic forms and structure, 91; popularity, 8; as possession stimulant, 112; regional style differences, 229–30n4; repertoire, 90–94, *92*; research lack, 229n3; research perspectives, 17–18; rhythmic patterns, 83–84, *84*; as ritual narrative, 114–15; as sacred folk music, 171; socialist ideology, 145–46; song changes, choices and linkage, 105; songscapes, 48, 93; speech tone effect, 143–44; spirit dance, percussion rhythms and, 116–19, *116*; spiritual literature, 91–94; sung text, 127–29; transformative power overview, 18–19; unsung songs, 151; vocal aspects, 90; vocal challenges, 143; Western-influenced pop v. tradition, 133–34; Western notation, 232n3. *See also* learning *chau van*

cheo (music theatre genre), 27, 32–33, 35, 202, 212–16. *See also* Ha Nam Cheo Troupe; *The Three Spirits*; Vietnam Cheo Theater

chu van, 35–36

collective-variative form, 48

Communism, 5, 17, 28, 126–27, 153. *See also* Ho Chi Minh; revolutionary *chau van*

composition, 147–48

Confucianism: female subservience to male family members, 177; gender and power, 156–58; institutionalization, 57; patriarchy, 22, 23; restriction of commercial success to men, 196

Connerton, Paul, 55

consciousness theories, 74–76

continuity v. change, 154. *See also* economic change and *len dong*; folklorization and *len dong*; history; modernity

copyright law, 147, 234n9

Csordas, Thomas, 56–57, 76

cultural nationalism: colonial history, 32; ethnic diversity, 125; globalization, 51–53; sacred site valuation and restoration, 61–62; socialism relationship, 33–34. *See also* Folk Culture Institute; Four Palace Religion; Mother Religion; revolutionary *chau van*

cultural phenomenology, 56–57

cultural revolution, 32–34

Cultural Thesis, 32, 52

Damasio, Antonio, 75, 112

Dan ca folk song, 33

Dan day lute, 14, 87, *88. See also* Moon lute (*dan nguyet*)

Dang Cong Hung, *88*; on backbone v. speech tone, 144; biographical information, 87–88; on *chau van* challenges for singer, 143; *chau van* notation, 137–40; documentary, 14; metaphors, 135, 136, 137; performer, 95; teacher, 132; on *The Three Spirits (Ba Gia Dong)*, 213; *The Three Spirits (Ba Gia Dong)* contribution, 207; traditional v. modern training, 144–45

Dang Xuan Khai, 41. *See also* Xuan Khai

Dao Nguyen, 35

"Deep Feelings for the Homeland" (Tham Tinh Que Huong), 35

Deep Listeners (Becker), 111–12

Department of Traditional Instruments (of Hanoi Music Conservatoire), 40, 43–44, 86

Diguet, E., 23, 24

Divine Utterances (Hagedorn), 212

Doan Duc Dan, 147, 148, 149

Doan (medium), *156*; afflictions, 67, 68; dancing, 224; documentary film, 15; "end-of-year ritual," 177–82; General Tran Hung Dao possession behavior and speech, 221; *hau vo* ritual, 109–10; madness, 69; mediumship legitimization, 30–31; Nguyet Ho possession behavior and speech, 217–18, 222; possession behavior and speech, 217–18; possession experience description, 76, 77; Second Mandarin possession behavior and speech, 223; "thanking ritual" (*hau ta*), 20, 217–24

Doan Nhung, 94

Doan Thi Diem, 22–23, 64

Doi moi era, 5, 52–53, 196–97

Dong Bong (as reference to mediums and mediumship rituals), 26

Dong Bong (Nhat Lang), 26–27

Dong co (term for effeminate male mediums), 172–73

Do Ngoc Vuong, 211
Dong Vinh, 23
Do Thien, 23, 185
Drummond, Lisa, 182
Duc (temple medium), 12
Du Hailly, 23
dulcimer (*dan tam thap luc*), 45
Durand, Maurice, 7, 22, 24–25, 91

Ea Sola, 87
economic change and *len dong*: distribution of *loc* (gifts), 192–95, *194, 195*; financial gain for mediumship, 191–92; flexibility and multiplicity, 200–201; goddess worship, 196–97; market economy effect, 196–201; mediumship expenses, 191–92; medium wealth and spirit identification, 198–99; overview, 190; Seventh and Tenth Princes' popularity, 199–200; thanking ritual, 220
economic reform, 5, 52–53, 196–97. *See also* market economy; renovation policy
embodied language, 72–73
embodiment, 56–57. *See also* embodied language
Emoff, Ron, 113
Endres, Kirsten, 158
Engendering Songs (Sugarman), 165
ethnopedagogy, 42
European dancing (*nhay dam*), 100–101

field research methodology and fieldwork, 9–11, 160–62, 220
Film and Theatre Institute, 206
First Mother. *See* Four Immortals; Lieu Hanh
The Five Spirits (*Nam Gia Dong*), 208–12
Fjelstad, Karen, 158, 163–64, 180
Folk Culture Institute, 6, 8, 9–10, 52, 86
folkloricization, 212, 216
folklorization and *len dong*: audiences, 213–14; authenticity issues, 211–13; example, *204–5t*; intentionality, 212–13; medium reaction, 214; overview, 191; purposes, 214; spirit possession, 212–16; theatricality v. spirituality, 215. See also *The Five Spirits* (*Nam Gia Dong*); *The Three Spirits* (*Ba Gia Dong*)
Folk music. *See* Dan ca folk song; folklorization and *len dong*

"For the Fighters at the Frontier" (Gui Anh Chien Sy Bien Thuy), 39
fortune-telling, 70–71
Four Immortals, 22–23. *See also* Four Palace Religion (Dao Tu Phu)
Four Palace Religion (*Dao Tu Phu*): as alternate female worldview, 158, 180–81; classification difficulties, 57–58; cultural nationalism, 62; evolution, 7, 62; history relationship, 62; male-female distinctions, 62–63; market economy, 197–98; mother spirits, 62; place relationships, 119–21; representation, 60–61, *60t*; root components, 57; sites preservation, 231n3; spirit hierarchy, 58; stories and poems, 59–60; Taoism relationship, 78; temple location significance, 61; as transplanted in America, 158; wars and struggles, 60–61; *A Westerner Loves Our Music* (documentary film) portrayal, 15. *See also* Three Palace religion
French colonialist modernism, 23–27, 147
Friedson, Steven, 55–56, 113
funeral music (*nhac dam ma*), 33

Gammeltoft, Tine, 68, 77, 180–81
gender and mediumship; *chau van* bands, 164–65; *chau van* instrumental sections and accompaniment to vocal line, 170; *chau van* musical examples, *167, 168; chau van* rhythms and vocal force, 169–70, 235n2n3; *chau van* role in engendering participants, 165–69; Confucian codes v., 156–58; culturally prescribed limits, 174–75; *dong co bong cau* (transgendering), 171; *dong co* characterization, 184–85; "family happiness" ethic and, 176–77; gender transversal in *len dong*, 155–56; men's "propensity" for *chau van* musicianship, 162–63; musical engendering characteristics, *170t*; musical performance, 165–66, 187–88; opposite gender possession, 155–56; overview, 19; performativity theories, 174; public perception of medium gender, 171–74; as reflection of Vietnamese society, 156; ritual role, 162–65; temple management, 164; third gender domain, 173–74; uses of mediumship, 178–80; women's "propensity" for mediumship, 162–63

gender cultural linkages, 119–21
gender issues in fieldwork, 160–62
Gender Trouble (Butler), 174
General Tran Hung Dao: as colonial power
    threat, 23, 24; Doan possession, 109–10,
    156; folkloric or theatrical presentations,
    210–11; Four Palace Religion (*Dao Tu
    Phu*) position, 25; historical importance,
    52, 63; Spirit Pantheon hierarchy position,
    58–59, 65–66
Gia Long code, 23
Gibbs, Jason, 8
Giran, Paul, 24
globalization, 51–53, 133–34, 153. *See also*
    cultural nationalism; market economy;
    market relations
Goddess of Mercy (Quan Am), 58

Hagedorn, Katherine, 212
Hamayon, Roberte, 74
Ha Nam Cheo Troupe, 34, 38, 203, 209
Hanoi Music Conservatoire, 33, 42, 49, 86.
    See also Department of Traditional In-
    struments
Hat tho (worship singing), 93
Hat Van (book), 74, 126, 150
"Hat Van Solo" (*Doc Tau Hat Van*), 42,
    43–44
Hau vo, 108–10
healing, 70–72
Heidegger, Martin, 55, 113
history of mediumship and music: ancient
    Vietnam, 22–23; antisuperstition cam-
    paign, 28–32; *chau van* music, 40–41;
    Confucian influence, 22, 23; cultural
    nationalism and globalization, 51–53; cul-
    tural revolution, 32–34; French colonial
    era, 23–27; matriarchy, 22–23; moder-
    nity v., 16–17, 21; musical structure-social
    structure relationship, 48–51; neotradi-
    tional music, 40–41; overview, 21–22;
    revolutionary *chau van*, 34–40; scientific
    pedagogy, 42–45. *See also* specific musical
    types and events
Hmong flute (*sao Hmong*), 122–23, 123
Hoa (medium), 67, 68
Hoang Kieu, 206–8
Hobsbawn, Eric, 210
Ho Chi Minh, 28, 33, 61
homeland theme, 44–45
homology theory, 50–51

homosexuality, 182, 183–84, 186–87, 235n4.
    See also gender and mediumship
Ho songs, 121
Hue music, 43
Hughes-Freeland, Felicia, 14

imperial court music (*nhac cung dinh*), 33,
    150
initiation. *See* mediumship
innovations, 148–50
interactive motivation (songscapes), 104–6
interactive network (songscapes), 99–102
interactive sound structure (songscapes), 104
interactive system (songscapes), 102–4
invocations, 72

Jade Emperor (Ngoc Hoang), 58

Kapferer, Bruce, 54–55, 113
Kathoey (Thai gendering category), 186
Kendall, Laurel, 163, 196
Khoat (medium), 176, 181–82
Kim Huong, 13, 14, 15
Kim Lien, 35, 37, 39
Kim Ma, 35–36, 38
Kleinman, Arthur, 68

Lai (medium), 67, 68, 69, 76, 113
Lan (*chau van* musician), 220
Lancker, Laurent Van, 13
Lanh Gang festival, 201–3
learning *chau van*, 131–34
Le Ba Cao, 14, 87–89, 89, 151
Le code, 23
Le Duan, 33
Le Minh Son, 51
Len dong: antisuperstition campaign, 29–30;
    atmosphere, 3–4; *chau van* interrelation-
    ship, 79–81; cultural nationalism, 51–53;
    distribution of *loc* (gifts), 192–95, 194, 195;
    as ethnic exchange vehicle, 126–27; folk-
    loricization, 216; gender and music per-
    formance, 187–89; gesture and rhythm,
    115–16; importance of music, 108–10,
    110–14; locations, 4; musical entrainment,
    118–19; as "national folk culture," 216;
    Phu Giay festival, 3; political sensitivity
    and access issues, 7–8. *See also* economic
    change and *len dong*; folklorization and
    len dong; songscapes; *The Three Spirits
    (Ba Gia Dong)*

Lesbians: An Embrace without Men (Bui Anh Tan), 187
Le Tuan Hung, 40
Le Tu Cuong, 95, 122–23, *123*
Lewis, I. M., 163, 164
Lieu Hanh, 2, 4, 22–23, 64–66, 209–10
Loi ("way" metaphor and Vietnamese "song"), 134–35
Long Chuong, 25, 26, 177
Luong Duyen, 203, 206
lute. *See* Specific lute types
Luu Huu Phuoc, 33
"Luu Thuy" melody, 202, 221

Malarney, Shaun, 9, 29, 158
Manuel, Peter, 22, 48, 50
market economy: capitalism and consumerism, 195; *chau van* independence, 134, 146; mediumship and gender realities, 175–77; overview of relationship to mediumship, 19–20. *See also* globalization
Marketing and Family (magazine), 184
market relations: communications technology, 146; goddess worship, 197–200; mediums' commercial activities, 196–97; mediumship flexibility, 200. *See also* globalization; market economy
"market socialism," 201. *See also* market economy; market relations
matriarchal system, 22
mediumship: afflictions, 67–69; "coming out" process, 66–69; economic factors, 175, *193*; embodied language, 72–73; everyday life, 175–79; expenses, 191–92; as family dynamics influence, 179–81; family happiness, 175–79; financial gain, 191–92; flexibility and multiplicity, 200–201; folklorization and performance, 204, 206; fortune-telling, 70–71; gender, 230n1; healing, 70–72; initiation ritual, 69–70, 231n6; madness, 69; marginalization and gender, 164; market economy effect, 196–201; as "national culture," 52–53; as "national folk culture," 216; photography, 219–20; possession states, 73–76, 231–232n7–13; self-imagery, 219; self-mutilation, 66; theater v., 215–16; trance, 74–76. *See also* Len dong; spirit possession experience
melody, 135–37. *See also* "backbone" metaphor; "way" metaphor
Merriam, Alan, 145

Ministry of Culture and Information, 4–5, 33, 61, 213
modernity: history v., 16–17; homosexuality, 184, 185, 235n4; sexuality and gender, 182–87; song form relationship, 48–49; tradition v., 223–24
modern national music, 40–41. *See also* Neotraditional music
monochord (*dan bau*), 41
moon lute (*dan nguyet*), *85*, 89; author performance, 12; description and tuning, 83; gender associations, 82–83; Lanh Giang festival, 202; leadership role in *chau van,* 102; "Que Ta," 45; as traditional, 41
Moon-Lute Text Book (Sach Hoc Nguyet), 42–43
"The Moon Remembers Uncle Ho" (Vang Trang Nho Bac), 35–36
Morris, Rosalind, 174, 185–86, 187, 218
mother goddess effigies, 59, *77*
Mother Religion (*Dao Mau*), 62. *See also* Four Palace Religion (*Dao Tu Phu*)
mountain songs, 122–25. *See also* "Xa" melodies
Mulberry Temple (Den Dau), 86, *95*, 151–52
musical change, 152–54
musical instruments. *See* Specific instruments
musical interaction (songscapes), 99–106
musical resurgence. *See* resurgence of music and religion
musical-ritual performance relationship overview, 17–18
music theater genres (*cheo, tuong, and cai luong*), 8, 27, 32

"Nam Dinh, My Hometown" (*Nam Dinh Que Toi*) (Kim Lien and Nguyen The Tuyen), 35
Nam Dinh Cheo Troupe, 34, 35, 39
Nam Dinh Folk Song and Dance Troupe, 86
neotraditional music, 40–41, 49–51. *See also* "Hat Van Solo," modern national music; "Que Ta" ("Our Native Homeland" or "Our Homeland"); reformed traditional music
new or renovated music (*cai cach* or *tan nhac*), 27
Nghiem Thi Dau, 222
Ngoc Dai, 51
Ngoc Hoang (Jade Emperor), 58

Ngo Duc Thinh, 6, 62, 74, 120, 215
Nguyen (medium), 67, 68
Nguyen Ngoc Thu, 95
Nguyen The Tuyen, 35, 36, 38
Nguyen Thi Hang, 94, 100, 101
Nguyen Thi Hien, 100
Nguyen Thi Lai, 94, 100
Nguyen Thuyet Phong, 8
Nguyen Trinh Thi, 235n4
Nguyen Trung Kien, 15–16
Nguyen Van Mui, 14
Nhac cung dinh (imperial court music), 33
Nhac dam ma (funeral music), 33
Nhac Viet: The Journal of Vietnamese Music, 8
Nhat Lang, 25, 26–27, 177
notation (Western), 42, 43–44

obsession, 73–76
opera. *See* Reformed opera
oral training. *See* learning *chau van*
Ots, Thomas, 77
"Our Native Homeland" or "Our Homeland" (*"Que Ta"*), 41

pear-shaped lute (*ty ba*), 83
pedagogy, 42–44
percussion (*bo nhac cu go*), 83, 85
performance theories, 206
performativity theories, 174
Perlman, Marc, 135–36
Pham Quang Dat, *85*, 86, 94
Pham Van Dong, 33
Pham Van Kiem, 147, 148
Pham Van Ty, *85*; biographical information,
   85–87; *chau van* notation, 137–40; on *The
   Five Spirits* (*Nam Gia Dong*), 211; innovation, 149; knowledge and spirituality, 90;
   Lanh Giang festival, 201–2; on male v. female *chau van* style, 170; metaphors, 135,
   136, 137; oral training, 131–34; performing musician, 15, 36, 39, 43, 94; Phu Giay
   video performance, 12; *The Three Spirits*
   (*Ba Gia Dong*) support, 213; traditional v.
   modern training, 144–45
Phan Ke Binh, 25, 100
Pho Duc Phuong, 154, 252n9
Phu Giay Festival: *chau van,* 1; description,
   4–5; *len dong,* 3–4; location, 1; Mother Religion, 12; significance of 1995 restoration,
   5–7; site, 2; video recording, 11–12. *See
   also* cultural nationalism

pitch, 142–43, 234n8
popular songs (*ca khuc*), 51, 147
"Presenting Lotus Flowers to Uncle Ho"
   (Mua Sen Dang Bac), 35–36, 38
prophecy. *See* fortune-telling

Quan Am (Goddess of Mercy), 58, 231n1
Quan Ho Folk Song Troupe, 33
"Que Ta" ("Our Native Homeland" or "Our
   Homeland") (Doc Tau Hat Van), 41,
   44–48, *46*, 230n4
Quoc Trung, 51
Qureshi, Regula, 80
Quyet (medium), 67, 68, 69, *175*
Quy (mediumship disciple), 222

RASA (world cultural arts organization),
   208
Rees, Helen, 50
reformed opera (*cai luong*), 27
reformed traditional music, 40–41
reform era, 5, 52–53, 196–97
relative pitch level, 142–143, *142t*
religion. *See* resurgence of music and religion
renovated or new music (*cai cach* or *tan
   nhac*), 27
renovation policy, 5, 52–53, 196–97. *See also*
   market economy
research methodology. *See* field research
   methodology and fieldwork
resurgence of music and religion, 5. *See also*
   cultural revolution; economic change and
   len dong
revolutionary *chau van*: creators and performers, 35; evolution, 39–40; purposes,
   34–35, 230–31n6; repertoire, 37; song
   texts, 35–37; structure, 48–49; structure of
   suites, 38; tempo and vocal forces, 38–39
Reyes, Adelaida, 8
Rice, Tim, 152
Richard, P. C., 23
ritual-musical performance relationship,
   17–18
ritual songscapes. *See* songscapes
Rouget, Gilbert, 73, 79, 111

Schechner, Richard, 206
Schutz, Alfred, 113
Second Lady (*Chau De Nhi*) songscapes, 94,
   97, 127, 128

Second National Congress of Culture, 32
Second Prince, 52
self-mutilation, 66
Serving the Spirits (Long Chuong), 26, 177
Shamanism. *See* mediumship
Silkstone, Francis, 134
sixteen-string zither (*dan tranh*), 41, 83, *85*
small gong (*thanh la*), 122
Socialism, 5, 32–34. *See also* Communism; revolutionary *chau van*
Somatic attention mode, 73, 78
song. *See* "backbone" metaphor; "way" metaphor
song borrowing, 150–51
song form, 48–49
songprint, 106–7
songscapes: *chau van,* 93; definition and overview, 18, 79; interactive motivation, 105–6; interactive network, 99–102; interactive sound structure, 105; interactive system, 99–102, 102–4; musical interaction, 99–106; place, gender, and ethnicity linkage, 119–21; Second Lady (*Chau De Nhi*), 94, 97; as sonic environments, 232n1; sung text relationship, 127–29; Tenth Prince (*Ong Hoang Muoi*), 94, 97–98; Third Mandarin (*Quan De Tam*), 94, 96–97; Third Princess (*Co Bo*), 94, 98–99
Soucy, Alexander, 158
South Korea, 196
speech tones, 234n7; 140–43, *140t*
Spirit Pantheon, 57–60; anthropomorphosis, 64, 231n2; gender distinctions, 63; hierarchy, 57–58; history relationship, 63, 65, 66; location associations, 60–61, *60t*; mandarins and princes, 63–64; mothers, 64–65; princesses and goddesses, 64–65. *See also* Four Palace Religion (*Dao Tu Phu*); specific spirits
spirit possession experience: aware possession, 73, 78; colonial political encounter relationship theory, 55; described by mediums, 56, 76–78; embodiment, 76–78; history relationship, 66; music relationship, 129–30; overview, 18; Taoism relationship, 77–78; theories, 54–55. *See also* Four Palace Religion (*Dao Tu Phu*); *Len dong*; mediumship; Spirit Pantheon
Stock, Jonathan, 143
Stokes, Martin, 119
Stoller, Paul, 55

The Story of the Goddess of Van Cat (Doan Thi Diem), 22–23, 64–65
strophic songs, 48, 90
Sugarman, Jane, 165
sung text, 127–29
Swindells, Rachel, 132–33
"System of the four," 186, 187
"System of the three," 185–86, 187

Ta Duc Thang, 39
Tai tu chamber music, 27
Taiwan, 196
Tanabe Shigeharu, 196
tan nhac (renovated or new music), 27
Taoism, 57, 58, 77–78
Taussig, Michael, 55
Taylor, Philip, 23, 62–63, 158, 196, 197
teaching. *See* pedagogy
Technique et Panthéon des Médiums Viêtnamiens (Durand), 7
temple altar, 59
Tenth Prince (*Ong Hoang Muoi*) songscapes, 94, 97–98, 127, 128
text (*chau van* songs), 127–29
Thailand, 185–86, 187, 218–19
Thang (medium), 31
Thang Noc Pho, 6
"Third Cinema," 16
Third Mandarin (*Quan De Tam*) songscapes, 94, 96–97, 127
Third Princess (*Co Bo*) songscapes, 94, 98–99, 127
Three Palace religion, 24, 25. *See also* Four Palace religion
The Three Spirits (*Ba Gia Dong*), 202–8; audience, 213–14; creation, 206–8, 235–36n2–3; international reception, 208; medium reactions, 214; national cultural policy, 207; purposes of, 214; ritual commonalities, 203; ritual v., 203–6; theatricality v. spirituality, 215, 235n1
three-stringed lute (*dan tam*), 202
Thuy Hoa (*ca tru* singer), 14
Thuy (medium), 52
tonal inflection, 141–142, *141t*
training and learning. *See* pedagogy
Tran Chung Sinh, 95
Tran family spirits, 58
Tran Manh Tuan, 51
Tran Minh, 206–7
Trinh Cong Son, 51

Trinh T. Minh-Ha, 10, 16, 230n5
Trong Kha, *85*, 86, 94
Trong Lang, 25, 185
Truong Chinh, 33, 34
Truong Manh Linh, *85*, 94
Tuong (music theatre genre), 27
Turino, Thomas, 145
Turner, Victor, 206
two-stringed fiddle (*dan nhi*), 202

unsung songs, 151

Vander, Judith, 106–7
Van (medium), 74, 76, 77
Van Quyen, 15
Vietnam Cheo Theater, 39, 87, 206, 207
Vietnamese Communist Party, 28–32
Vietnamese Dancers Association, 206
"Vietnamese Magic and Religion" (Giran), 24
Vietnamese Television (VTV), 11, 14, 182–85, 208
Vietnamese women, 157–58. *See also* Confucianism; gender and mediumship
Vietnam Music Copyright Protection Agency, 234n9
Vietnam National Music School, 33. *See also* Hanoi Music Conservatoire
Vinh (*chau van* musician), 220
vocal melodies, 140–43. *See also* "backbone" metaphor; *chau van*; "way" metaphor
Voice of Vietnam radio, 11, 38, 39
Vuong (spirit priest), 220–21

Wade, Peter, 125
Waterman, Christopher, 113
Water puppetry (mua roi nuoc), 8
"Way" metaphor and Vietnamese "song," 134–35, 144
"Welcoming Vietnam's Great Victory" (song), 36
Weller, Robert, 196
A Westerner Loves Our Music (documentary film), 12–16, 19, 178–79
Western notation, 42, 43–44
women, 157–58. *See also* Confucianism; gender and mediumship
"The World of Witchcraft of *Dong Co*" (magazine article), 184
A World Without Women (Vietnamese television drama), 182–84, 187
worship singing (*hat tho*), 93

"Xa" melodies, 120–26, 129
"Xa Mua Moi" (*chau van* song), 224
"Xa Quang" melody, 124
"Xa Tay Nguyen" melody, 123, 124
Xuan Hinh, 39, 235n4
Xuan Khai, 42–43, 86. *See also* Dang Xuan Khai
Xuan (medium), 67–68, 76, 77

Yin and yang, 70, 71, 89, 159, 188–89
Yung, Bell, 143

Zito, Angela, 159

BARLEY NORTON is a senior lecturer in ethnomusicology in the Music Department at Goldsmiths College, University of London. He received a PhD in ethnomusicology from the School of Oriental and African Studies, University of London, in 2000. He is a performer of the Vietnamese *dan nguyet* and *dan day* lutes, and his research on Vietnamese music and culture was the subject of a documentary called "A Westerner Loves Our Music" (Nguoi Tay Me Nhac Ta), which was made by Vietnamese Television (VTV).

The University of Illinois Press
is a founding member of the
Association of American University Presses.

Composed in 10.5/13 Adobe Minion Pro
with Meta display
by Jim Proefrock
at the University of Illinois Press
Manufactured by Thomson-Shore, Inc.

University of Illinois Press
1325 South Oak Street
Champaign, IL 61820-6903
www.press.uillinois.edu